Albert Schmitz
Edith Schmitz

TOOLBOX

ENGLISH
for
Technical Purposes

2
Coursebook

Max Hueber Verlag

Folgende Symbole werden verwendet:

 für Texte auf der Cassette

für Texte auf der CD (hier Text 2)

Das Werk und seine Teile sind urheberrechtlich geschützt.
Jede Verwertung in anderen als den gesetzlich zugelassenen
Fällen bedarf deshalb der vorherigen schriftlichen Einwilligung
des Verlages.

| 3. 2. 1. | Die letzten Ziffern |
| 2000 99 98 97 96 | bezeichnen Zahl und Jahr des Druckes. |

Alle Drucke dieser Auflage können, da unverändert, nebeneinander
benutzt werden.
1. Auflage
© 1996 Max Hueber Verlag, D-85737 Ismaning
Sprachliche Durchsicht und Beratung: Eileen Anne Plümer
Verlagsredaktion: Cornelia Dietz, München
Zeichnungen: Paul Netzer, Berlin
Umschlaggestaltung: Alois Sigl, München
Herstellung: Erwin Schmid, München
Druck und Bindung: Ludwig Auer, Donauwörth
Printed in Germany
ISBN 3-19-002417-0

Vorwort

Toolbox 2 ist ein modernes Lehrwerk, das sich für Lernende mit Vorkenntnissen eignet, die sie entweder durch die Arbeit mit **Toolbox 1** erworben haben oder durch etwa drei- oder vierjährige anderweitige Beschäftigung mit der englischen Sprache.

Toolbox 2 wendet sich an alle, die mit technisch orientierter Sprache zu tun haben. Das lebendige Unterrichtsmaterial baut ganz auf der Praxis auf und stammt im wesentlichen aus folgenden Fachgebieten:
- Automobilbau
- Transport und Verkehr
- Energie und Umwelt
- Fördertechnik
- Werkstoffe (Metalle und Kunststoffe)
- Testverfahren
- Industrieroboter / Elektronik
- Computertechnik (Programme, virtuelle Realität)

Toolbox 1 und **Toolbox 2** eignen sich zur Vorbereitung auf das ICC Certificate „English for Technical Purposes".

Toolbox legt besonderen Wert auf den Umgang mit der modernen technischen Sprache, sowohl im mündlichen als auch im schriftlichen Bereich. Alle vier Fertigkeiten (Hören, Lesen, Sprechen, Schreiben) werden gleichermaßen geübt:

- Hören
  Die Cassetten/CDs zum *Coursebook* enthalten Hörverständnisübungen zu jeder Unit; zur Kontrolle befinden sich die entsprechenden Tapescripts im Anhang des *Teacher's Book*. Zum *Workbook* wird eine gesonderte Cassette mit weiteren Hörverständnisübungen angeboten (Tapescripts im Anhang).

- Lesen
  Die Lektionstexte bieten Einführungen in das jeweilige Fachgebiet, ergänzt durch zahlreiche Illustrationen. Mit fortschreitender Arbeit finden die Kursteilnehmerinnen und Kursteilnehmer mehr und mehr Originaltexte aus Broschüren, Fachartikeln und Prospekten.

- Sprechen
  Ein wichtiges Element sind die lebensnahen Dialoge, Telefongespräche und Diskussionen, die die Sprache so zeigen, wie sie heute verwendet wird. So werden die Lernenden optimal auf die Kommunikation mit Geschäftspartnern und -partnerinnen und Berufskollegen und -kolleginnen vorbereitet.

- Schreiben
  Schriftliche Übungen (z.B. Briefe, Notizen, Berichte) helfen den Lernenden bei der Einübung des Stoffes.

Verfasser und Verlag

Contents

Unit	Title of Unit	Subject of Dialogue	Language Functions ▶ A Look at Grammar	Page
1	Engineering as a career	Making an appointment	Assuring or confirming ▶ "Own" / "-self"	6
2	Cars and driving: safety features	At the Coventry office	Accepting / rejecting suggestions ▶ Interrogative pronouns	14
3	Transportation problems	The job interview (1)	Questioning ▶ Relative pronouns and clauses	22
4	Energy efficiency	The job interview (2)	Expressing possibility / capability ▶ "–ever"	28
5	An APM in action	The job interview (3)	Comparing ▶ Expressions with "go"	32
6	"Conveyors International"	A look at the shop floor	Drawing conclusions ▶ Expressions with "get"	36
7	Aluminium extraction	Back in the office	Expressing pleasure / displeasure ▶ "used to" / "didn't use to"	42
8	Aluminium extrusion	First day at work	Expressing necessity / obligation ▶ The use of articles	46
9	Working with steel	Finding a flat in Coventry	Giving advice / warning people ▶ Adverbs of degree	50
10	Applying for a job	Inviting friends and colleagues	Expressing a condition ▶ "Need" / "Needn't"	54

Testing Your Language – Part One ... 64

Unit	Title of Unit	Subject of Dialogue	Language Functions ▶ A Look at Grammar	Page
11	Testing and finishing (1)	Travelling to the plant	Classifying something (1) ▶ Continuous forms	68
12	Testing and finishing (2)	At the company car park	Classifying something (2) ▶ Reported speech	74
13	Plastics in daily use	Driving home	Classifying facts by time ▶ Expressions with "take"	78

Unit	Title of Unit	Subject of Dialogue	Language Functions ▶ A Look at Grammar	Page
14	The Docklands Light Railway	Conversation at the pub	Expressing your wishes ▶ Simple past perfect	82
15	Cleaning the air	Planning a trip to London (1)	Expressing indifference ▶ Conditional sentences	86
16	Working with a machining center	Planning a trip to London (2)	Satisfaction / dissatisfaction ▶ "As" / "because" / "since"	92
17	A helping hand (1)	At Heathrow Airport	Requesting / ordering ▶ Expressions with "do" and "make"	98
18	A helping hand (2)	Let's go to a museum	Requesting / giving permission ▶ -ing form (1)	102
19	Bits and bytes: PRO-CEDE for windows	At the Science Museum (1)	What is it like? ▶ -ing form (2)	108
20	Bits and bytes: Images and cyberspace	At the Science Museum (2)	Expressing belonging ▶ Expressions with "mind"	116

Testing Your Language – Part Two.. 124

… and finally: Not Yet the End – A science fiction story by Fredric Brown........................ 130

Appendix 133

A technical dictionary – words and phrases.. 134
Not Yet the End – words and phrases 164
American English vocabulary 166
List of common prefixes / List of common suffixes... 168/169
Pronunciation of mathematical expressions 170
Signs and symbols / Greek alphabet 171
Prefixes for the SI system / Fuel consumption / Engine power 172
The chemical elements 173
Paper sizes / Roman numerals 174
Common substances used in production and manufacturing 175
Denominations above one million 176
Guide to English pronunciation 177
Grammar and subject index 178

1 Engineering as a career

The Industry

This is a leaflet introducing you to Engineering – an industry which is not only important to each and every one of us, but is one which provides careers opportunities offering challenge, excitement and satisfaction.

Engineering is at the forefront of technological change. Not only does it use the latest techniques, it researches, designs and develops them.

Engineering makes most of the things that are essential to our modern way of life: cookers, stereos and motor cars – aircraft, power stations and hospital equipment – and rarely seen things like water mains, oil rigs and telecommunications equipment.

Engineering also makes most of the things other industries need – sanding machines and chisels for the Furniture Industry, microphones and staging for the Entertainment Industry, lifts and keys for the Hotel Industry, radar and cameras for the Defence Industry, combs and scissors for the Hairdressing Industry, terminals and printers for the Computer Industry, portable tools and ladders for the Building Industry, turbines and instruments for the Energy Industry, and so on …

1

Questions on the text. Have a look at the text on the left and answer these questions:

a. What does the engineering industry offer, according to the text?
b. What does it mean when they say "engineering is at the forefront of technological change"?
c. What kind of things does engineering produce?
d. Give some examples of different industries that are influenced by engineering.

2

Study the "Language Functions" below and put in *assure, confirm* or *sure*:

a. Have you made all the necessary reservations? – Yes, I have. I asked the hotel to … them as soon as possible.
b. Can you … the reports about the accident?
c. Let's make … that nothing goes wrong.
d. Can you … us that there will be no delay?
e. You're … to find what you're looking for in that toolbox.

LANGUAGE FUNCTIONS:

Assuring or confirming

That's right. / You're right.

Absolutely.

We can assure you that your application will be considered.

Seriously, I think we should give her a chance.

I can confirm that.

I'm sure they will send my application to their Coventry office.

We do try to make sure that all documents are sent back to the applicants.

3

Listening comprehension and note-taking.

Making an appointment

Listen to the dialogue and take notes of what the two people are saying. Try to answer the following questions:

a. What does Audrey say about a written application?
b. When will the job interview take place?
c. Where did Audrey send her written application?
d. How does Ms Penrose describe the office building where the interview will take place?

1 A LOOK AT GRAMMAR:

"Own" / "-self" / "-selves"

OWN

I'd like to have my own computer.
ALSO: I'd like to have a computer of my own.
Don't use my computer – use your own.
I saw it with my own eyes.
Own brand goods are sometimes cheaper.
   (= goods on sale in a shop with the name of the shop on the packaging, not the name of the manufacturer)
That was an own goal!
   (= in soccer, a goal scored against her/his own team)
She did all the work on her own. *(= alone, without help)*

NOTE: "Own" is also used as a verb: How many cars does she own?
   (= How many cars belong to her?)

-SELF / -SELVES

I'm trying to teach myself algebra.
You have to do that yourself!
She was able to introduce herself in English.
He helped himself to another drink. *(= he took another drink)*
Help yourself! *(= take what you want!)*
The envelope was there, but the letter itself was missing.
We can't repair the computer ourselves.
You and John will have to clean the motor yourselves.
They wrote the minutes themselves.
Do you think you can manage by yourself? *(= without help)*

This is a self-winding watch. *(= it winds itself)*
He usually fills the tank of his car at a self-service petrol station.
A self-contained portable electric lamp is operated by an electric battery and is designed to be carried about by its user.
A self-centring chuck is a lathe-chuck for cylindrical work in which the jaws are always maintained concentric.
A self-lubricating bearing is a powdered-metal bearing having a special structure and a lubricant which is released gradually during the movement of the bearing.
If you do something out of self-interest, you do it for your own benefit and not to help other people.
A self-addressed envelope(SAE) is one on which you have written your own name and address (such an envelope will be used for a reply addressed to yourself).
   NOTE: SAE can also mean: stamped addressed envelope.

4

Make sentences according to the example below:

	plan the software	repair the machines	develop special programs	check the figures	service the equipment
I	X		X		X
Mary	X	X			X
Rudolph		X			X
Vicky			X	X	X

My colleagues and me: What we do ourselves …

EXAMPLE: Mary – She plans the software, repairs the machines and services the equipment herself.

Now go on …

5

Discussion / group work.

a. For some jobs, you need only a few weeks' training. Can you give some examples?

b. There are other jobs which take several years of study and quite a lot of experience. Can you name some? Which of these jobs would you like to have if you could choose?

c. Which field of engineering, do you think, has the best chances for the future?

d. Jobs which involve very hard or dangerous work are often badly paid. What do you think about this?

e. What do you think is the best basis: a university education, or an apprenticeship and some further training?

f. What is the role of in-company training? What sort of training programmes should a company offer, do you think?

g. What do you think about training courses in foreign countries? Are they a useful alternative?

h. What is the best way to learn a foreign language? (Language school? Courses in foreign countries? Work in an English-speaking country? Reading? Listening to TV and radio?)

1. What do you want from a job?

Different people want different things from jobs. Some prefer security even if the wages are not very high and others consider a high wage is worth the risk of being in a less secure job.
A lot of people say they are looking for job satisfaction, but what makes a job satisfying is different for each individual. So it is not enough to say you want job satisfaction, you have to find out what satisfies you.
Look through the different aspects of jobs listed below. There are examples to give you the idea of what might be important to some people.
Write down the things that are important for *you* to have in a job. There may also be aspects which you would definitely *not* want in a job. Write these down as well.

JOB ASPECTS	THINGS I WOULD WANT	THINGS I DEFINITELY WOULD NOT WANT
PHYSICAL CONDITIONS		
Examples: extreme heat or cold a clean work place noise good lighting		
CONTACT WITH OTHERS		
Examples: working alone being part of a group dealing with the public		
TYPE OF SUPERVISION		
Examples: easy to ask supervisor for advice closeness of supervision allowed to use initiative		
WHAT THE JOB ITSELF INVOLVES		
Examples: seeing the results a job I can do well satisfies my interests		
PAY		
Examples: getting enough to live on getting a high wage being paid by results		
HOURS		
Examples: fixed hours (for example, 9-5) working overtime some flexibility about hours		
PROSPECTS		
Examples: chance of promotion job security		
LOCATION		
Examples: town or country easy travel to work a particular area or town		

6
What's your field of work? Talk about your job.

- Aerospace Engineering
- Automation
- Automotive Engineering
- Building Construction
- Chemical Engineering
- Civil Engineering
- Computers
- Data Processing
- Electrical Engineering
- Electronics
- Mechanical Engineering
- Metallurgy
- Mining
- Nuclear Engineering
- Papermaking
- Petroleum Engineering
- Plastics
- Process Engineering
- Railways and Traffic
- Telecommunications
- Textiles
- TV / Radio / Video
- Toolmaking

7
Note-taking. Listen to the two telephone messages on the recording (message a and message b) and write down the relevant information on a separate memo sheet.
Put in today's date.

8
Group work.

Have a look at the drawing below.
Where does the whole thing begin?
What happens when you let the mouse get out of its cage?
Discuss the whole process in groups of three or four.
One person in the group writes down the whole process.
After about twenty minutes or so, the groups compare their results.

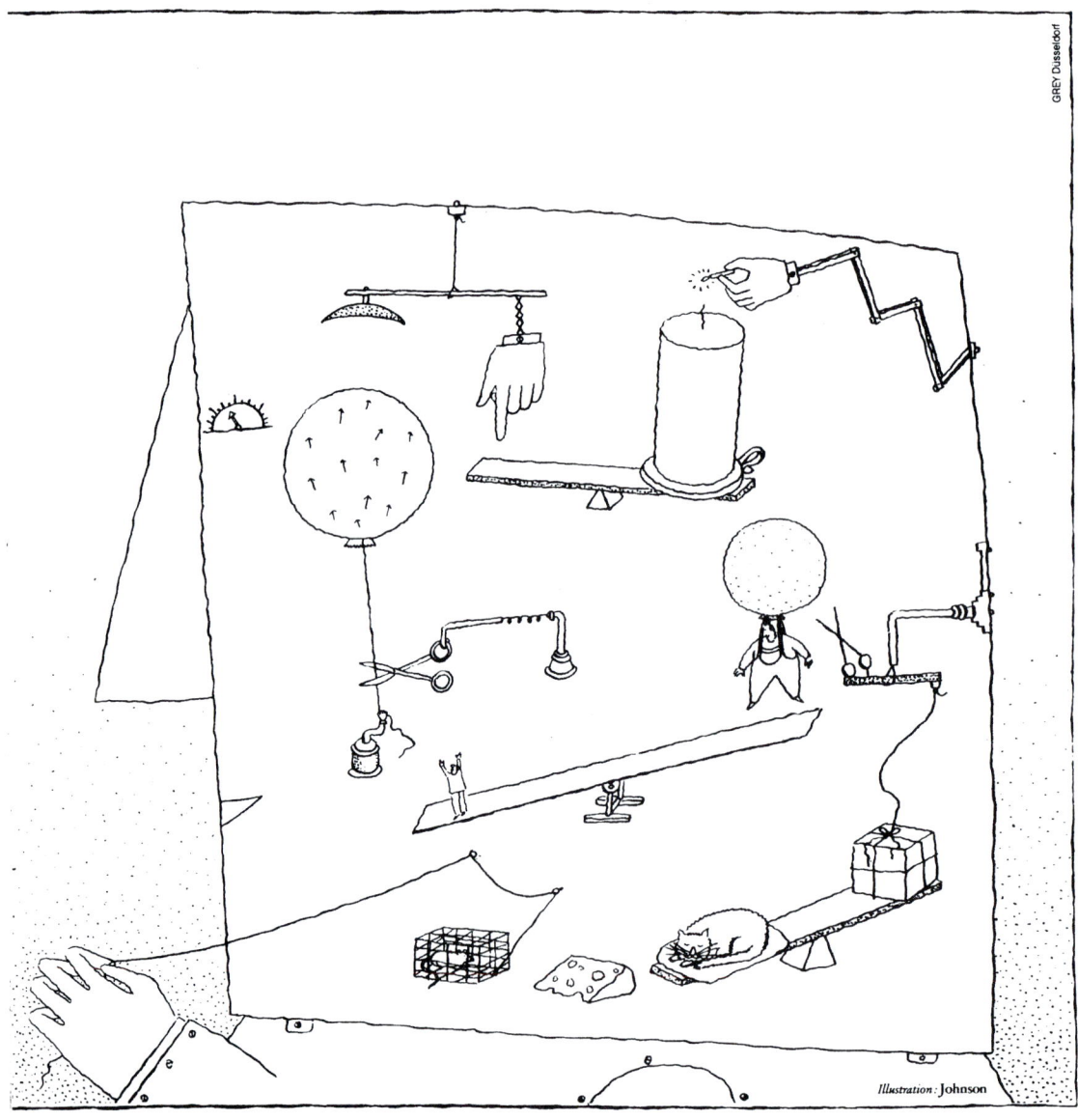

9

Discussion / group work.

Some jobs are more stressful than others. The following list was published in an American newspaper some time ago and shows the most and least stressful jobs. Do you agree?

Eight most stressful jobs	Eight least stressful jobs
Inner-city school teacher	Forest ranger
Policeman	Musical-instrument repairer
Air traffic controller	Architect
Firefighter	Natural scientist
Waiter / waitress	Piano tuner
Assembly-line worker	Barber
Customer service representative	Industrial machine repairer
Newspaper editor	Craftsperson

10

Put in the correct form with -*self*/-*selves*:

a. Can you install the modem …?

b. We can test the virus killer program … .

c. Can the technicians solve the problem …?

d. I can translate the report … .

e. I think she's able to write the documentation … .

f. They wanted to write the report … .

g. He cut … with a knife.

h. Did she do all the maintenance work …?

'The trouble is, it's been programmed to cut a longer lawn.'

2 Cars and driving: safety features

1

Listening comprehension.

You are going to hear two telephone conversations (A and B).

Listen carefully and write down the missing information for A and for B:

A: Caller's name / Caller's company / Reason for call / Number of caller / Who will call back?

B: Caller's name / Caller's company / Who does the caller want to speak to? / Reason for call / Who will help the caller?

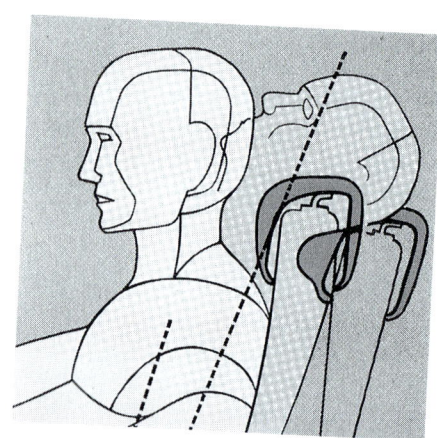

Tests on dummies have demonstrated that the head restraint has excellent energy-absorbing properties. For the best possible protection, the head restraint should be set level with the back of the head.

LANGUAGE FUNCTIONS:

Making / accepting / rejecting suggestions

Let's have a look, shall we?

Why don't you go right in?

What about a cup of coffee? – I'd rather not.

If you like, you can have a seat and wait a few minutes.

If I might make a suggestion …

We might as well wait here – I think she'll be down in a few minutes.

Shall I call her first? –
    Yes, I think that's a good idea.
    I don't think that's such a good idea.
    Yes, go right ahead.

2

Vocabulary and comprehension.

Have another look at the sentences under "Language Functions" and combine one sentence part from A with another from B:

A I really don't think

    Let's use the laser printer,

    Shall I call her office?

    We might as well wait here –

    What about

    What about a drink at the pub?

    You can sit down here

B a short walk to the new plant?

    I'd rather not – I'm driving today.

    if you like.

    I think she'll be down in a minute.

    that's such a good idea.

    That would be a good idea.

    shall we?

3
Questions on the text and discussion.

Have a look at the "Early Bird" repair order below and answer or discuss these points:

a. Who is this form for?

b. What kind of services can you check off?

c. Do you think these services are all necessary at the same time? Which do you usually need? Do you do some of them yourself? Which?

d. How can you pay the invoice?

e. What do you do with the repair order when you have filled in all necessary information?

"EARLY BIRD" REPAIR ORDER

Welcome to ALDRIDGE MOTORS SERVICE DEPARTMENT. We're pleased that you are taking advantage of our Early Bird Service. Please fill out the information requested below and check off services needed.

Name: .... Make of Car: ....
Address: ....
.... Reg. No. ....
Phone number you can be reached on today: ....
What time do you expect to pick up your car? ....

PLEASE CHECK OFF SERVICES NEEDED:
- ❏ 1500 K/1 MONTH SERVICE
- ❏ ... KM COUPON SERVICE
- ❏ LUBE AND OIL CHANGE
- ❏ CLEAN MOTOR
- ❏ TUNE UP MOTOR
- ❏ TYRE BALANCE
- ❏ FRONT WHEEL ALIGNMENT
- ❏ OIL FILTER CHANGE
- ❏ AUTO TRANSMISSION SERVICE
- ❏ CHECK AND ADJUST BRAKES
- ❏ AIR CONDITIONING SERVICE
- ❏ OTHER ....

Will you pay by: CASH ❏   CREDIT CARD ❏   CHEQUE ❏
I hereby authorize the above work.
Signature: .... Date: ....

PLACE KEYS AND ANY LETTERS INTO ENVELOPE AND PUT ENVELOPE INTO CHUTE. THANK YOU.

LETTERBOX LOCATED AT SERVICE RECEPTION OFFICE AT SOUTHERN END OF BUILDING.

ALDRIDGE MOTORS SERVICE 272 1684

4

Warm-up discussion / group work.

a. What do you think are the safest cars in the world? Is it possible to call one car safer than the other? If so, why?

b. Is there a difference in quality between cars from different countries? (Japan, USA, Germany, France, Italy, Sweden, Korea …)

c. Which part of the car is the most important as far as safety is concerned? (Wheels? Body? Steering? Brakes?)

d. What can be done to make driving safer? (What can the driver do? What can the manufacturers do?)

e. Should the city centres be kept free of cars? (Advantages? Disadvantages?)

f. How can the traffic situation be improved?

Safety steering column
The three-section steering column is designed to collapse in stages in a frontal collision. The upper section is telescopic and the lower section is jointed and fitted with a patented Saab sheet-metal bellows that crumples under abnormal stress. The steering gear is located low and far back in the engine compartment, so that it is well protected by the engine itself.

Head restraints
In a rear-end collision, the seat backs must rapidly absorb the reverse impact of occupants heads and bodies, particularly the whiplash effect. Therefore the front and outer rear seats are fitted with strong, adjustable head restraints, built up on sheet-steel frames and covered with soft foam padding.

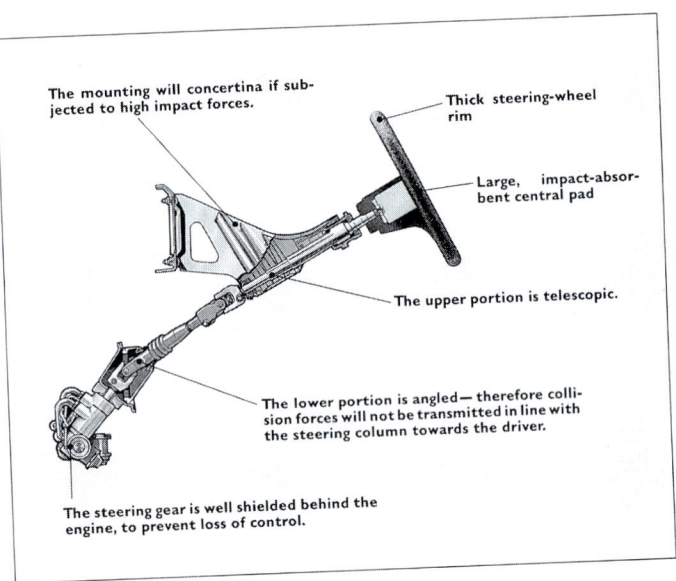

The mounting will concertina if subjected to high impact forces.

Thick steering-wheel rim

Large, impact-absorbent central pad

The upper portion is telescopic.

The lower portion is angled — therefore collision forces will not be transmitted in line with the steering column towards the driver.

The steering gear is well shielded behind the engine, to prevent loss of control.

5

Reading comprehension.

Have a look at the drawings and text above and decide whether these sentences are TRUE or FALSE.

	TRUE	FALSE
a. Tests have shown that the head restraint is very useful.	☐	☐
b. The lower part of the steering column is telescopic.	☐	☐
c. The steering wheel rim is impact-absorbent and thick.	☐	☐
d. The steering gear is located in front of the engine.	☐	☐

A LOOK AT GRAMMAR:
Interrogative pronouns

WHO
Who saw you?
Who helped you with the maintenance work?
Who did you see at the conference?
Who do you think I should call?

NOTE: "Who" is used for questions about persons, not things.

WHICH
Which engine are you going to use?
Which of the suppliers are you going to call?
Which of you knows the right answer?
Which cities in Canada do you know?

NOTE: "Which" is used for questions about persons or things out of a specified group, often followed by "of".

WHAT
What is your problem?
What people did she meet in Bristol?
What Canadian cities have you visited?
What are you interested in?

NOTE: "What" is used for persons or things in a general way.

WHOSE
Whose screwdriver is this? *(= who does it belong to?)*
Whose computer did you work on?
Whose car did you repair first?
I wonder whose book this is.
Whose telephone rang? – Mine did.

NOTE: "Whose" asks about possession (Who is the owner? Who does it belong to?). The owner is usually a person and the answer we expect is somebody's name or a form such as "mine", "hers" etc.

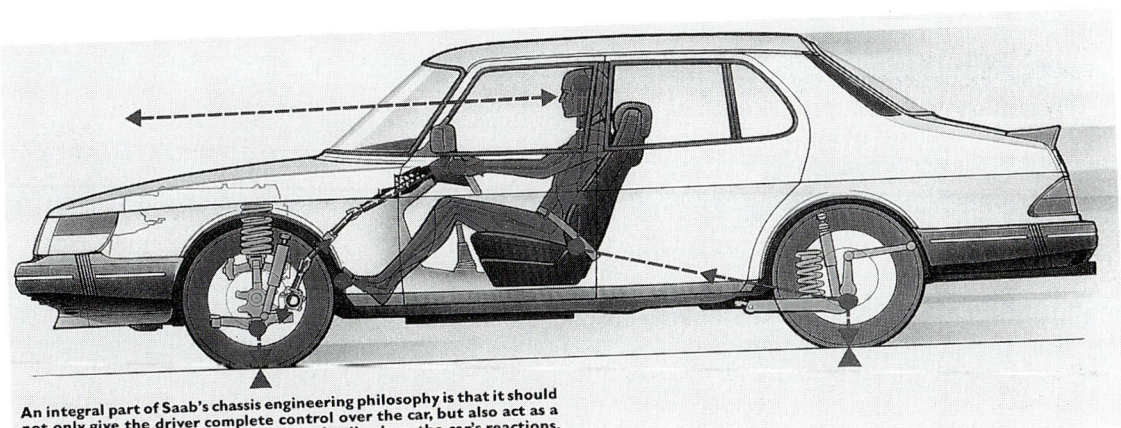

An integral part of Saab's chassis engineering philosophy is that it should not only give the driver complete control over the car, but also act as a responsive medium, supplying constant feedback on the car's reactions.

6

What / where / which / who
Ask questions and give answers, using the right form of the following verbs:
be / discover / invent / make.

EXAMPLE: Which (or: what) animal has the largest ears? – The African elephant.

animal with the largest ears	Alexander Fleming
famous American inventor and manufacturer	Henry Ford
electric light bulb	African elephant
colder – North Pole or South Pole?	moon
oldest parliament in the British Isles	Number 10, Downing Street
our closest neighbour in space	Thomas Alva Edison
penicillin	???

7

Reading comprehension / Questions on the text.
Have a look at the drawing with the short texts on the right and answer the following questions:

a. Which part of the car, they say, has been designed with the help of a CAD program?

b. What do they say about the engine location?

c. What have they done to improve the side protection?

d. How many crumple zones are there?

e. What is the reason for locating the fuel tank in that position?

f. What measures have they taken to make the roof construction safer?

g. What does the text say about seat belts?

h. What is special about the design of the front seats?

i. Why is the steering column collapsible?

j. What does the steering wheel centre pad do?

k. What general measures have been taken to make the interior safer?

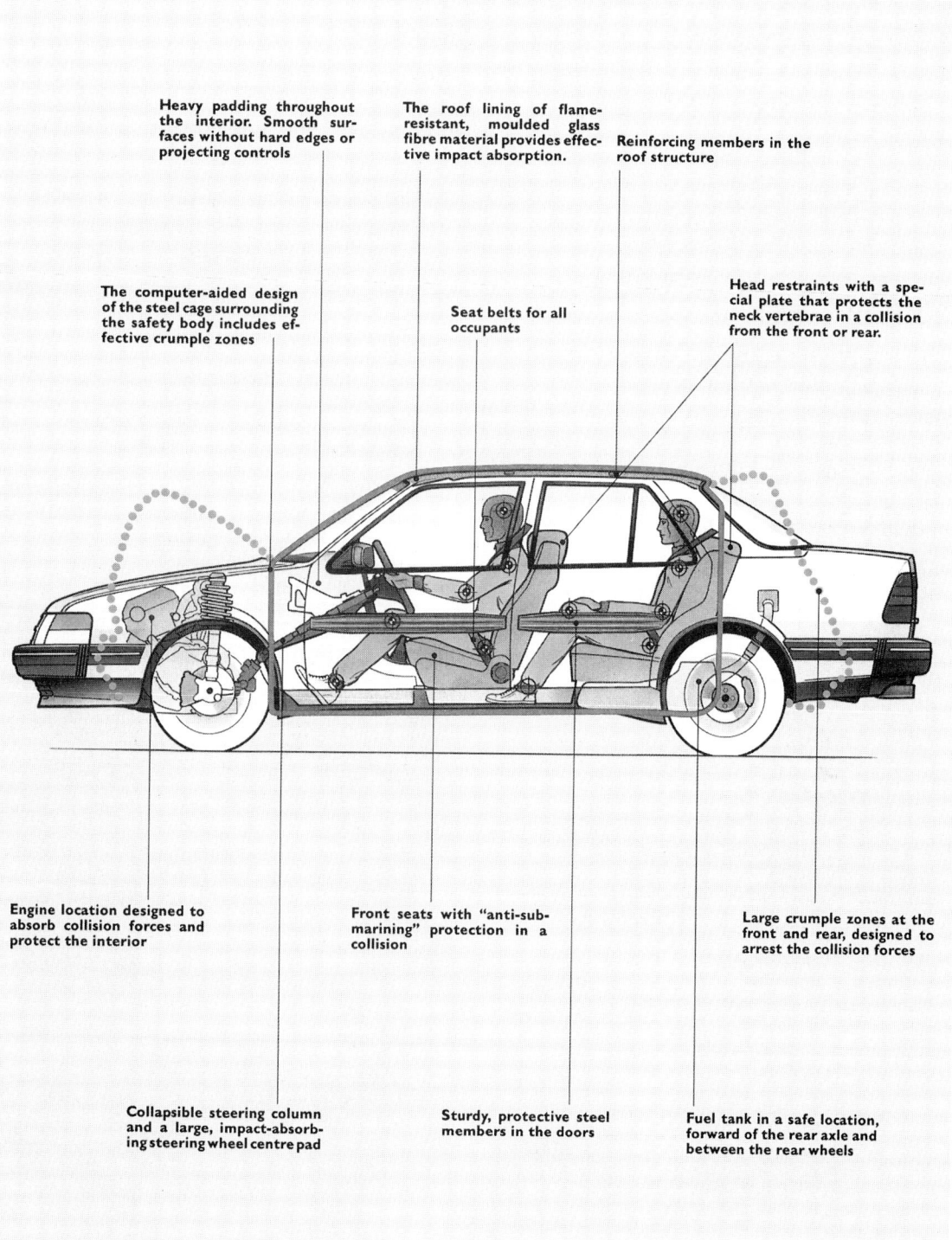

Heavy padding throughout the interior. Smooth surfaces without hard edges or projecting controls

The roof lining of flame-resistant, moulded glass fibre material provides effective impact absorption.

Reinforcing members in the roof structure

The computer-aided design of the steel cage surrounding the safety body includes effective crumple zones

Seat belts for all occupants

Head restraints with a special plate that protects the neck vertebrae in a collision from the front or rear.

Engine location designed to absorb collision forces and protect the interior

Front seats with "anti-submarining" protection in a collision

Large crumple zones at the front and rear, designed to arrest the collision forces

Collapsible steering column and a large, impact-absorbing steering wheel centre pad

Sturdy, protective steel members in the doors

Fuel tank in a safe location, forward of the rear axle and between the rear wheels

8

Put in a suitable preposition.

a. Engineering is ... the forefront of technological change.
b. Can you send the application ... our Birmingham office?
c. She helped herself ... another drink and went to the other room.
d. The head restraint must be set level ... the back of the head.
e. Do you think you can manage ... yourself or do you need help?
f. She did all the work ... her own.
g. She likes jobs where she has to deal ... the public.
h. You should discuss the whole process in groups ... three or four.
i. I'm not interested ... chemistry.

10

Listening comprehension.

At the Coventry office

Listen to the dialogue and answer the following questions:

a. What's the reason for Audrey's call?
b. Who is Ms Penrose?
c. Is Ms Penrose in the receptionist's office?
d. When is Audrey's interview?
e. Where is Ms Penrose's office?
f. Does Ms Penrose know about Audrey's arrival? Who has informed her?
g. What's the number of the room Audrey has to go to? Is it far away?

9

Pair work.

Student A: customer – has just collected his car
Student B: service technician at Aldridge Motors Service

Student A complains about bad service (What was wrong?) – Student B answers / finds excuses or reasons:

– work done by inexperienced colleague
– some colleagues on holiday
– could not get the correct spare parts
– bad construction – it's the car company's fault

Repeat this procedure with other students.

11
Discussion.

Working in the office or on the shop-floor ...

What are the advantages/disadvantages?

3 Transportation problems

When it comes to transportation, Japan offers more challenges than many other countries: It has a lot of mountains and huge population concentrations. Is that the reason why the Japanese have been great innovators in transportation systems? Some years ago, they introduced high-speed "bullet" trains, or "shinkansen", and one of the world's first monorail lines. The latest development is Maglev, a magnetic levitation system which uses a linear motor. Companies in Europe and the USA are also developing such train systems.

Maglev systems offer the advantages of very high speed (maybe 400 or 500 kph) and economical travel because the train is held above the ground by magnetic force, thus eliminating friction. The linear motor also uses magnetic force to propel the train. Several different systems have been developed, among them urban and regional transportation systems to be used between big cities, or maybe from one airport to another.

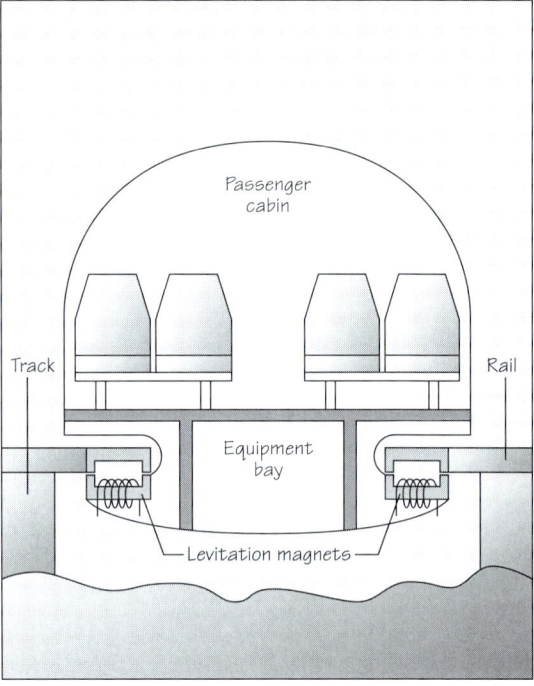

Below the carriages are permanent magnets which fit under the track. The force of attraction pulls the carriages above the guideway. Linear motors in the guideway generate a travelling magnetic field which interacts with the magnets under the vehicles to pull them along. Small guide wheels keep them on the track.

All systems, some people say, cause environmental problems – and these will have to be solved first.

1
Reading comprehension.
Have a look at the text about transportation systems on the left and try to answer the following questions:

a. What country offers a lot of challenges in the field of transport? (Why?)
b. Is the train the Japanese call "shinkansen" a Maglev train?
c. Who is developing Maglev trains?
d. What are some of the advantages of magnetic levitation?
e. Is there only one system?
f. What do you find below the carriages?
g. What does the text say about environmental problems connected with transport systems?

> **LANGUAGE FUNCTIONS:**
>
> **Questioning**
>
> What do you think?
>
> What's your opinion on this?
>
> Would you agree with me?
>
> Have you seen our new products – they're on show on the second floor.
>
> Can we leave the matter there then?
>
> I wonder if you could help me – I urgently need some information on one of the applicants for the job.
>
> I wonder if you could tell me something about your previous job.
>
> Can you give me any further information about my duties?

2
Listening comprehension.

The job interview (1)

Listen to the dialogue and write down the part of Audrey Bell.

Ms Penrose:	Yes, come in.
Audrey:	…
Ms Penrose:	Yes – You're Ms Bell, aren't you – Audrey Bell?
Audrey:	…
Ms Penrose:	Glad to meet you. Have a seat. Did you have any trouble finding our office?
Audrey:	…
Ms Penrose:	Oh, that's all right. It's only a few minutes anyway … well, let's see … I've got your CV here – looks very good, by the way – and I'd like to ask you a few questions …
Audrey:	…
Ms Penrose:	Particularly about your experience with CIM …
Audrey:	…

3

Listening comprehension.
Listen to the text about transportation systems and Maglev trains and decide whether the sentences below are TRUE or FALSE:

According to the text …   TRUE   FALSE

a. There will be more people in the world in the next few years.   ☐   ☐
b. In future, less money will be spent on rapid transit systems.   ☐   ☐
c. Companies in the transportation field have to face a lot of
   competition.   ☐   ☐
d. Lack of noise is one of the arguments the companies offer.   ☐   ☐
e. Conventional transportation systems are usually heavier than
   Maglev systems.   ☐   ☐
f. Maglev trains are easy to maintain.   ☐   ☐
g. The Maglev system is not very safe – it is dangerous if there
   is a motor failure.   ☐   ☐

4

Put in *at, for, in, on* or *up*:

a. One student … each group is responsible … the minutes.
b. What's your opinion … this?
c. I urgently need some information … Maglev trains.
d. Mr Hamilton's office is … the second floor, I think.
e. Small guide wheels keep the vehicles … the track.
f. The letterbox is located … the southern end of the building.
g. What time do you expect to pick … your car?
h. Our company makes lifts … the hotel industry.
i. These designs are the basis … all our new products.
j. Our new conference room can hold … to 150 people.
k. It's too expensive – prices went … again last year.
l. Are you interested … virtual reality?
m. That knife is … cutting paper.
n. Is this letter … me or … Kathy?

5

Group work. A brain-storming session – speaking and writing.
The groups think about a new transport system. Speak about the various advantages and disadvantages of rapid transit systems. Among other points, you should take the following into consideration:

- Cost?
- Maintenance?
- Capacity?
- Efficiency?
- Speed?
- Noise?
- Safety?
- Energy?
- Environment?

One student in each group is responsible for the "minutes" – she/he writes down all the important points and arguments. This can form the basis for a later class discussion.

6

Grammar repetition.
Make sentences according to this example:

tools / Audrey –
Whose tools are these? –
I think they're Audrey's.

a. office / Ms Penrose

b. idea / John

c. suggestion / Mr Hamilton

d. cup of coffee / I

e. seat / receptionist

f. printer / our chief engineer

g. car / my neighbour

h. pen / my colleague

i. dictionary / Helen

j. bag / Michael

3 A LOOK AT GRAMMAR:

Relative pronouns and clauses

WHO or **THAT**	That's the technician who/that repaired the laser printer. She's the woman who/that lives next door. Is this the man who/that gave you the operating manual?
WHICH or **THAT**	This is the photo which/that shows the new plant in Birmingham. This is the dictionary which/that I always use in the office. These are the tools which/that arrived this morning.
WHOSE	She's the woman whose bike was stolen yesterday evening. This is the machine whose motor was repaired last week. This is the woman whose dog bit me when I opened the door.

NOTE: "Who" is used for persons, "which" for things; both can be replaced by "that", as in the examples above.

It is very important to remember that sometimes a relative clause is necessary ("defining") and sometimes not ("non-defining"):

- *People who/that work with computers should learn how to use CAD programs.*
  Here, the sentence (the clause) "who work with computers" is necessary, it defines the meaning of "people". Without the clause, the sentence would be relatively meaningless (*The people should learn how to use CAD programs* – Which people? Who is meant?).

A non-defining clause is not absolutely necessary:

- *Our chief technician, who lived in Bristol before he came here, speaks English and French.*
  If you leave the clause out, you get *"Our chief technician speaks English and French"* which is a meaningful, complete sentence. In non-defining clauses, commas are used, and it is not possible to use "that".

It is important to remember that the use of commas may change the meaning of a sentence:

- The management which promises to increase wages and salaries will be popular.
- The management, which promises to increase wages and salaries, will be popular.

The first sentence refers to any management which may come into power in the future. The second sentence refers to the popularity of the management that is actually in power at the moment. Whatever it does, this management will be popular. Among other things, it promises to increase wages and salaries.

7

Structures and grammar.
Have a careful look at the grammar explanations on page 26. Make sentences according to the following example:

EXAMPLE: Who's very efficient? – technician / repair our car / last week

The technician who repaired our car last week is very efficient.

a. Who works with computers? – Mr Smith / be in London / last Monday
b. Who speaks Japanese? – engineer / introduce the new system / at the conference
c. Which machine cost a lot of money? – paper machine / break down / two days ago
d. Who is interested in the new software? – technicians / install the unit / Tuesday last week

8

Prepositions.
Have another look at the "Language Functions" of this unit. After that, complete the sentences below by putting in a suitable preposition:

a. I wonder if I could have some more information … the magnetic levitation system.
b. Are your new three-way catalytic converters … show during the exhibition?
c. She wasn't able to tell me anything … the power failure at the production plant.

9

Vocabulary.
Complete the sentences below by putting in *cause(d)* or *keep/kept*:

a. We're still trying to find out what … the accident.
b. We sold our old printers but we … the plotter.
c. Could you all … quiet for a minute? I'm trying to make a phone call to England.
d. If you … trying, I'm sure you will be successful.
e. The delay in delivery was … by bad planning.

10

Writing exercise.
Write a short letter to a friend of yours in an English-speaking country and tell him/her about the traffic situation in your area. (Cars? Roads? Buses? Trams? Trains? Bikes? City centre? Your ideas? …)

4 Energy efficiency

- Cracks in the ceiling
- Unwanted heat loss from ventilation
- No insulation on walls and roof
- Single glazed windows
- Old heating systems / old radiators

- Double glazing
- External doors draughtproof
- Modern heating system
- New radiators in all rooms
- Roof insulated with mineral fibre (50 mm)
- Roof hatch insulated with 75 mm mineral fibre

1
Discussion. On the left you can see an unhappy house owner, on the right a happy one. Have a look at the points mentioned as well as the text and diagram on the next next page. What sort of problems does the unhappy house owner have? Discuss the problem of energy efficiency and try to find other points that can be improved when an old house or flat is renovated.
How can energy be saved by using the right kind of fuel for a house or flat?

If you want to make your home energy efficient, heat loss from too much ventilation is an important factor. The strategy should be to reduce unwanted air leakage, which can represent as much as 25 per cent of the total heat loss from a typical British home. Ventilation rates in old houses are often around two air changes per hour. Where windows fit badly, ventilation rates may be even higher. The diagram below shows the unwanted leakages paths into and from a typical house and also where it is important to maintain essential ventilation. As can be seen from the diagram, there are a lot of potential air leakage points – many are impossible to correct in an existing building, although gaps around components (doors, windows, roof hatches, for instance) can be sealed.

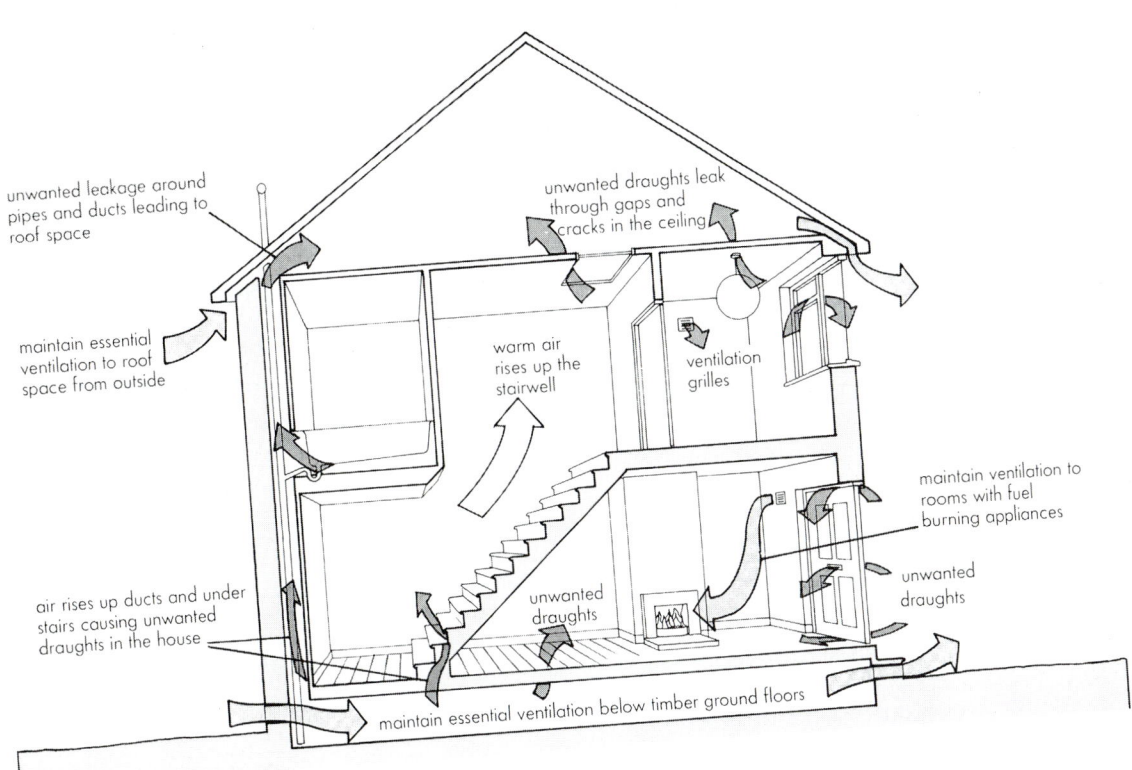

4 A LOOK AT GRAMMAR:

"-ever"

- However difficult it is, we must repair the machine as soon as possible.
  (= it doesn't matter how difficult it is)
- Whatever troubles you may have, feel free to call us.
  (= it doesn't matter what …)
- You can buy whichever car you like best.
  (= it doesn't matter which …)
- Whoever comes to our reception office should be welcomed.
  (= it doesn't matter who …)
- Wherever you are, call us.
  (= it doesn't matter …)

2

Complete the sentences below by putting in a form with *-ever*:

a. … the arguments against it, we must have a new computer network.

b. I know there are a lot of systems on the market, but … we buy, it must be energy efficient and easy to maintain.

c. Yes, it's expensive, but … it costs, we must have it for the new plant in Birmingham.

d. … operates the new CNC lathe, must be very experienced.

e. … complicated the problem is, we must find a way to solve it within the next few days.

3

Technical vocabulary.

Under a. and b. you will find the explanations of two words from the drawings on the right. Can you find the correct words?

a. A … is a piece of soft material placed between two surfaces so that steam, gas, oil or other substances cannot escape.

b. The first commercial synthetic rubber was developed in the USA in 1931. The substance is called "polychloroprene" but it is better known under its trade name … .

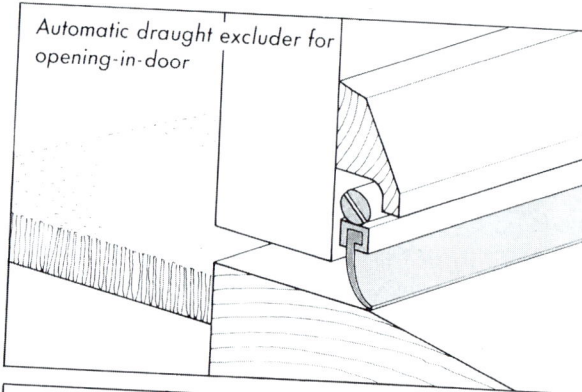

Automatic draught excluder for opening-in-door

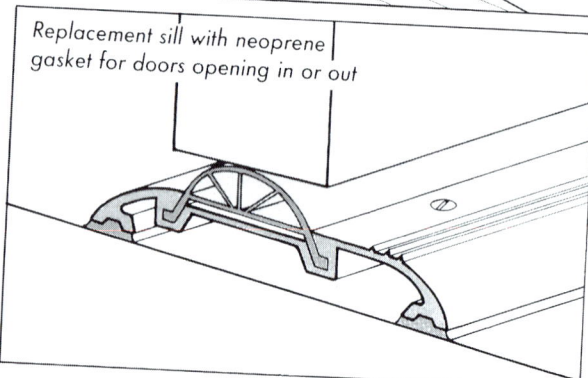

Replacement sill with neoprene gasket for doors opening in or out

4

Listening comprehension.
You will hear five short texts about different points to consider when you renovate a house or flat.
Take notes of what is said about a. pipe insulation; b. reflective foil; c. electric heating; d. showers; e. future systems.

5

Have a look at the "Language Functions" below and complete the four sentences by putting in one of the following expressions:

could be a bit difficult / I can assure you / quite impossible / she may be a bit late

a. I'm quite sure she'll do her best to be on time next Monday, but … I'm afraid.

b. Of course we will make every effort to deliver the machine tools next week, but it … .

c. … that we will use the best material we can find.

d. I know they want a discount of 20%, but I told them it was … .

LANGUAGE FUNCTIONS:
Expressing possibility / capability

I may be a bit late.

It could be a bit difficult.

That's quite impossible.

Yes, that's a possibility.

There might be a possibility to increase your salary after a couple of months.

Some of the work may be routine but I can assure you there will be plenty of new things – plenty of challenges, you know.

We could have used a different process – a cheaper one, maybe – but I think anodising is the best for this part.

6

Listening comprehension.

The job interview (2)

Listen to the dialogue and answer the following questions:

a. What does Ms Penrose say about the company's extrusion presses?

b. Does Audrey like to work with computer controlled machines?

c. What does Ms Penrose say about their managers and computers?

d. What kind of things does the company produce or do?

e. What does Audrey want to see at the end?

f. Who will show Audrey around?

5 An APM in action

1
Listening comprehension and note-taking.
Have a look at the picture below. Listen to the text about an APM system and write down what the machine can do and what it is used for.

A LOOK AT GRAMMAR:

Expressions with "go"

- This clock does not go. (= *does not work*)
- Let's go over it again. (= *let's check it again*)
- Let's go for a walk. (= *let's walk*)
- These colours go well with the office furniture. (= *these colours can be used very well with the office furniture*)
- That tower looks just about ready to go. (= *it might fall down any minute*)
- These bikes go for fifty pounds. (= *are sold for …*)
- This chip goes here, you see – into this slot. (= *it must be put in here*)
- You will go hungry if you don't take enough food with you. (= *become hungry*)
- Go ahead! (= *go on*)
- When the explosives go off, that wall will come down. (= *explode*)
- When that fuse blows, all the lights will go out. (= *stop burning*)

2

Have a look at the sentences below. In each sentence, you can replace the verb with *go*, sometimes together with a preposition. Can you do this? The verbs are underlined.

a. These computers <u>are sold for</u> $2,540.

b. This road <u>leads</u> to Liverpool and Manchester.

c. Would you like me to explain our system to you? – Yes, please <u>do</u>.

d. The fire <u>stopped burning</u> and all of a sudden it got very cold.

e. When all that dynamite explodes, the whole building will <u>come down.</u>

f. The screwdriver <u>fits in</u> here, you know.

g. These colours <u>can be used</u> very well with all our office furniture.

h. That tower in Pisa looks just about ready to <u>fall.</u>

i. This is much too complicated – I'm afraid it won't <u>work.</u>

j. I think we should <u>check</u> our plans again – there must be something wrong.

Life in the country …

3

Pair work. Have a look at the drawing and text on the right and ask one of the other students:

a. What is the APM used for?
b. What do you have to pay for in your community?
c. What is the APM key pad used for?
d. How does the machine show that it has correctly registered the transaction?
e. What does the text say about the size of the display screen?
f. What does the display screen show?
g. Can you explain in English what an allotment garden is?

4

Listening comprehension and pair work.

The job interview (3)

Listen to the dialogue and decide whether the following sentences are TRUE or FALSE:

	TRUE	FALSE
a. Audrey could start next week.	☐	☐
b. She didn't finish college.	☐	☐
c. She will get the job.	☐	☐
d. She doesn't want to work overtime.	☐	☐

Work with another student. One of you writes down the part of Ms Penrose, the other the part of Audrey (listen again to the interview).

Imagine you are the people in the job interview and play the situation.
Use the following expressions:

finish college / if that's all right / well, I don't know / I'll manage / I don't mind / familiar with this kind of work / Have you ever worked with this system?

LANGUAGE FUNCTIONS:

Comparing

Your qualifications are much better than I expected.

There's more work involved than you think.

Such a machine costs more than a hundred thousand pounds.

Can you start earlier? – Well, I don't know ... I think Tuesday would be the earliest.

This extrusion press is similar to the one you saw yesterday.

Is this the kind of job you are looking for?

What sort of computer system did you work with?

That's the best job I have ever had.

5

KEY PAD

The key pad is used to control a menu display and select the accounts to be paid as well as to enter the value of cheques deposited. The digital display combined with an audible 'click' reassures customers that the machine is registering their transaction.

```
Use keypad to select
    payment options

1 Community Charge
2 House Rent
3 Garage Rent
4 Allotment Rent
9 RETURN CARD
```

DISPLAY SCREEN

A large, well lit screen gives clear instructions to guide customers through the account options such as Community Charge, Rent or Mortgage. As each note or coin is accepted, the value is updated on the screen. Large characters and a Liquid Crystal Display (LCD) ensure that it can be easily read, even in bright sunlight or at night.

AUTOMATICALLY THE BEST SOLUTION

6 "Conveyors International"

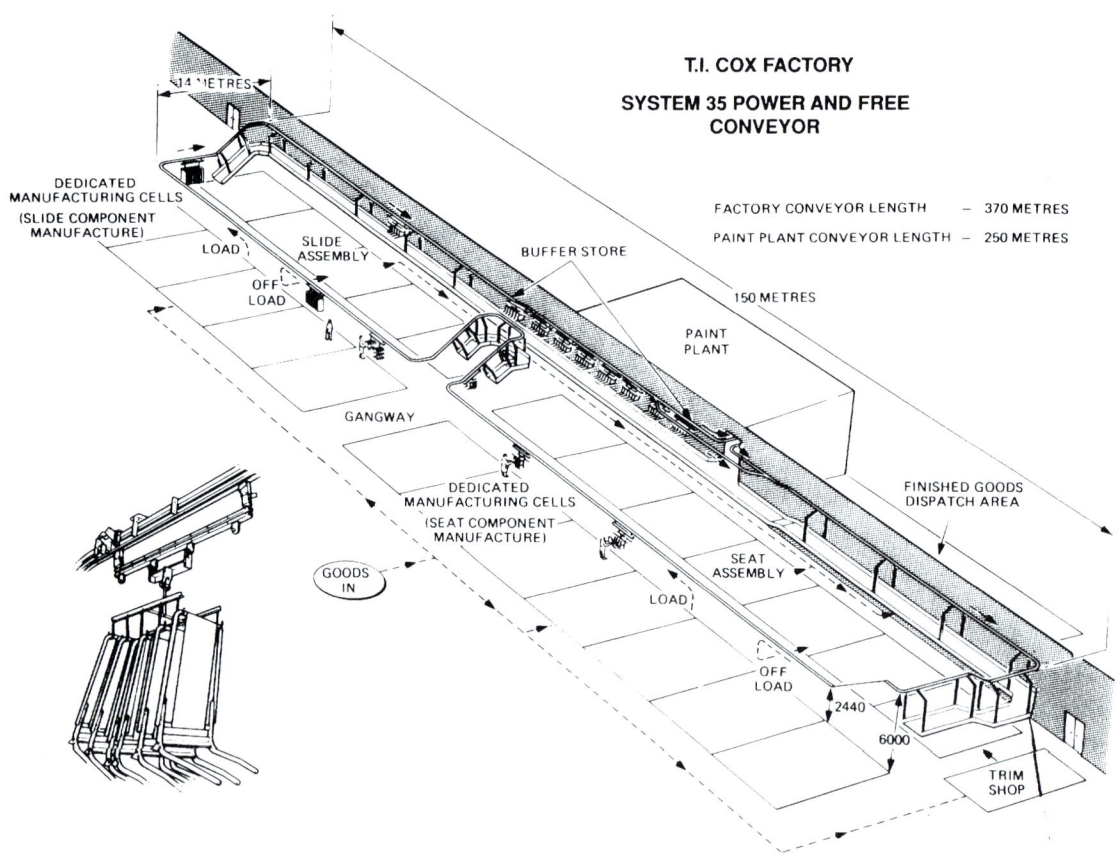

The overhead conveyor layout at the TI Cox factory comprises two integrated Power-and-Free circuits controlled by a Siemens PLC. Illustrated here is an overall view of the plant, showing the relative position of the main circuit, dedicated manufacturing cells and the electrophoretic paint plant, which houses the second circuit.

6

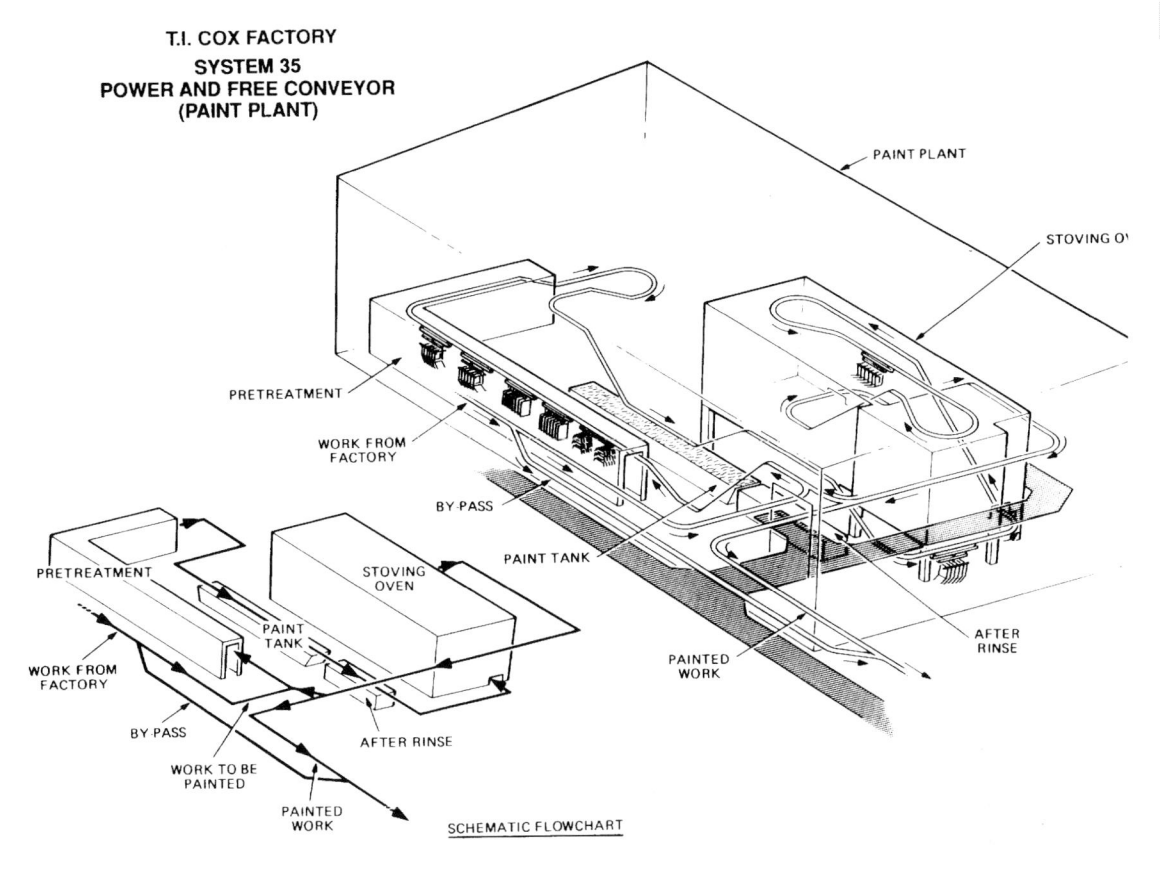

**T.I. COX FACTORY
SYSTEM 35
POWER AND FREE CONVEYOR
(PAINT PLANT)**

PAINT PLANT
STOVING O[VEN]
PRETREATMENT
WORK FROM FACTORY
BY-PASS
PAINT TANK
PAINTED WORK
AFTER RINSE

PRETREATMENT
STOVING OVEN
PAINT TANK
WORK FROM FACTORY
BY-PASS
AFTER RINSE
WORK TO BE PAINTED
PAINTED WORK

SCHEMATIC FLOWCHART

1
Listening comprehension.

Listen to the recording. You will hear two short texts describing a conveyor system for a car seat manufacturer. Decide which text (a or b) belongs to which drawing (above or on the left).

▲ *An automatic power-and-free system for the assembly/finishing of gearbox parts.*

37

6
Conveyors International

Conveyors International is a leading force in the world of overhead handling. A talent for innovation, coupled with the application of sound precision engineering techniques and dependability in the field, has gained the company an enviable reputation across manufacturing industry. And it's a reputation that continues to grow!

Systems designed and installed by CI can be found in applications ranging from microelectronics assembly and the manufacture of foodstuffs, to large-scale garment storage, the finishing of aluminium extrusions and the production of large steel fabrications.

CI's range of standard overhead conveyors offers maximum operational flexibility and accommodates a broad range of needs. For special purposes, the company's design department prides itself on finding cost effective solutions to the trickiest handling problems. Whatever your overhead conveying requirement, CI can handle it!

2

Questions on the text. Have a look at the text and the drawing on the left and answer these questions:

a. Where can CI conveyor systems be found?
b. What do they say is their special talent?
c. Why does the company have "an enviable reputation"?
d. What sort of companies use CI conveyor systems?
e. If a company has special problems, which department is responsible?
f. What kind of applications can you see in the drawing?

3

Writing exercise: Leaving a message to a colleague.

You have to make a visit to a company in a nearby town. Before you leave the office, you write down a message for your colleague:

a. The copier in your office is out of order. Ask your colleague to phone the manufacturing company and tell them to send somebody to repair the copier as soon as possible. You have already tried to phone them but the line was busy.

b. Tell your colleague about what time you will probably be back at the office. Ask her/him to make a note of all incoming phone calls and messages.

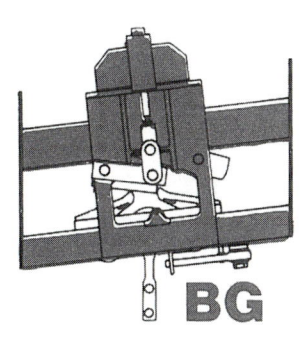

Stop-station on free-track.
Bloqueur gravitaire sur voie-libre.
Sperre für Freibahn.

4

Listening comprehension.

A look at the shop floor

Listen to the dialogue and decide which answer (a or b) is correct:

A The woman in the dialogue has
   a. a lot of experience with aluminium products.
   b. hardly any experience with aluminium products.

B The extrusion press they have in the company
   a. has just been bought and is brand-new.
   b. is old but can still produce good quality.

C Their CIM system
   a. is used for the manufacturing process.
   b. will be put into operation later.

6 A LOOK AT GRAMMAR:

Expressions with "get"

- If you add up all the figures, you will get 1,000. *(= reach by calculation)*
- Do you get my point? *(= do you see what I mean?)*
- When do I get to see the new plant? *(= when do I have a chance ...)*
- I'll get the technician to show you the paper machine. *(= I will tell the technician to show you ...)*
- We must get it repaired! *(= we must find somebody to repair it)*
- The police got him last month. *(= caught him)*
- This train is very slow – when will we get to Glasgow? *(= arrive in)*
- Let's get going! *(= let's start)*
- Do you understand what I'm getting at? *(= ... what I want to say)*
- I can't tell you at the moment, but I'll get back to you. *(= I'll speak or write to you again later)*
- We must get on with our work! *(= we must continue our work)*

5

Complete the sentences below by putting in *get* or *got*:

a. It's quite important that you ... the report typed by Monday.

b. I've ... more than enough work on my desk.

c. My son is hoping that he will ... a mountain bike for his birthday.

d. Yesterday evening we... home very late.

e. First you will have to go and ... permission from our chief engineer.

f. Did you ... the trolley designs last week?

g. It's very important that you ... him to go with us.

h. Ask Mary – I think she's ... a very good English-German dictionary.

i. It's no problem to find it – I've ... all the maintenance reports on file.

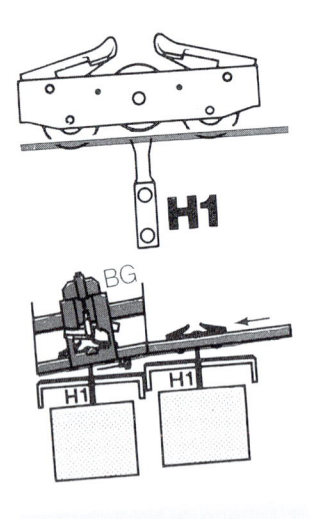

H1 – the basic trolley

LANGUAGE FUNCTIONS:

Drawing conclusions

These are the report's main conclusions.

She came to the conclusion that something had to be done.

This extrusion press is fairly old. I'm afraid downtime will be a big problem. – That means our output will decrease, doesn't it? – Yes, I'm afraid it does.

This proves we need a new extrusion press – and soon.

In that case, we'll have to start planning – we have to allow about four months for delivery.

6

Have another look at the "Language Functions" on the left and complete the sentences with a suitable verb (*come, decrease, do, plan* or *prove*):

a. Could you … me a favour?

b. We'll have to … the amount we spend on advertising.

c. All our tests … that this machine is the best.

d. I like to … my summer holiday as early as possible.

e. Most of our machine tools … from Sweden and Norway.

f. For the examination, you'll have to … all the arithmetic problems on that page.

g. Electric motors … in many sizes – from very small to quite big.

7

Into or *onto*?

a. The cat jumped … the table.

b. They walked through the big door … the building.

c. When you heat it, water changes … steam.

d. Don't worry, we'll look … the matter.

A CLEAN DESK IS A SIGN OF A SICK MIND!

7 Aluminium extraction

OBTAINING ALUMINIUM

The extraction of aluminium from bauxite is carried out in two distinct stages. The first stage involves producing alumina from bauxite. Depending upon where it is mined, bauxite has a variety of impurities in its make-up, generally oxides of iron, silicon and titanium. By crushing the bauxite and dissolving it in a hot solution of caustic soda, the impurities can be removed leaving a sodium aluminate solution which is then decomposed into pure alumina trihydrate and caustic soda. The trihydrate separates out from the caustic soda and is passed through high temperature rotary kilns to drive off the chemically combined water content to leave alumina powder.

The second stage involves reducing the alumina to metallic aluminium in electrolytic cells containing molten cryolite, at temperatures between 950° and 1 000°C. The alumina dissolves in the liquid through which a high DC current of 40 to 180 kA is passed at a low voltage (4 to 5V). This causes the alumina to split into aluminium and oxygen. The aluminium sinks to the bottom of the cell and the oxygen rises to the anode combining with the carbon from which the anode is made, to form carbon dioxide. The molten aluminium is siphoned off periodically, and the alumina is kept constantly topped up to keep the process continuous □

1
Questions on the text.

Obtaining aluminium:

a. What kind of impurities can you find in bauxite?

b. How can these impurities be removed?

c. What do you have at the end of the first stage?

d. What is the temperature used in the second stage of the extraction process?

e. What kind of current is used in the second stage?

f. What does the alumina split into?

g. What happens then with the aluminium?

2
Read the text above again and decide whether a or b is correct:

1. Titanium is
   a. a metallic element.
   b. an oxide of aluminium.

2. Caustic soda is
   a. made from silicone.
   b. strongly alkaline in water.

3. DC current
   a. changes direction very often.
   b. flows in one direction.

A LOOK AT GRAMMAR:

"Used to" / "didn't use to"

USE(D) TO
+ Infinitive

I used to play soccer when I was younger.
 (= ... but now I don't play it any longer)
She used to smoke a lot but she finally gave it up.
We didn't use to have computers when we started our business.
Did you use to live in Bristol? *(= in the past)*
Didn't they use to make their own components?

NOTE: In these sentences, "use(d) to" refers to something that happened in the past, or was a habit in the past.

USED TO
+ -ing form

I'm used to getting up early – I do it every day.
 (= it's normal for me)
When you travel to England, you should get used to driving on the left. *(= you should learn to drive on the left)*
She'll get used to it. *(= she will learn to live with it)*
She isn't used to working overtime.
 (= it's not normal for her, she hasn't done it very often)
Are you used to working night shifts?

NOTE: Here, "used to" means "familiar with".

In all these sentences, you can also use "accustomed to":
We must get used to working with computers / We must get accustomed to working with computers.

Aircraft windshield frame

7

3

Listening comprehension, note-taking and pair work.

Back in the office

Listen to the dialogue once or twice. One student writes down what Ms Penrose says, the other writes down what Audrey says. Read the dialogue aloud and play the situation.

While listening to the dialogue, pay attention to the following details:

a. Was Mr Mill helpful?

b. What about the old press?

c. Are they using CIM?

LANGUAGE FUNCTIONS:

Expressing pleasure / displeasure

I do like the new design.

I like the look of their latest product.

I'm very happy with the new job.

I feel wonderful here.

What I don't like is the constant noise in this room – we'll have to do something about it.

If there's one thing I hate it's listening to his complaints.

All right, that's enough – we don't have time to discuss this now.

Stop it! Why don't you wait until the managing director is back – it's not my business.

4

Have another look at the grammar explanations on page 43 and the "Language Functions" on the left. Complete the sentences below by putting in the correct form of *use(d)*:

a. It takes a while to get … to the new designs.

b. I'm surprised to see you smoking – you didn't … to.

c. Didn't they … to build their sports cars by hand?

d. She … to read a lot of science fiction stories, but she never gets the time now.

e. What they don't like is working under pressure – they can't get … to it.

f. When was the last time you … the CAD program?

g. Munchies? That nice little coffee shop, you mean? Yes, I know it very well. I … to go there a lot when I was in London.

5
Listening comprehension and note-taking.

Listen to Alice and Henry talking about aluminium foil. Write down how aluminium foil is used nowadays.

6
Expressing your feelings and ideas – How do you say it?

a. You are in a meeting. Some colleagues start smoking. What do you say?

b. You think it's time for a break. How do you say this?

c. Somebody has explained technical details, but you have not understood all the points he has made. How do you ask him for more information?

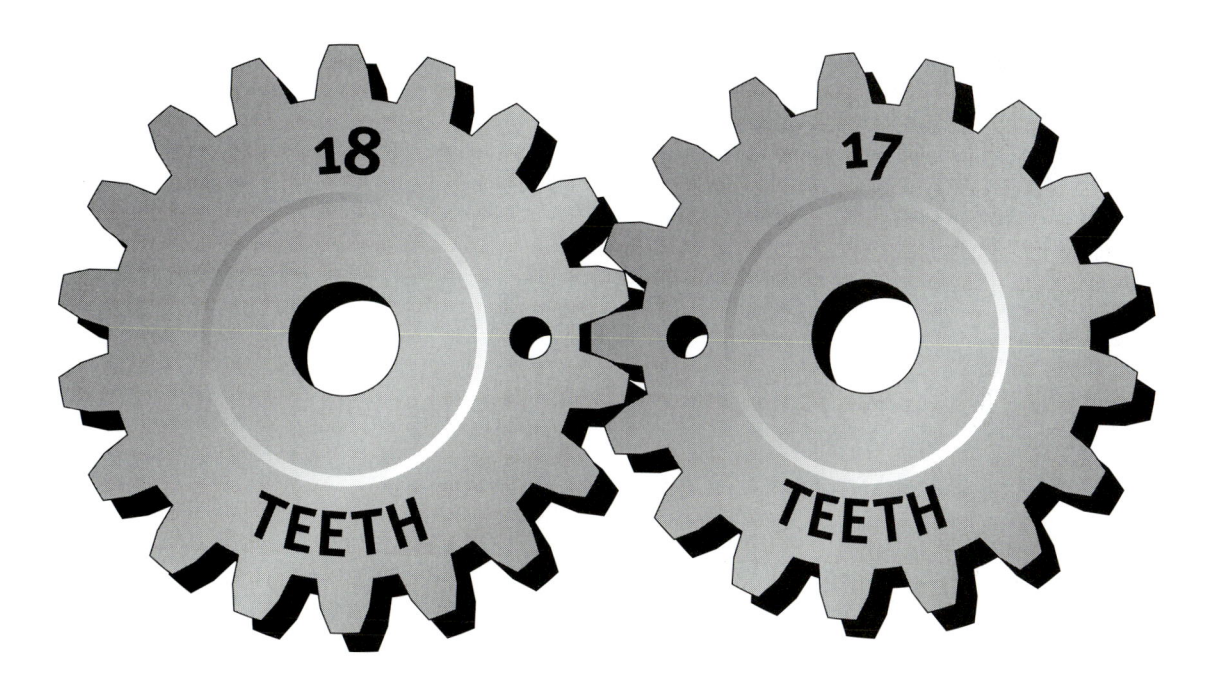

Here are two gear wheels. One of them has 18 teeth, while the other has 17. Each of them has a mark in the form of a circle which denotes their starting position. How many revolutions does each wheel undergo before the starting circles come to face each other again?

8 Aluminium extrusion

Volume production commences

Final evaluation and approval

1

Listening comprehension and group work.

a. Have a look at the illustrations and text on this and on the next page. After that, listen to the conversation (Linda and Peter, two young technicians, are asking Mr Bellows some questions about aluminium extrusion in four different fields of application).

b. Each group chooses one or two fields (aviation / car industry / conveyors / packaging) and takes notes of what is said in that particular field.

c. One student in each group writes down the notes and reports the result to the whole class.

d. The results are discussed, and each student can mention additional points, particularly general benefits of aluminium extrusion.

e. The whole class listens again to the conversation and tries to find some points that might have been missed.

Two important areas where aluminium is used are conveyor systems and car frames. Some cars will have 100% extruded aluminium frames, some experts say. The use of aluminium will reduce weight and cost – normal steel frames, for example, currently involve over 2000 welding points, aluminium frames would reduce that number to about 40.

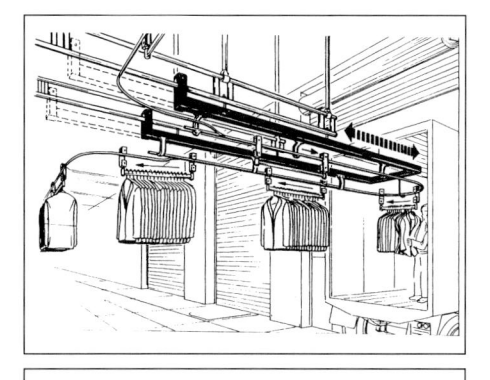

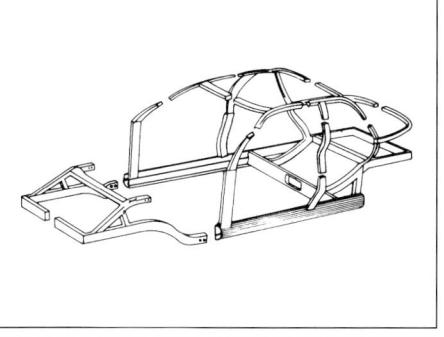

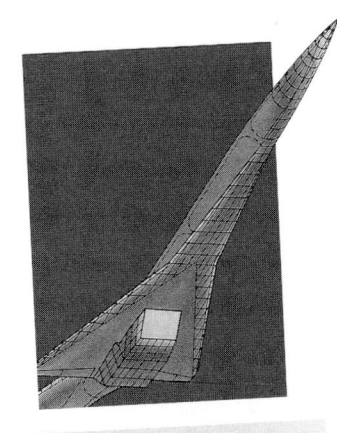

Advanced material systems will be developed as an integral part of the design process for such applications as the national aerospace plane and aseptic packaging to preserve food supplies for developing countries.

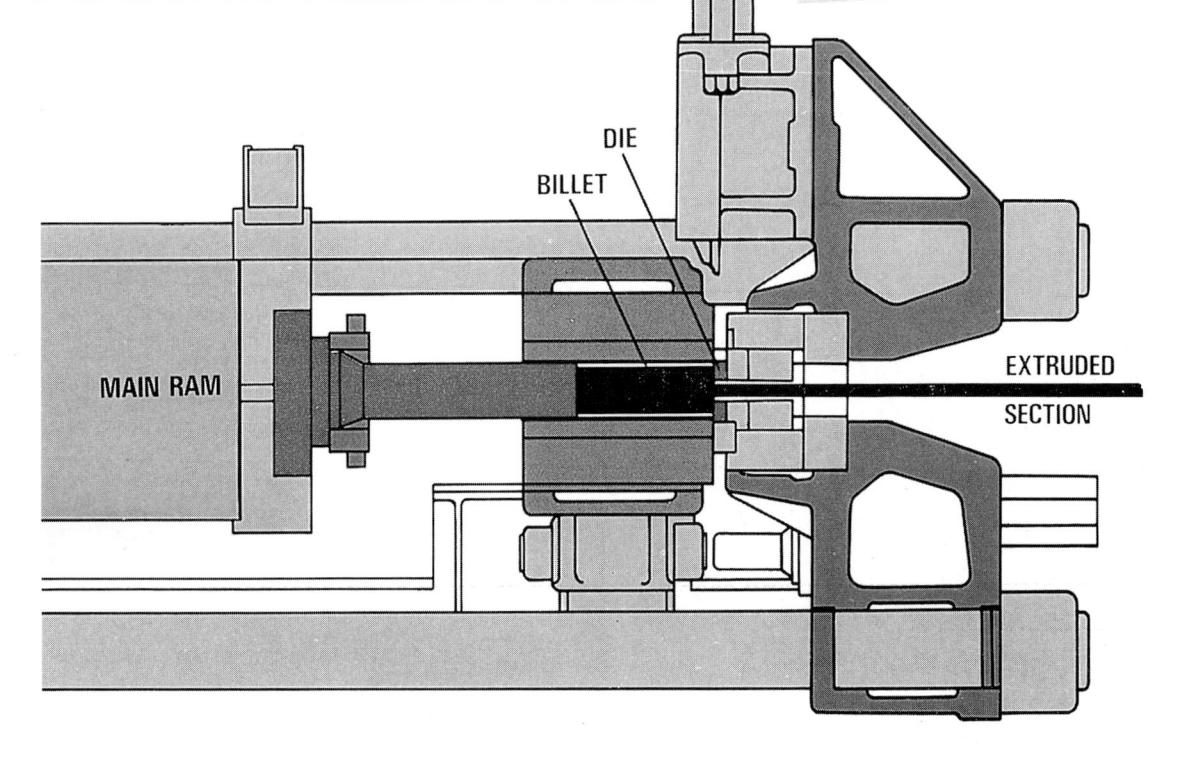

MAIN RAM

BILLET

DIE

EXTRUDED SECTION

8 A LOOK AT GRAMMAR:

The use of articles with "double", "half", "quite", "such", "twice"

- They sold the generator at double the price. (= *two times as much*)
- They used more than half a ton of packing material.
- That was quite a surprise. (= *really a surprise*)
- Quite a few people came to our international sales conference. (= *many*)
- She was such an experienced saleswoman. (= *very experienced*)
- That was such an interesting film! (= *very interesting*)
- Have you ever seen such a beautiful car? (= *a car as beautiful as that*)
- Such a dictionary is difficult to find. (= *a dictionary like that*)
- The new motor must be serviced twice a year. (= *two times a year*)
- Take these pills twice a day. (= *two times a day*)
- She earns twice the money now. (= *a hundred percent more than before*)

2

Put in *double*, *half* or *such*:

a. I must warn you – … a job does not pay very well.

b. You should have called me … an hour earlier.

c. I'm having … a hard time learning that new computer language.

d. This is not the only story of a computer virus infection – … cases are reported every week.

e. You're blocking the road. Why don't you park your car … a metre to the left?

f. It was … a surprise!

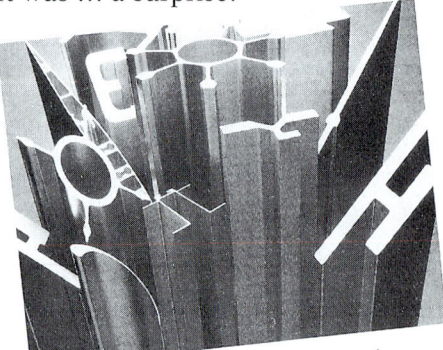

A selection of high strength aluminium extrusions for defence and aerospace applications

3

Grammar repetition. Find the correct form of the words in brackets:

a. We (have) an interesting conversation with Mr Bellows yesterday morning.

b. Can you tell me where I can (find) the recycling plant?

c. When she (arrive) at the workshop that morning, the others were already waiting for her.

d. I'm very tired – I (type) letters all day.

e. I (know) John since he was ten.

f. She (go) to the conference last week because she wanted to get some useful information on aluminium extrusion.

g. He (not finish) the accident report yet.

h. The new security system (be) in operation since last Monday.

i. Charles (be unemployed) since he lost his job as a drilling-machine operator.

j. I (wait) for that letter since Tuesday.

LANGUAGE FUNCTIONS:

Expressing necessity / obligation

We need a new table to put the fax machine on.
Do I have to use this fax machine?
The carburettor needs repairing.
We must finish the job.
I'm afraid we can't do without a renovation programme – it's got to be done.
You needn't wait – there's another fax machine in Mr Mill's office.
A new copier may be needed.
He tried to avoid answering my questions.

5

Have a look at the "Language Functions" above and put in *got* or *must*:

a. I'm afraid it's … to be translated.

b. … they make so much noise?

c. I … remember to clean that laser printer.

4

Listening comprehension.

First day at work

Listen to the dialogue and write down the part of Tim:

Audrey: You're Tim – Tim Gilbert, aren't you?

Tim: …

Audrey: Thank you.

Tim: …

Audrey: Yes, thank you, I'll do that. Could you tell me where I can find a fax machine? I have to send a small drawing to a Bristol office – one of the new window profiles, you know.

Tim: …

Audrey: Yes …

Tim: …

Audrey: Thank you. I'll take care of it right away.

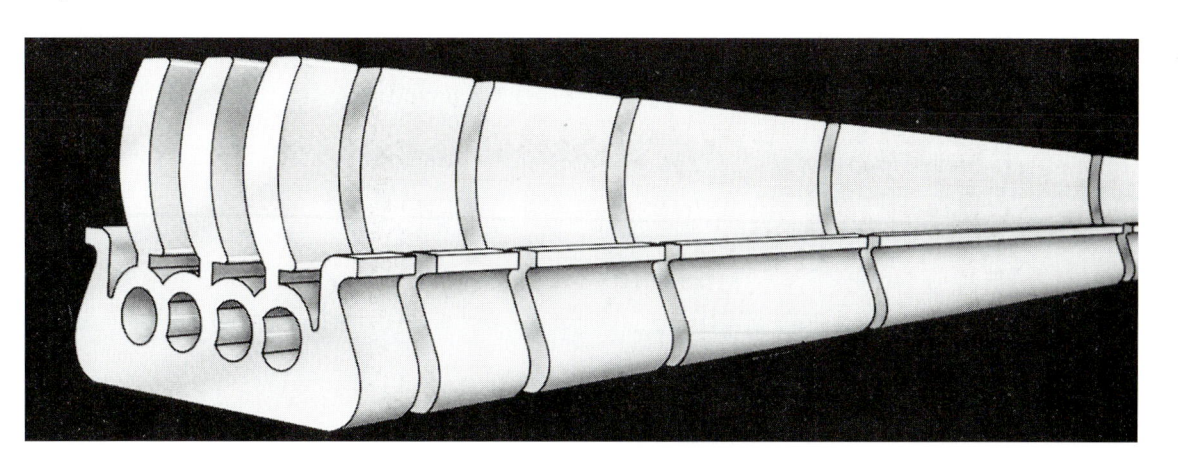

9 Working with steel

Figure 1

t = sheet thickness in mm
d = weld diameter [d = 5√t]
Note: All dimensions shown are the minimum.
* For sheet thicknesses ≤ 3.0 mm.

Figure 2
Examples of rivets used in sheet metal fabrication

Steel drive pin rivet is set by a single hammer blow.

Blind rivets are ideal for limited access installations. Minimum back-up clearance is needed.

Semi-tubular and full tubular rivets before and after setting.

Full Tubular

Semi Tubular

Figure 3

Types of clinched sections

1

Listening comprehension, group work and note-taking

Have a look at the illustrations on this page and the text on the next page. Galvatite, a zinc coated steel, is a product of British Steel.

On the recording, you will hear a text about the many different methods of joining steel together, such as mechanical fixing or welding. Listen to the text once or twice and take notes of the methods mentioned.

Compare the results of each group.

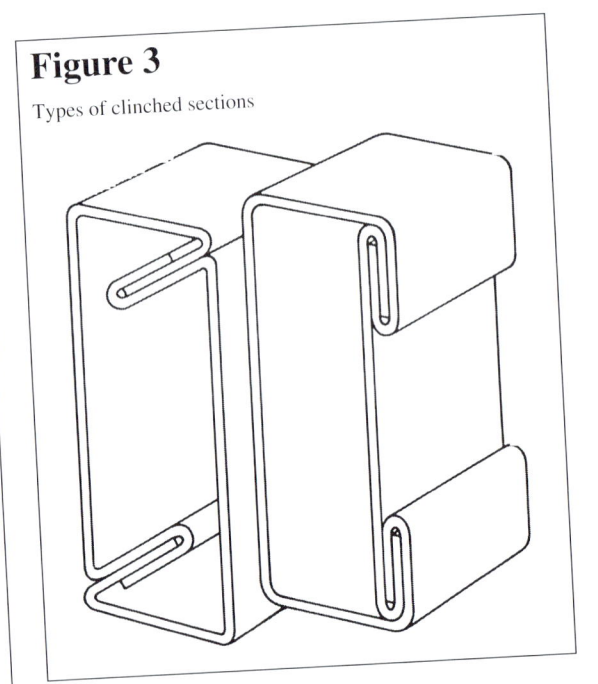

Galvatite can be welded using conventional fusion and resistance welding techniques:

SPOT WELDING

The distance from the edge of the component to the centre of the weld should not be less than 1.25d, where d is the initial weld diameter (figure 1). The use of edge distances less than the recommended values will have a negative influence on weld quality.

SEAM WELDING

It is generally considered that the resistance seam welding of zinc coated steel is a critical process. Conventional seam welding of zinc coatings is therefore not recommended. However, some new methods are now available using a number of techniques which allow effective seam welding without the problems of previous methods.

PROJECTION WELDING

Galvatite can be projection welded satisfactorily, provided that projection dimensions and welding machine settings are controlled closely.

STUD WELDING

This is a high speed, semi-automatic process in which the connection is produced by an arc between the metal stud and the workpiece. The metal stud and workpiece are then brought together under pressure.

FUSION WELDING

Fusion welding processes can be used to join the various types of Galvatite. Techniques and procedures used are similar to those used for uncoated steel, such as gas welding, manual metal-arc welding, and metal active-gas welding (MAG). These processes can result in a certain amount of damage to the zinc coating in the area of the weld, but this can be minimised by the choice of process and welding conditions. For example, coating damage is much less with metal active-gas welding than in either gas or manual metal-arc welding.

LASER WELDING

While resistance welding is the most favoured technique for the assembly of sheet metal structures, there are opportunities for using alternative technologies such as laser welding. A typical example is the welding of automotive floor pans.

9 A LOOK AT GRAMMAR:

Adverbs of degree

FAIRLY   The report she sent us was fairly good.
He's a fairly good salesman.

NOTE: In these sentences, *fairly* means "OK, but not perfect". *Fairly* is more negative than *quite*.

QUITE   Her lecture on mechanics was quite good.
He handles the new computer quite well.

NOTE: Here, *quite* means "not bad at all, but still less than perfect".

Stop! The container is quite full!
I am not quite finished with my report.

NOTE: Here, *quite* indicates 'completely', 'absolutely'.

PRETTY   She was pretty tired after the meeting. (= *very tired*)
That will cost you a pretty penny! (= *quite a lot of money*)
I'm pretty sure they'll do it. (= *quite sure*)

NOTE: *Pretty* in this sense is informal British English.

RATHER   I'm feeling rather tired. (= *more than a little tired*)
We're having rather cold weather for May. (= *quite cold*)
That's rather good. (= *quite good*)

NOTE: *Rather* is usually stronger than *quite* or *fairly*. It is also used in some special forms:
- I'd rather go home. (= *I would prefer to go home*)
- It costs about ten dollars, or rather, ten dollars and sixty cents. (= *more exactly*)

Typical automotive pressings involving stretching and deep drawing

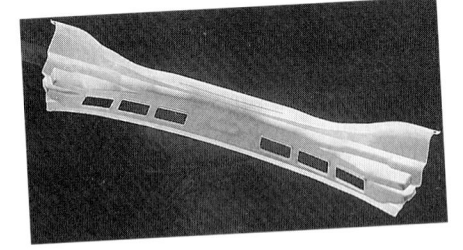

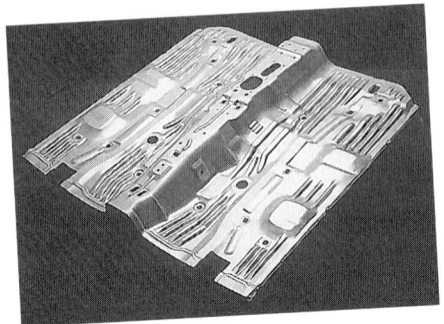

52

2
Writing exercise.
Do you remember what you have learned about aluminium in Unit 7 and Unit 8? Write a short summary with all the facts you remember. (Extraction? Uses? Properties?)

3
Have a look at the grammar explanations of this unit (page 52) and the "Language Functions" below and put in *quite* or *very*:

a. Be careful when you go down those stairs – the ceiling is … low.

b. There was … a large crowd waiting outside the theatre.

c. She still hasn't … finished the report, has she?

d. Here's the computer print-out you wanted. – Thanks … much.

LANGUAGE FUNCTIONS:

Giving advice / warning people

If I were you, I wouldn't go to that agency.

Be careful! That plug is damaged.

Mind your head! The ceiling is very low.

Mind that step – it's loose.

Make sure you get that fax through by six o'clock.

We'd better be careful – there's a storm coming.

I can't really recommend that.

They really shouldn't take so much money for this flat.

I don't think you should stay in Bristol.

4
Listening comprehension.

Finding a flat in Coventry

Listen to the dialogue between Tim and Audrey and mark the sentences below with TRUE or FALSE:

	TRUE	FALSE
Audrey …		
a. has a lot of problems in her company.	☐	☐
b. has already found a flat in Coventry.	☐	☐
c. has had a look at the local newspaper.	☐	☐
d. wants to go to an estate agency and then ask around in the company.	☐	☐

Listen again and find the correct sentences for the ones you have marked wrongly.

10 Applying for a job

1
Written exercise / discussion.

On the next three pages, you will find an application form as it is used by many international companies.

On a separate sheet of paper write down your own data you would need to fill in a form like this (you may use your imagination). Discuss the purpose of such forms:

- Are they really necessary?
- Why do companies use such forms?
- What do you think about the information they want? Is it too much?
- What kind of information do you think companies have a right to get? (Why?)

ic

INTERNATIONAL PETROLEUM COMPANY PLC. • EXPLORATION AND PRODUCTION

Application Form

Application for employment in Indonesia

PLEASE COMPLETE THE FORM, SIGN AND RETURN IT TO:

IC EMPLOYMENT SERVICE
PO Box 5399
Edinburgh EH6 8AY

	Last	First	Middle
FULL NAME (block letters)			

ADDRESS (block letters)

	Area Code	Number		Area Code	Number
PHONE (home)			**PHONE** (work)		

NATIONALITY

DATES AVAILABLE FOR INTERVIEW

JOB HISTORY
Please give details of your most recent employment first. There is additional space on the next page if you wish to add more information.

CURRENT (OR MOST RECENT) EMPLOYER'S NAME AND ADDRESS	TYPE OF BUSINESS			May we contact the company? Yes ☐ No ☐
	Month/Year	From	To	NUMBER OF YEARS
POSITION	NOTICE PERIOD			CURRENT ANNUAL SALARY (exclusive of bonus and benefits)
DUTIES / RESPONSIBILITIES (Please include details of particular skills or specialised experience)	REASON FOR LEAVING			

PREVIOUS EMPLOYER'S NAME AND ADDRESS	TYPE OF BUSINESS			May we contact the company? Yes ☐ No ☐
	Month/Year	From	To	NUMBER OF YEARS
POSITION	FINAL ANNUAL SALARY	REASON FOR LEAVING		
DUTIES / RESPONSIBILITIES (Please include details of particular skills or specialised experience)				

10

GENERAL INFORMATION

| DATE OF BIRTH | Month | Day | Year | AGE | Do you hold a valid driving licence? | Yes ☐ | No ☐ |

| FAMILY STATUS | Single ☐ | Married ☐ | Legally Separated ☐ | Divorced ☐ | How many legal dependants do you have (including wife)? |

| | SPOKEN | | WRITTEN | | |
| Are you fluent in English? | Yes ☐ | No ☐ | Yes ☐ | No ☐ | Please give details of other language skills |

| Have you previously applied for employment with IC? | Yes ☐ | No ☐ | If yes, when and to whom? |

ON WHAT DATE WOULD YOU BE AVAILABLE FOR WORK?

FOR THOSE WHO HAVE WORKED IN INDONESIA BEFORE

| EMPLOYER & ADDRESS | From   To |
| | Month/Year |

EDUCATION

SECONDARY Name of School	Qualifications obtained				
TECHNICAL COLLEGE Name of College	Certificates and diplomas awarded			Number of Years	Year Awarded
APPRENTICESHIP Company and location	Describe field			Number of Years	Final Year
UNIVERSITY / POST GRADUATE STUDY Name(s)	Specialisation	Degree	Class	Number of Years	Year Awarded
	Specialisation	Degree	Class	Number of Years	Year Awarded

| OTHER TRAINING OR COURSES
Place | Description of training or courses (including dates and duration) |

10

FORMER EMPLOYERS AND ADDRESSES	TYPE OF BUSINESS	POSITION	FROM Month/Year	TO Month/Year	NUMBER OF YEARS

LEISURE INTERESTS AND ACTIVITIES

ADDITIONAL INFORMATION
Please use this space for any additional job or other information you think may be of interest.

I apply for employment with IC, and certify that the statements in this application are true. I authorise the Company to seek any information desired in connection with the application, and agree to undergo a medical examination on request.

SIGNATURE OF APPLICANT

DATE   Month   Day   Year

10

2

Listening comprehension.

On the recording, you are going to hear three young people – Sarah, Andrew and Simon – talking about their jobs, training and future plans. Make a table like the one below and put in the information (in short form).

	SARAH	ANDREW	SIMON
Present job / workplace			
Training			
Future plans			

A LOOK AT GRAMMAR:
"Need" / "needn't"

- The laser printer drums need cleaning. *(= must be cleaned)*
- Does she really need to go? *(= is it really necessary …)*
- I think we need to call in an expert. *(= it is necessary to …)*
- Do you still need the dictionary I gave you yesterday?

- You don't need to bring sandwiches – we can go to a café.
  ALSO: You needn't bring sandwiches – we can go to a café.
- We didn't need to go to the supermarket because we had plenty of food.

NOTE: It is very important to remember that *mustn't* and *needn't* have completely different meanings: You mustn't wear a hard hat *(= it's forbidden to wear a hard hat)*. You needn't wear a hard hat *(= it's not necessary to wear a hard hat)*.
Must I do it? – No, you needn't *(= it's not necessary)*.

3
Have a look at the grammar explanations above and complete the sentences below by putting in *mustn't* or *needn't*:

a. Electric appliances … be exposed to rain or moisture.

b. To reduce the risk of electric shock, the back cover of the TV … be removed unless the power cord is disconnected.

c. You … return the operating manual until tomorrow morning.

d. Children … be allowed to put anything into an electric socket.

e. The electric plug … be touched with wet hands.

f. The voltage conversion is automatic – it … be set by hand.

Working on the building site …

10 Looking at an application and a CV

103 Sydney Street
London SW3 6NJ

The Manager
Lemmington Motors PLC
24 North John Street
Liverpool L2 9RP   October 27, 19..

Dear Sir/Madam

In response to your advertisement in today's *Daily Herald* I am writing to apply for the post of Assistant Motor Mechanic.

As you will see from my enclosed curriculum vitae I have already completed a one-year course in mechanical welding and I have some fundamental knowlegde of mechanics. I am particularly interested in this position as I am keen to learn more about the engineering side of the business.

If you think that I might be suitable, I would very much welcome the opportunity of coming to Liverpool to talk about the job.

Yours sincerely
Kevin Harrington
Kevin Harrington

CURRICULUM VITAE

NAME:	Kevin Harrington
DATE OF BIRTH:	May 2, 19..
ADDRESS:	103 Sydney Street London SW3 6NJ
TEL.NO:	71-354 2265
EDUCATION:	St. Paul's Comprehensive School, Kensington London Polytechnic
EXAMINATIONS:	GCSE in English, Maths, Biology, French and Physics
	Diploma in Mechanical Welding
INTERESTS:	Writing programs for computers Swimming and tennis
AVAILABILITY:	Immediate

The Manager
Lemmington Motors PLC
24 North John Street
Liverpool L2 9RP

4

A puzzle with numbers

In the pyramids on the right, the number in one box is equal to the sum of the two numbers in the boxes just beneath. For example, in the first three squares, "A" is equal to "B" plus "C". Complete all the numbers in each of the pyramids.

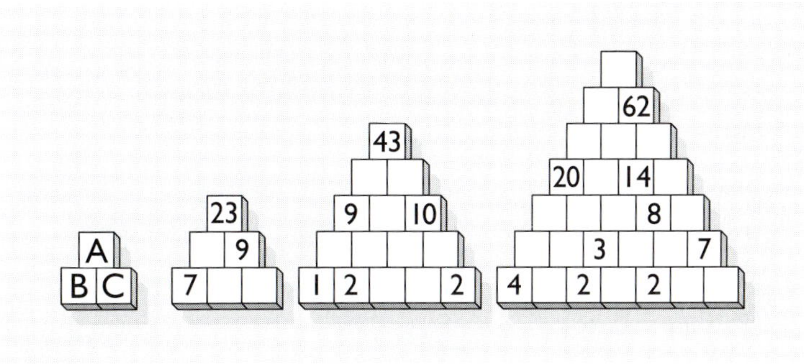
A
B C
23
9
7
43
9 10
1 2 2
62
20 14
8
3 7
4 2 2

5

Written exercise.

Have a look at the advertisement on the right.
Write a letter of application and a CV or data sheet.

Use expressions like

a. in reply to …

b. I refer to …

c. I would like to apply for …

d. I completed …

e. I graduated from …

f. I attended …

g. I look forward to …

h. I'm interested in …

We require the services of an

AUTOMATION SPECIALIST

to plan the implementation of our automation programme; to define the details of automatic functions; and to manage the automation project paying special attention to equipment quality and system integration with other control systems.

The successful applicant must have a university degree, with at least five years' practical experience.

Please send CV to:
CALEX ENGINEERING PLC
19 Church Street
Warwick DT43 5BS

6

Have a look at the "Language Functions" below and complete these sentences by putting in *had* or *would*:

a. If it were not so cold, the snow … melt.

b. If we … shown her the report, she … have called the maintenance department right away.

c. If I were you, I … not invite him to the housewarming party.

d. If I … … enough money, I … have bought a sports car.

e. She told us that she … return soon.

f. … you hand me that screwdriver, please?

g. Tomorrow afternoon? No, I'm sorry, but that … be too late.

7

Listening comprehension.

Inviting friends and colleagues

Listen to the dialogue and decide which of these statements is TRUE or FALSE:

	TRUE	FALSE
a. Audrey has found a nice flat.	☐	☐
b. The housewarming party is at a local hotel.	☐	☐
c. It is quite difficult to find a nice flat.	☐	☐
d. One of the people lives in a company apartment.	☐	☐
e. The company always helps them to find a flat.	☐	☐
f. Ms Penrose has got a flat she wants to rent.	☐	☐

LANGUAGE FUNCTIONS:

Expressing a condition

If you come, I'll help you.

If you had invited him, he would have come.

I'll stay in Bristol unless I can find an apartment here.

I'll be angry if I'm not invited to the housewarming party.

If you had had a look at the local newspaper, you would have found an apartment.

We shouldn't wait too long with our renovation programme.

The snow will melt unless the weather gets colder.

If unprotected, steel corrodes.

8

Put in *any* or *some*:

a. He doesn't drink ... alcohol, not even beer or wine.

b. ... of the books he gave me last week were quite interesting.

c. There were ... letters on my desk when I arrived.

d. I'd like ... information about that new CPU.

9

Have another look at the grammar explanations of this unit (p. 59) and make sentences according to this example:

EXAMPLE: Must we oil the machines today? (next week)
– No, you don't need to oil the machines today, you can oil them next week.

a. Must we write all the reports now? (Monday or Tuesday)

b. Must she speak with the chief engineer today? (tomorrow afternoon)

c. Must we test the brakes this morning? (when you are at the garage tomorrow)

d. Must I check the milling machines right away? (later)

e. Must they replace the chip before they start work? (afterwards)

"What do you mean, you're tired?"

Testing Your Language   Part One

A. Reading comprehension

Below are the specifications for four different radio cassette recorders. Read the questions first. Then scan the specifications given, and choose the radio cassette recorder which is most suitable, according to the information given. Mark the correct answer (a, b, c or d):

Model A

Type	Stereo multiband radio cassette recorder
Circuitry	95 transistors, 65 diodes, 17 ICs, 7 LEDs, 1 FET
Power source	Batteries, DC 13.5 V (UM-1 x 9)
	Back-up power supply (for tuner memory) DC 3 V (UM-3 "AA" dry cell x 2)
	AC 110 – 120 V/220 – 240 V (switchable)
	50 – 60 Hz
	Car battery (thru car adaptor)
Output	28 W maximum (14 W + 14 W)
Power consumption	42 W
Speakers	140 mm cone (2)
	50 mm cone (2)
	170 mm Passive Radiator (1)

Tape Recorder Section

Built-in microphones	Electret condenser microphones (2)
Tape speed	4.8 cm/sec
Recording system	AC bias
Erasing system	AC erase
Recording time	90 minutes (C-90 cassette, both directions)
Frequency response (AUX)	LH tape: 35 – 12,500 Hz
	CrO_2 tape: 35 – 13,000 Hz
	METAL tape: 35 – 16,000 Hz
Signal-to-noise ratio (AUX)	54 dB (LH tape, Dolby NR OFF)
	65 dB (METAL tape, Dolby NR ON, PEAK LEVEL)
Wow and flutter	0.038% (WRMS)

Radio Section

Frequency ranges	FM: 87.5 – 108 MHz
	MW 525 – 1,605 kHz
	LW 150 – 285 kHz
Antennas	Whip antenna for FM
	Ferrite bar antenna for MW and LW and LW External antenna terminals for FM
Dimensions (W x H x D)	588 x 325 x 163 (mm)
Weight	8.6 kg
Accessories	AC power cord 1
	Cassette tape 1

The specifications and external appearance of this set are subject to change without prior notice.

Model B

Type	Stereo multiband radio cassette recorder
Circuitry	27 transistors, 19 diodes, 6 ICs, 5 LEDs, 1 FET
Power source	Batteries, DC 9 V (UM-2 x 6)
	AC 220 V 50 – 60 Hz
	Household AC power (thru AC adaptor)
Output	5 W maximum (2.5 W + 2.5 W)
Speakers	92 mm cone (2)

Tape Recorder Section

Built-in microphones	Electret condenser microphones
Tape speed	4.8 cm/sec
Recording system	AC bias
Erasing system	AC erase
Recording time	90 minutes (C-90 cassette, both directions)
Frequency response	Normal tape: 35 – 12 500 Hz
	METAL tape: 35 – 16 000 Hz
Signal-to-noise ratio	54 dB
Wow and flutter	0.17% (WRMS)

Radio Section

Frequency ranges	FM:	87.5 – 108 MHz
	MW:	525 – 1 605 kHz
	SW:	5.9 – 18 MHz
	LW:	150 – 285 kHz
Antennas		Whip antenna for FM and SW
		Ferrite bar antenna for MW and LW
Dimensions (W x H x D)		380 x 120 x 76 (mm)
Weight		2 kg
Accessories		AC adaptor 1
		Cassette tape 1
		Dial window label 1
		(BL type only)

The specifications and external appearance of this set are subject to change without prior notice.

64

Testing

Model C

Cassette Tape Used	Normal: C-30, C-60, C-90
Tape Speed	4.8 cm/sec.
Track System	Four-track two-channel stereophonic
Recording System	AC bias
Erasing System	Multipolar magnet erasing
Frequency Response	60 Hz to 12 kHz
Receiving Frequency	FM: 88 MHz to 108 MHz
	SW: 5.9 MHz to 15.4 MHz
	MW: 526.5 kHz to 1606.5 kHz
	LW: 145 MHz to 270 kHz
Intermediate Frequency	FM: 10.7 MHz
	LW/MW/SW: 460 kHz
Antenna	FM/SW: telescopic antenna
	LW/MW: ferrite-core antenna
Speakers	100mm (dia.) dynamic x 2
	15 mm (dia.) piezo-electric type x 2
Jacks	[MIC] jack x 2, Impedance
	200 ohm to 2 kohm
	[PHONES] jack x 1
Power Supply	AC 220 V – 240 V, 50Hz
	DC 9 V IEC R14 ("C" cell) x 6
Power Consumption	14 W
Dimensions	(W) 500 mm x (H) 135 mm x (D) 104 mm
Weight	2.7 kg (without batteries)

Specifications are subject to change for improvement.

Model D

Speakers	8 cm x 2
Tuner section	
Frequency ranges	FM 88 – 108 MHz
	MW 540 – 1600 kHz
	LW 150 – 350 kHz
Antennas	Telescopic antenna for FM
	Ferrite core antenna for MW & LW
Tape recorder section	
Track system	4-Track 2-Channel stereo
Frequency response	100 – 12,000 Hz
Wow & flutter	0.15 % (WRMS)
Fast wind time	Approx. 150 sec. (C-60 cassette)
Amplifier section	
Power output	Max. 2.8 W (1.4 W + 1.4 W) at 8 Ω
	2.4 W (1.2 W + 1.2 W) at 10 % THD
Input jack	Mic x 1, 0.7 mV (–62 dBV), 200 Ω ~ 2 kΩ
Output jack	Headphone x 1 (22 mW/32 Ω, 8 ~ 32 Ω)
Power supply	DC 9 V (6 "R6" batteries)
	AC 220–240 V/110–120 V, 50/60 Hz
Power consumption	9 W
Dimensions	
Open	450(W) x 165(H) x 77(D) mm
Closed	330(W) x 165(H) x 77(D) mm
Weight	Approx. 1.8 kg (without batteries)

Design and specifications subject to change without notice.

---

1. Which radio cassette recorder has the worst frequency response (normal tape)?
   a. Model A
   b. Model B
   c. Model C
   d. Model D

2. Which radio cassette recorder has the lowest weight (without batteries)?
   a. Model A
   b. Model B
   c. Model C
   d. Model D

3. Which radio cassette recorder has no short wave (SW)?
   a. Model A
   b. Model B
   c. Model C
   d. Model D

4. Which radio cassette recorder has five speakers?
   a. Model A
   b. Model B
   c. Model C
   d. Model D

Testing

B. Listening comprehension

You are going to hear four sentences about Lufthansa training facilities. Decide whether the following statements are TRUE or FALSE:

			TRUE	FALSE
1.	a.	Besides Lufthansa employees, staff from other airlines can also be instructed at the training facilities in Bremen, Berlin and Frankfurt.	☐	☐
	b.	Lufthansa has given up its training facilities in Bremen, Berlin and Frankfurt.	☐	☐
2.	a.	Pilots and inflight personnel are trained in these courses, which are available in five languages.		
	b.	Pilots and inflight personnel must be able to speak or – at least – understand five languages.	☐	☐
3.	a.	The technology they use at the training facilities is not state-of-the-art but ranges from computer systems to simulators.	☐	☐
	b.	They use the latest flight simulator and the most sophisticated computer systems.	☐	☐
4.	a.	A lot of crews are being trained but not at the schools in Bremen, Phoenix and Tucson.	☐	☐
	b.	At the training schools in Bremen, Phoenix and Tucson a lot of crews are being trained.	☐	☐

Testing

C. Listening comprehension

PUTTING FASHION ON THE RIGHT TRACK

22

The text you are going to hear explains a garment handling system installed at a factory in England. Mark the correct answer with a cross (a, b or c):

1. According to the text, the conveyor system at Solihull is
   a. as large as all the other CI conveyor systems.
   b. larger than some other CI conveyor systems.
   c. the largest CI conveyor system ever installed.

2. The Solihull conveyor system
   a. must have a new distribution system.
   b. sends all the clothes to the main frame computer.
   c. uses trolleys to transport the clothes.

3. The main frame computer is used to
   a. calculate the capacity of the system.
   b. link the conveyor systems to the trolleys.
   c. record the data of each trolley.

4. At the moment, the Solihull conveyor system
   a. can handle less than 400,000 clothes.
   b. consists of manually operated devices.
   c. has a capacity of more than 400,000 clothes.

11 Testing and finishing (1)

1 Listening comprehension.

Have a look at the text and the illustrations on the right and on the next page. Luke, Catherine, and Michael are talking about finishing – what should or should not be done.

Make a tick (✓) under "OK" if the design of this particular part is all right.

Design considerations	Avoid	Design preference	OK
Rolling edges Design so that plating solutions cannot be trapped			
Hollow articles Provide drain holes in hollow articles			
Corners They should have radii of at least 1mm			
Edges They should be smoothed out as much as possible			
Fins Space them as widely as possible and round their edges			
Ribs They should be smooth in section and spaced as widely as possible			
Slots Eliminate sharp edges and corners of slots			
Bends Inside curved surfaces should have a minimum radius of 12.5mm			
Blind holes If these are essential, they should be shallow with well-rounded corners or edges			

Metal finishing is very important – it should be considered as a final manufacturing process planned at the design stage of a product.

Plating is a very precise way of metallically coating an article so that it will resist corrosion, wear longer or simply look better. There are two principal methods: electroplating or by chemical immersion. Articles are suspended on wires in vats or, if they are too small for individual treatment, rotated in barrels. Both are wet processes and a first rule is that the article must be capable of immersion, draining and quick transfer from one liquid to another. However, because plating liquids contain water, do make sure that process temperatures are never higher than about 100°C.

There are some important points that should be considered during the design stage:

- deep holes in the article may be a problem;
- surfaces that are not to be plated should be identified so that they can be masked;
- articles for vat plating should include points where they can be securely attached to the wires;
- the article should be designed to allow less important surfaces to be uppermost during plating (particles may settle on some surfaces causing roughness and possibly lower corrosion resistance).

The illustrations on the left show some guidelines for designing with electroplating in mind.

Where plated articles have to be fitted together – as on screw threads – allowance must be made for the coating thickness. Where coatings thicker than 10 µ are required, special allowance has to be made.

The strength and hardness of the material to be plated must be considered, for certain plating processes will affect its mechanical properties. High-strength steels (normally above 1000 N/mm^2), for example, may become brittle during the plating process.

Electroless nickel plating is smooth, non-porous, easy to clean and has a good corrosion resistance in most environments.

11

LANGUAGE FUNCTIONS:

Classifying something by location or direction (1)

Where does this module go? – It goes under the control board, I think.

The component you gave me last week doesn't go into this slot.

Which box do these transistors go into?

All the ladders stood against the wall.

I'm sure this button must be pressed first, and that one last.

When I arrived, the technicians had already gone away.

We drove along the High Street.

2

Have a look at the grammar explanations of this unit (p. 71) and the "Language Functions" on the left and find the correct form of the words in brackets:

a. The operating manual you (give) me last Monday is very complicated.

b. When I came into the workshop this morning, all the ladders (stand) against the wall.

c. We've (be/use) this kind of plastic ever since it was first produced.

d. When she arrived at the building site, the workers (already/go) away.

e. When I first met Mr Everston, he (be/work) for British Steel for twenty years.

f. I've (be/try) to get her on the phone every day for the past two weeks.

Communication problems ...

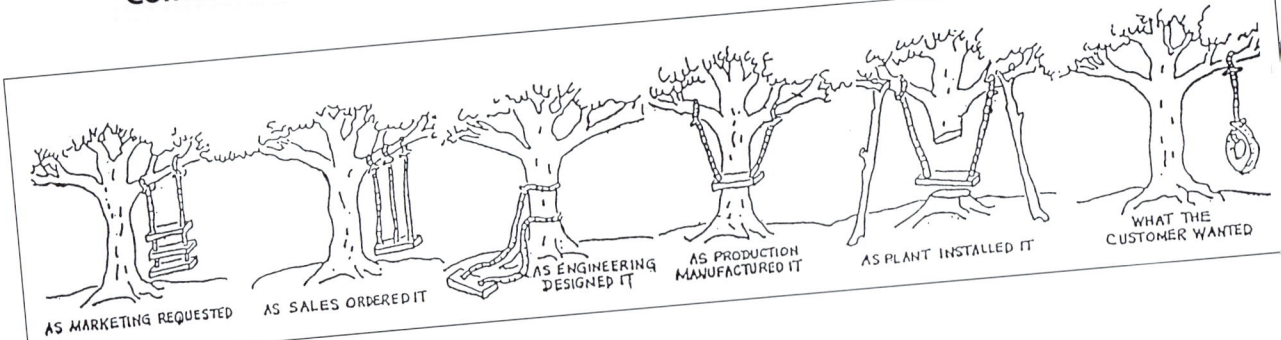

AS MARKETING REQUESTED   AS SALES ORDERED IT   AS ENGINEERING DESIGNED IT   AS PRODUCTION MANUFACTURED IT   AS PLANT INSTALLED IT   WHAT THE CUSTOMER WANTED

A LOOK AT GRAMMAR:
Present perfect continuous / Past perfect continuous

- It's been raining all day.
- How long have you been learning English?
- She's been waiting here for twenty minutes.
- I've been phoning her every day for the past week.

NOTE: This form is used to emphasize that an activity has been going on for a long time. It is not always necessary that the activity is still going on at the time of speaking.

In a similar way, this form may also be used for activities going on during an earlier past:

- Yesterday he was very tired – he had been writing reports all day.

Some words like *learn, live, rain, sit, sleep, wait, work* ("continuity words") express continuous activity more than others and thus are often used with the perfect continuous form. Words which describe a situation and not an activity do not normally have the continuous form:

- I've known her since Christmas.
- I haven't seen her since she left the office an hour ago.
- We've been good friends for many years.
- I've been here for two hours now.
- She's been in the workshop since nine o'clock.

"Continuity words" can have both forms (no difference in meaning but the continuous form puts more emphasis on the on-going activity):

- I've been working for IBM for ten years.
- I've worked for IBM for ten years.
- When I first met her, she had been working for VW for fifteen years.
- When I first met her, she had worked for VW for fifteen years.

Working at the assembly plant ...

3

Listening comprehension and note-taking.

Travelling to the plant

Listen to the dialogue once or twice. Work in pairs – one of you concentrates on the part of Peter, the other listens carefully to what Manfred says. On a separate sheet of paper write down the missing information:

Peter: Very nice of you to … .

Manfred: … – it's … , really.

Peter: I've only been here … , so I really don't know … .

Manfred: Well, I don't know Zurich … – I'm from Austria, … .

Peter: Yes – Linz, … .

Manfred: Yes.

Peter: But … you speak the … . The little … .

Manfred: Where … ?

Peter: London, … .

Manfred: Ah, here we are – … .

Peter: … ?

Manfred: … – that big grey building with … .

4

Have another look at the grammar explanations of this unit (p. 71) and make sentences (the first sentence gives you a little help):

Why were they very tired?

a. … work all day. (Because they had been …)

b. … learn technical English from morning to night.

c. … write technical reports all day.

d. … wash cars from nine to four.

e. … repair fork-lift trucks all morning.

f. … talk to the boss for hours.

g. … make phone calls from ten to three.

h. … talk to English customers all day long.

i. … program computers from nine to six.

5
Discussion / language practice.

What are the people in the two photos doing?
Why should they be careful?
What dangers can you see?
Why are there warning signs?

12 Testing and finishing (2)

TUBE FURNACES

Many processes including gas analysis, material testing, ceramic firing, continuous strip heating, and thermocouple calibration demand the use of a tube furnace.

With maximum temperatures of 900°, 1000°, 1200°, 1500° and 1600°C, in a variety of standard tube diameters and lengths, Carbolite tube furnaces offer precise temperature control and uniformity, rapid heating and cooling, reproducible performance and operating economy.

Major benefits:

- Efficient – low thermal mass insulation materials, the latest micro-electronic circuitry and high quality heating elements all combine to provide excellent temperature uniformity and rapid heating/cooling.
- Safe – All furnaces are fitted with an outer mesh which promotes natural air cooling of the case and protects the operator from the risk of burns.
- Accurate – Carbolite tube furnaces are available with a wide choice of the latest microprocessor based temperature controllers and programmers each carefully selected to ensure maximum reliability and performance.

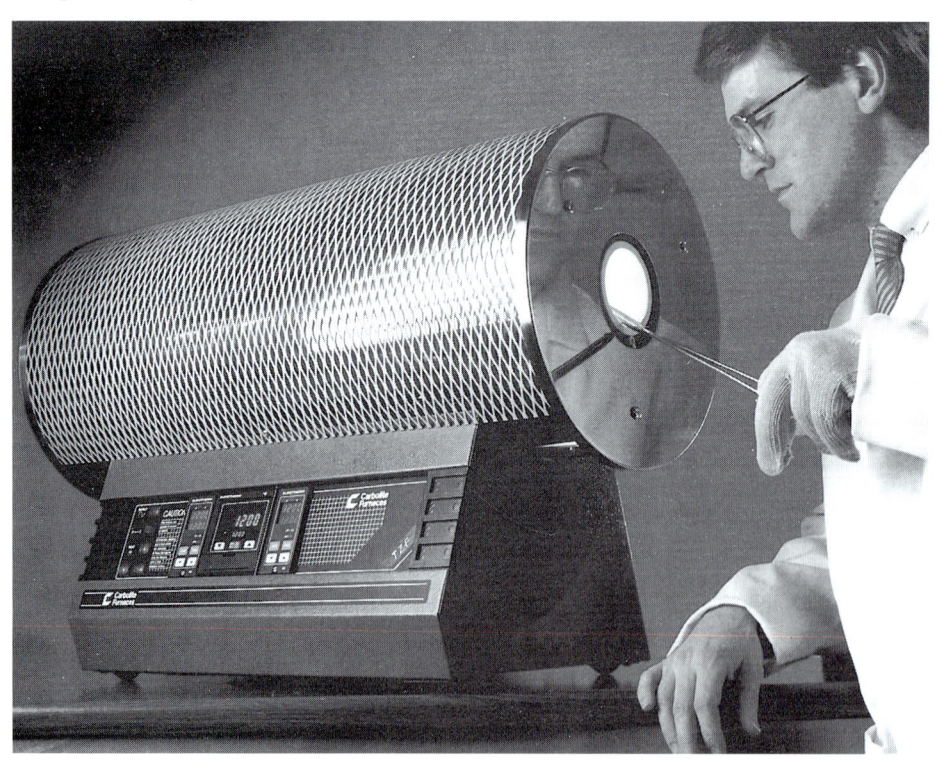

1
Questions on the text.

Have a look at the text and the photo on the left and answer these questions:

a. For what sort of processes are tube furnaces used?
b. Have all tube furnaces got the same maximum temperature?
c. What differences are there in size and diameter?
d. Why is it important to have "reproducible performance"?
e. Why are the tube furnaces described here so efficient? (What do you think about the arguments used here?)
f. Why have the tube furnaces been equipped with an outer mesh?
g. What does the text say about temperature controllers and programmers?

3
Have a look at the "Language Functions" on the right and put in *turn* or *start*:

a. It's very important to … a dish antenna in the right direction.
b. To … the engine, you have to … the crank.
c. Before you … the process, all control instruments must be checked.
d. At the beginning of the operation, the big wheel … very slowly anti-clockwise.
e. Is it a good idea to … a discussion on politics?
f. We were doubtful about the equipment's usefulness from the … .

2
Listening comprehension and pair work.

At the company car park

Listen to the dialogue and report what you heard to another student.

LANGUAGE FUNCTIONS:

Classifying something by location or direction (2)

Details of the proposed extension of our plant are given in the table below.

Before we start up the machine, these two wheels must be brought back into alignment.

To open the bottle, you have to turn the lid anti-clockwise.

The warning light is located at the bottom.

For good reception, the antenna should be mounted on the roof.

The door fits flush into the frame.

The emergency switch is situated below the voltmeter.

12 A LOOK AT GRAMMAR:

Reported speech

- "I can see the problem." → She says she can see the problem.
- "Have the tools been cleaned?" → She wants to know if the tools have been cleaned.

- "I can see the problem." → She said she could see the problem.
- "Have the tools been cleaned?" → She wanted to know if the tools had been cleaned.

NOTE: Usually, there is a tense change if the verb used for reporting ("say", "want") is in the past tense, but this is not a rule. Tense changes are often used when there is a longer interval between the original words and the reported speech. Usually, the past perfect is used to report something that was in the present perfect:

- "She has lived in Brussels for years," Mr Miller said. → Mr Miller told me that she had lived in Brussels for years.

If the original sentence was in the simple past, it is not always necessary to change the reported speech to the past perfect:

- "I lived in England in the 1980's," Mr Evans said. → Mr Evans said that he lived/had lived in England in the 1980's.

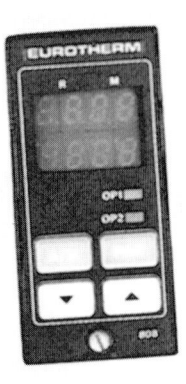

4

Listening comprehension and discussion.

Ms Jackie Bellingham has recently had some problems with a camcorder shop. She has written the letter below to the Helpline Editor of "Camcorder World" in Adelaide. Listen to the answer and report to another student what the editor said. Discuss the problem.

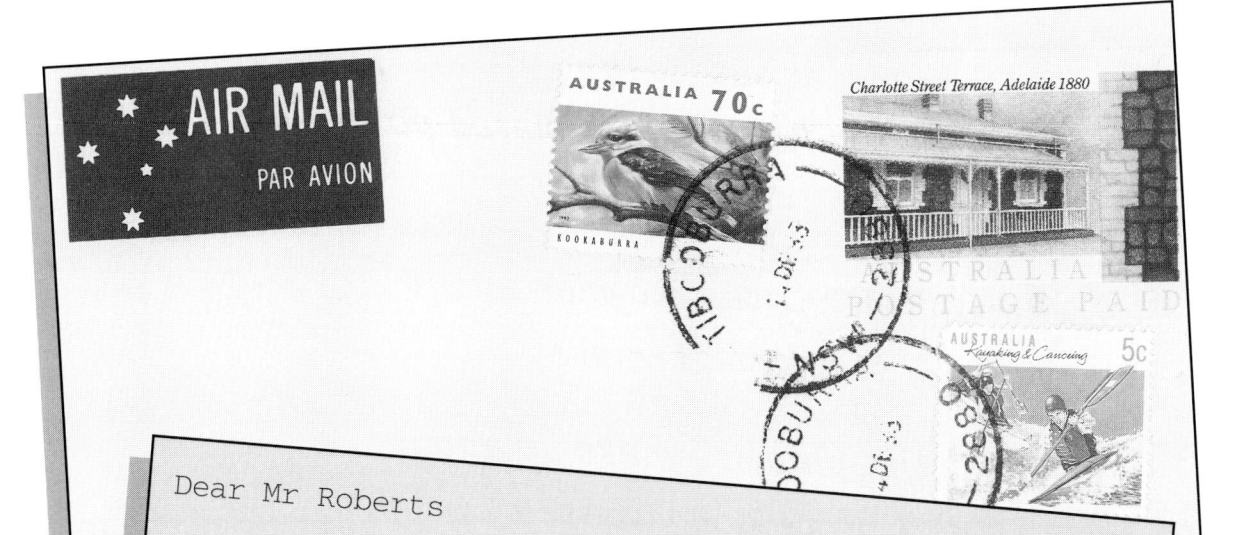

Dear Mr Roberts

My camcorder leads a busy life, and one of the screws which secures the lid of the battery compartment worked loose and disappeared.

A replacement screw, ordered via a dealer, cost $8.46! How can the shop justify this? At that price, a complete set of screws would cost $120! The screw is smaller than a matchhead.

Is this a record? Are all dealers like that?

Sincerely

Jackie Bellingham
Jackie Bellingham

13 Plastics in daily use

> The average Parisian throws away about ... (a) pounds of trash a year.
>
> In Germany, about ... (b) landfill sites have been declared potentially dangerous.
>
> The United States recycles about ... (c) % of its solid waste.
>
> In the US, plastics make up about ... (d) % of its solid waste by weight.
>
> ... (e) of pounds of used plastics are recycled successfully.

1
Listening comprehension and discussion.

Have a look at the text on the right and the sentences above. You are going to hear a text about waste management problems and plastics. Listen carefully to the recording and write down the correct figures of the sentences above. After that, discuss the waste problem (recycling, incineration, landfills – other methods).

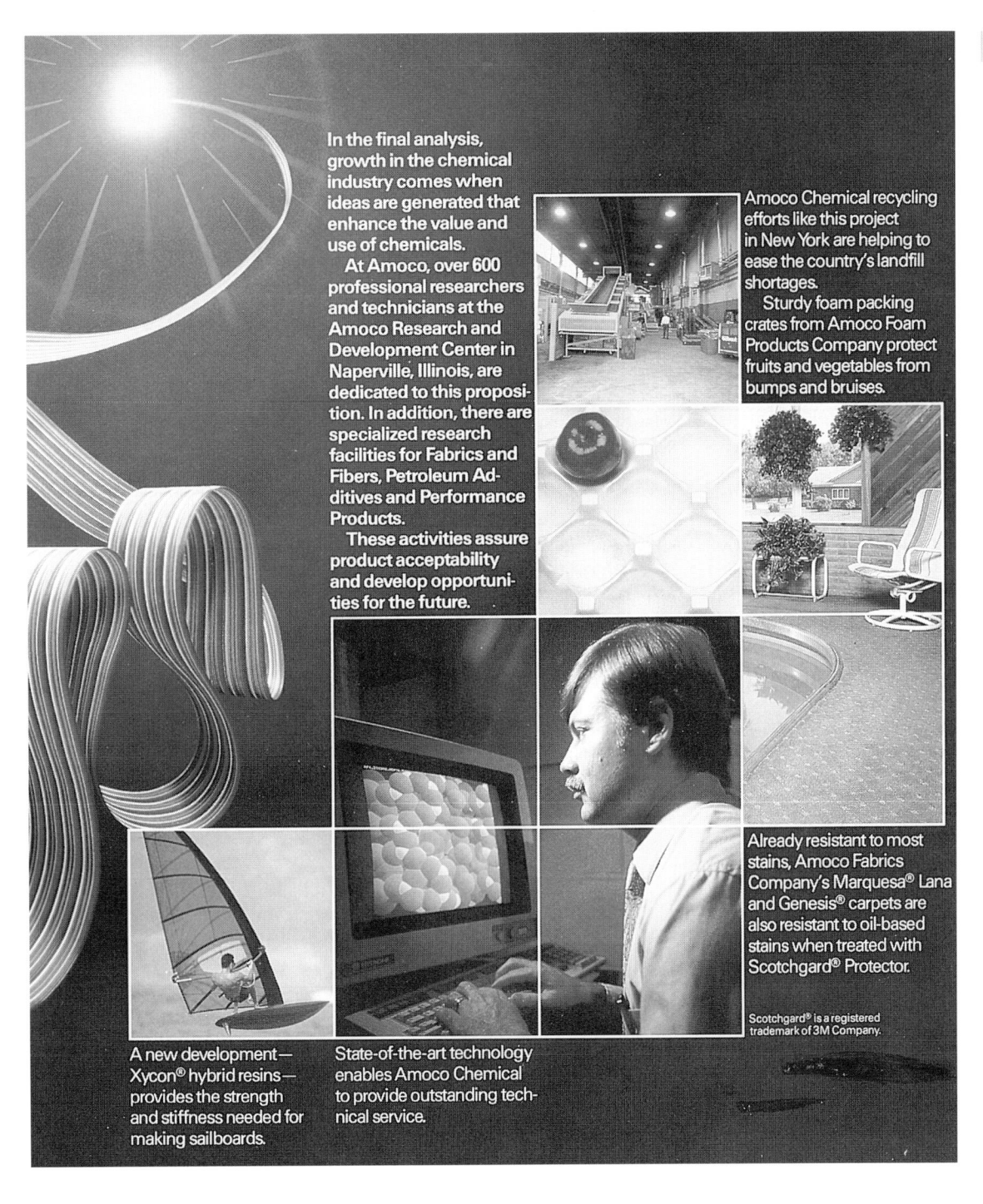

In the final analysis, growth in the chemical industry comes when ideas are generated that enhance the value and use of chemicals.

At Amoco, over 600 professional researchers and technicians at the Amoco Research and Development Center in Naperville, Illinois, are dedicated to this proposition. In addition, there are specialized research facilities for Fabrics and Fibers, Petroleum Additives and Performance Products.

These activities assure product acceptability and develop opportunities for the future.

Amoco Chemical recycling efforts like this project in New York are helping to ease the country's landfill shortages.

Sturdy foam packing crates from Amoco Foam Products Company protect fruits and vegetables from bumps and bruises.

Already resistant to most stains, Amoco Fabrics Company's Marquesa® Lana and Genesis® carpets are also resistant to oil-based stains when treated with Scotchgard® Protector.

Scotchgard® is a registered trademark of 3M Company.

A new development— Xycon® hybrid resins— provides the strength and stiffness needed for making sailboards.

State-of-the-art technology enables Amoco Chemical to provide outstanding technical service.

13 A LOOK AT GRAMMAR:

Expressions with "take"

- I'll take the blame for the accident. *(= I'll accept responsibility)*
- It takes money to live in a big town. *(= you need money ...)*
- If you're not sure, take a reading on the dial. *(= get information by looking at the dial)*
- He can't take criticism. *(= can't accept)*
- I can't take a letter in shorthand. *(= can't write down a letter in shorthand)*
- I'll take your word for it. *(= I believe what you say)*
- Our conference room is too small – we can't take more than 80 people. *(= can't accept)*
- How long will it take? *(= how much time will it need?)*
- The flight from Bristol to Stuttgart takes two hours. *(= lasts two hours)*

2

Have a look at the grammar above and the "Language Functions" on the right and put in *get*, *go* or *take*:

a. These colours ... very well with our new office furniture.

b. When the explosives ... off, the whole building will come down.

c. It will ... a lot of time to grease all the machines in the workshop.

d. Nearly all the reports we ... are in English.

e. We must ... the machining centre assembled as soon as possible.

f. We'll inform you as soon as we ... the spare parts for the machine.

g. I think we'll ... this finished by Monday morning.

h. The trouble is that all the work we ... from our central office must be finished within a day or two.

i. I'm afraid we'll have to ... over the production figures again.

j. First we will have to go and ... permission from the board of directors.

k. I'm afraid I don't ... the meaning of this letter.

l. How long will the flight to London ... ?

m. We must ... this batch finished within the next fifteen minutes.

n. I'd like to ... for a walk now.

LANGUAGE FUNCTIONS:

Classifying facts by time

When's your appointment? – On Tuesday at 3 o'clock. – Well, you have plenty of time, then.

Put the grease gun on the workbench when you've finished greasing.

On receipt of the spare parts, we noticed that several items were missing.

This batch must be finished within the next two days.

Most of the work we get must be finished within a given period of time.

Before assembling the machine, we should make sure that we have all the necessary parts.

3
Listening comprehension.

Driving home

Listen to the dialogue and write down the part of Peter:

Peter: …

Manfred: And how did it go?

Peter: …

Manfred: That's terrific.

Peter: …

Manfred: Yes, I can imagine. I still remember my first day.

Peter: …

Manfred: Yes, that would be great.

Peter: …

Manfred: Hmm … yes, I think so … there's a small pub off Kreuzstrasse – should be OK, I think.

Peter: …

Manfred: Fine. I'll park the car in front of my flat – we can walk from there.

Recycling today for a cleaner tomorrow.

14 The Docklands Light Railway

1
Group work, writing and discussion.

Have a look at the texts and photos on this and the next page.
Write down the most important points of the ATO and ATP systems.
Discuss why such systems are important.

THE OPERATIONS AND MAINTENANCE CENTRE

The Operations and Maintenance Centre (OMC)

The Operations and Maintenance Centre (OMC) houses all the administrative functions of the DLR, the control centre and the maintenance facilities. It is a modern building situated close to Poplar passenger station.

The OMC has a workshop area with accommodation for three articulated vehicles. One track, allocated to heavy maintenance, has lifting jacks and turntables to facilitate the removal of bogies.

14

The Docklands Light Railway (DLR) is a fully automatic electrically powered railway which runs between the City of London and the Docklands area. The operation of the DLR depends on two systems: the automatic train operation (ATO), and the automatic train protection system (ATP).

The ATO computer on each train contains two alternative programs to drive it from one station to the next. Each program contains instructions like "accelerate to 60 km/h, hold that speed for 600 metres, then brake and stop after a total distance of 945 metres". One program is for the minimum journey time, the other is an energy saving program and takes about 10% longer (saving some 30% energy in the process). Normally the slower program is used but, if a train is late, it is instructed to switch to the faster program until it has caught up with the timetable.

The ATP system is separate from the ATO system. It has two functions: to ensure that the trains observe speed limits and to prevent unsafe train movements (for example, to prevent two trains entering the same track section). The speed limits are controlled by signals from a pair of cables laid in the track. A 470 Hz signal is transmitted along the cables and picked up by the train. If the speed is too high, the emergency brakes are applied.

Control of the OMC is from two VDUs in the control room. The supervisory, control and data acquisition system (SCADA) enables the controller to identify the state of each circuit breaker, monitor the power consumption of the system and receive alarm and trip indications. Each circuit breaker on the 11kV and 750V dc systems can be controlled by a **mouse** or via the keyboard. All events are logged and are recorded on a printer.

Power control (SCADA) screens. The left hand screen is showing a system overview and the right hand screen is showing the DC switching diagram for Poplar substation. Control can be from the keyboard or from a "mouse".

14 A LOOK AT GRAMMAR:

Simple past perfect

- We cleaned the conference room as soon as our guests had left.
- The meeting had already started when the sales engineer arrived.

NOTE: This form is mainly used to show which of two events happened first. Remember: It is not used for a single event that happened some time ago in the past:

- The engine was installed last week. (**not**: ... had been installed ...!)

2

Listening comprehension and note-taking.

There's been an accident outside the OMC. Listen to the conversation and write down the information for the form on the right.

3

Listening comprehension and written exercise.

Conversation at the pub

Listen to the dialogue between Manfred and Peter and answer the following questions in writing:

a. Why are they meeting at the pub?

b. Do they like the pub?

c. How often has Manfred been to Britain?

d. Where will they go?

e. Where will they stay in London?

DOCKLANDS LIGHT RAILWAY

PRELIMINARY ACCIDENT REPORT

NAME: ....

FIRST NAME: ....

DATE OF ACCIDENT: ....

TIME OF ACCIDENT: ....

PLACE OF ACCIDENT: ....

....

POSITION IN COMPANY: ....

....

TYPE OF INJURY: ....

....

IN HOSPITAL? ....

IF YES, WHERE? ....

LANGUAGE FUNCTIONS:

Expressing your wishes

We'd like a copy of the printout.

We'd like to have a look at all the available data before making a decision.

We'd like to know if they can meet the deadline.

We'd greatly appreciate your comments.

We'd appreciate it if you could send us the components as soon as possible.

We only wish we could have helped you.

If only the price of the raw materials were not so high!

I wish to make a complaint.

4

Have a look at the picture above and complete the text below by putting in a suitable preposition:

It is now clear that the best-known picture ... (a) Scotland's Loch Ness Monster "Nessie" (see illustration ... (b)) is not a real photo. First published ... (c) 1934, the black-and-white photograph shows a long-necked creature moving through the waves.

But just before his death a few years ago, Christian Spurling admitted ... (d) two British researchers that the whole story was made up ... (e) his stepfather and a handful of friends – one of them Christian Spurling.

He told the researchers that he had made Nessie's head and neck ... (f) of various materials, mounted them on a lead-weighted, wind-up toy submarine, and put them on the water.

15 Cleaning the air

1

Listening comprehension / group work or pair work / note-taking / discussion.

You are going to hear a text about air conditioners in RVs (= recreational vehicles as, for instance, motorhomes). Groups of two or more students work together, listen to the recording and take notes. After that, they report the results to the class.

Discussion: Are air conditioners a good idea (RV? / Home? / Office? / Workshop? / Factory? / Hotel? / Airport? / Lab?)

2

Discussion / group work.

Are you handy with tools ???

Which of these things can you do without asking for help?

check the tyre pressure ☐	change a tyre ☐
connect wires to a plug or socket ☐	replace a spark plug ☐
change oil in a car ☐	build a hi-fi loudspeaker ☐
make a wooden shelf ☐	tune a car engine ☐
develop your own photos ☐	install an electric cooker ☐
tile a foor ☐	wallpaper your flat ☐
repair a bicycle puncture ☐	put a film in your camera ☐
make a technical drawing ☐	hang a picture on the wall ☐
repair a dripping water tap ☐	repair a transistor radio ☐

Which of these skills do you think are most important? Where did you learn them? Should everybody be able to do these things?

3
Listening comprehension and note-taking.

Planning a trip to London (1)

Listen to the dialogue between Peter and Manfred and answer the questions.

a. When is Peter planning to go to London? Does he know exactly?
b. Who is Jane?
c. Where can Peter stay for a few days when he is in London?
d. Where does Peter's sister-in-law live? How far is it to London?

LANGUAGE FUNCTIONS:

Expressing indifference

Does it make a difference?

What's the difference?

What difference does it make?

It doesn't make the slightest difference whether we use this or that material.

I can't see much difference between the two diagrams.

You can choose whatever tool you want – it's all the same to me.

The deadline must be met, whatever the cost.

Which of these sandwiches would you like? – I don't mind.

I know there is a problem, but it doesn't concern me.

That problem doesn't concern you.

Don't concern yourself with these problems.

There is no cause for concern.

4
Grammar repetition: Have a look at the "Language Functions" on the left and the text **Are you handy with tools?** on page 86 and find the best word:

a. I don't care if all the test pieces are … the same size.
   1 even   2 exactly   3 mostly

b. I can't hear the difference … the two loudspeakers.
   1 at   2. between   3 within

c. You can show them the difference by … of a diagram.
   1 kind   2 means   3 method

d. Getting … of garbage costs millions of dollars every year.
   1 away   2 off   3 rid

e. Can you … a bathroom?
   1 roof   2 tile   3 wall

f. My car had a … yesterday.
   1 punch   2 point   3 puncture

g. That car engine must be …
   1 taped   2 tiled   3 tuned

Air Conditioning: For New and Existing Systems

Industrial Air, Inc. is proud to have served the Industrial southeast for more than twenty years. Over the years, we have provided services for both small and large organizations, many in Forbes Magazine's list of top 100.

The size of jobs completed has ranged from small to in excess of five million dollars (completed in less than one year).

We have worked hard at increasing our capabilities so that we might better serve our customers. The areas we now serve are: air conditioning and filtration for applications ranging from hi-tech clean rooms to textile production areas, process piping, and metal fabrication.

Our facilities are located in Greensboro, North Carolina, but we have representatives throughout the southeast ready to travel to your location when the need exists.

We at Industrial Air, Inc. are very much humbled by the faith which you, our customers, have placed in us, and we intend to make every possible effort to continue earning that trust.

If you are not yet one of our many fine customers, give us a chance. We would like to add your company's name to our list of satisfied customers.

A. Reese Hunter,
President

A LOOK AT GRAMMAR:

Conditional sentences

GENERAL CONDITIONS
He never apologises if he is late.
If this goes on, our company will go bankrupt.
If the factory closes, we will all be unemployed.
The doctor will see you if you come at ten.

NOTE: The if-clause can go before or after the main clause.

UNLIKELY CONDITIONS
She would pass the examination if she worked harder.
If you needed money, you could get it from the bank.
He wouldn't be happy if he couldn't work overtime.

PAST CONDITIONS
I would have tested the components if I had had the necessary equipment.
If they had not put so much chromium in, the steel would not be stainless.
She might have written the report if you had asked her.
If you hadn't parked your car here, the police wouldn't have given you a ticket.

5

Have a look at the grammar above and the text on the left and put in *if, now, when* or *yet*:

a. ... will the air conditioners for our labs arrive?

b. Please write to us if you are not ... one of our customers.

c. I would have written to Industrial Air ... I had wanted more information.

d. They ... serve the following areas: air conditioning and filtration.

e. ... you had sent the components for the filtration units by airfreight, they would have arrived much earlier.

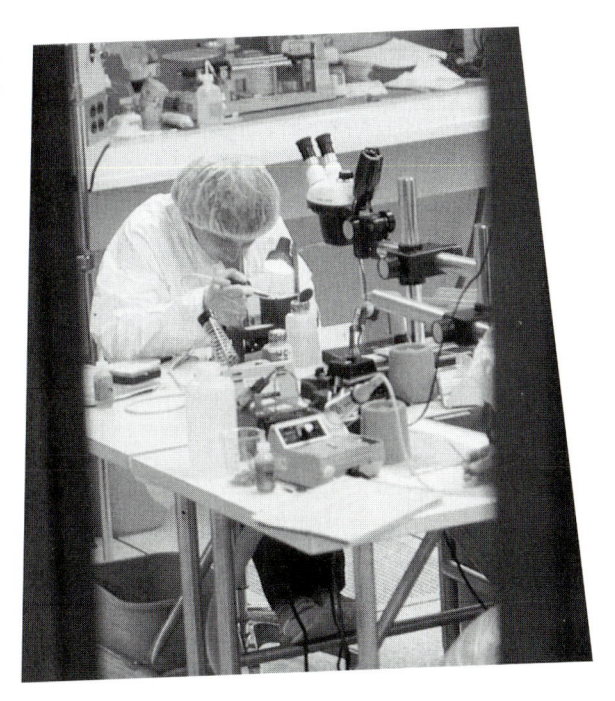

Working in the central lab ...

6

Describing a technical process. Have a careful look at the drawing on this and the following page. You can see a proposal for a complete air conditioning system. Describe the process you see – the passage of air from the beginning to the end – using the expressions given in the drawing.

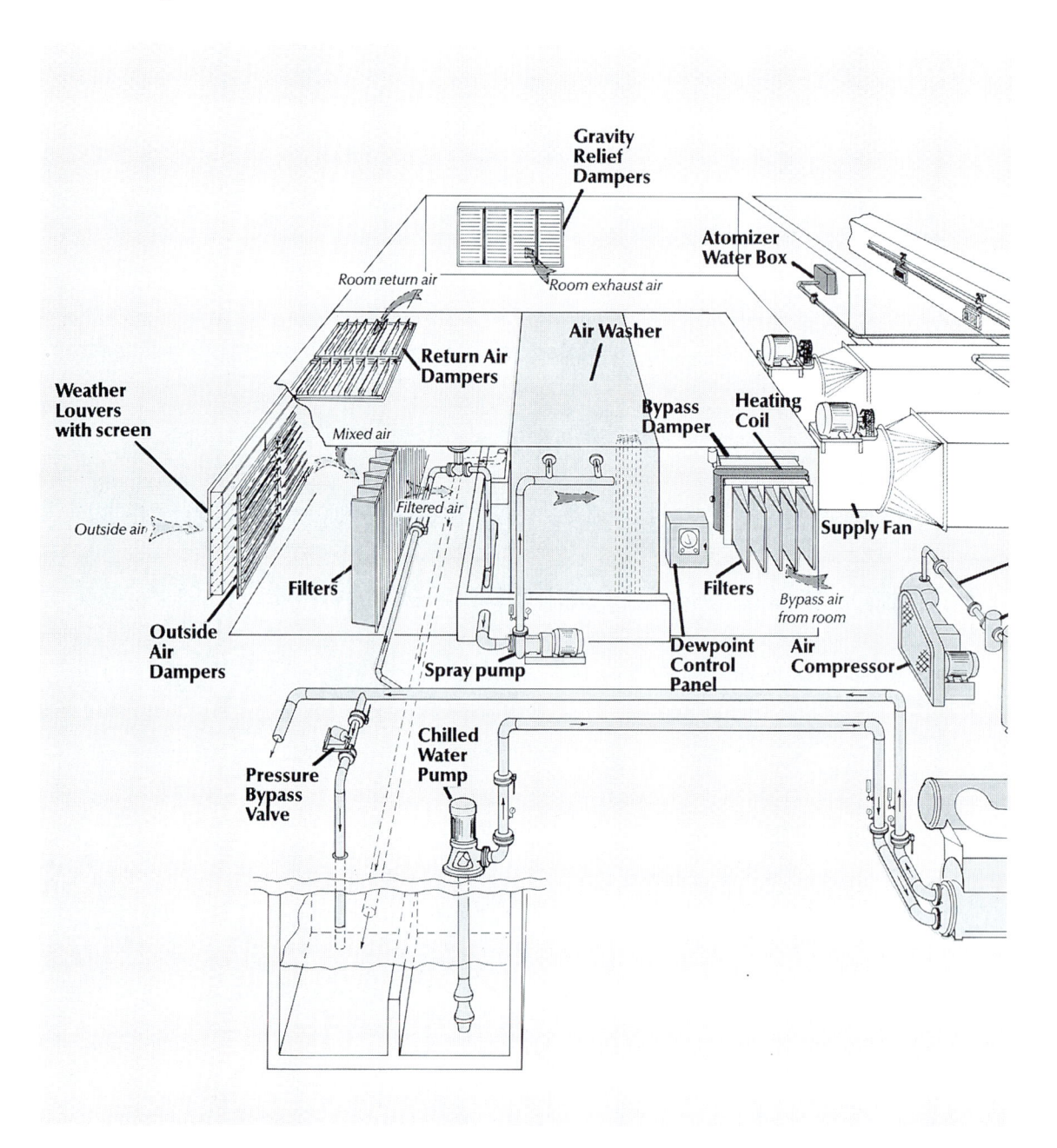

90

In addition to new installations, we modify and expand existing systems to meet your growing or changing air requirements.

Our engineers' efforts have resulted in several patented methods and components which can allow upgrading of your existing system to meet your current air requirements, saving significant cost over a new system.

Call an Industrial Air representative for an evaluation.

Industrial Air designs, manufactures, installs and services a wide range of air systems, from simple make-up or ventilation units to complex process air systems requiring extremely critical control of humidity, temperature and pressure.

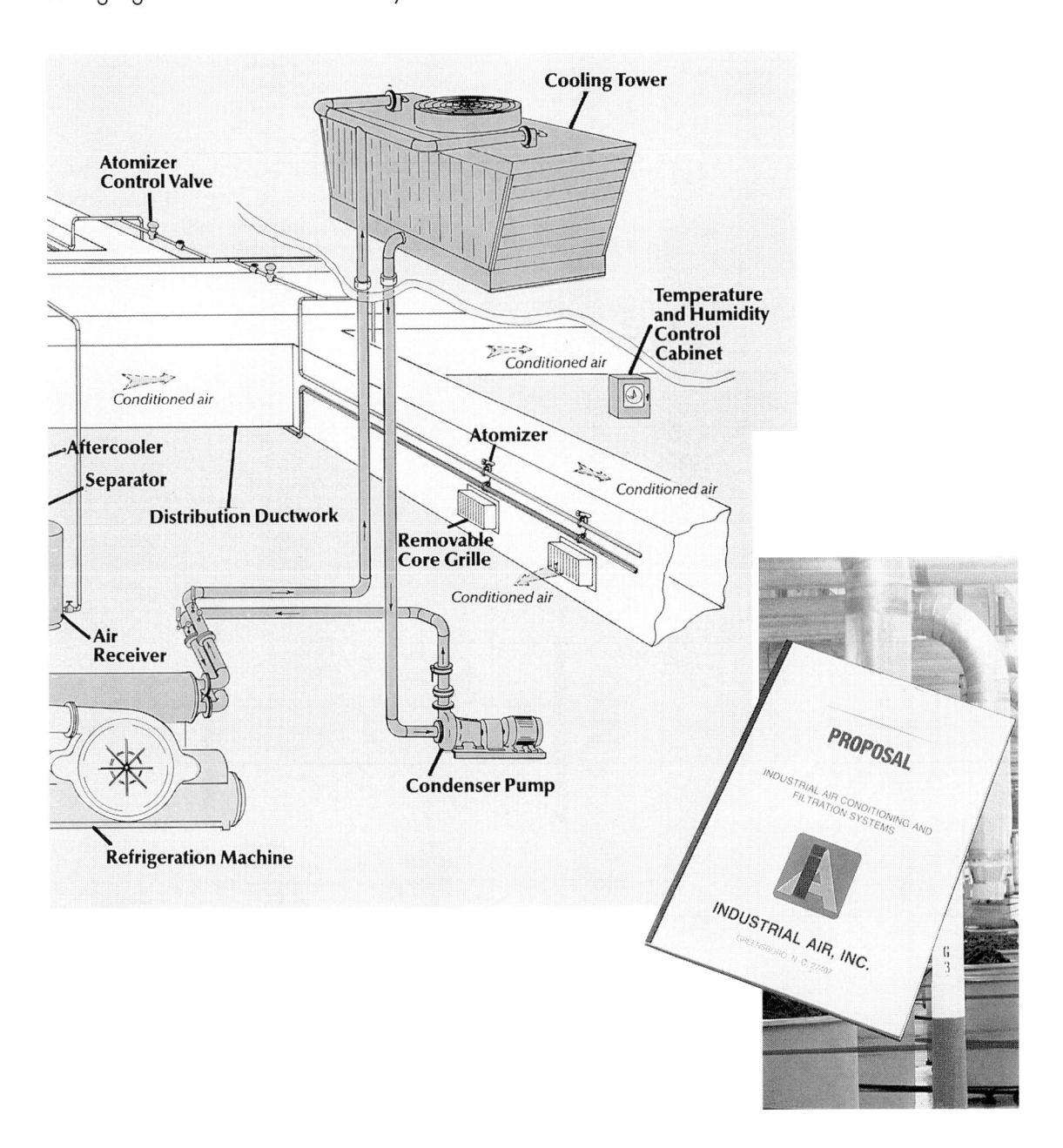

Labeled diagram components:
- Cooling Tower
- Atomizer Control Valve
- Temperature and Humidity Control Cabinet
- Conditioned air
- Aftercooler
- Separator
- Distribution Ductwork
- Atomizer
- Removable Core Grille
- Air Receiver
- Condenser Pump
- Refrigeration Machine

PROPOSAL
INDUSTRIAL AIR CONDITIONING AND FILTRATION SYSTEMS
INDUSTRIAL AIR, INC.
GREENSBORO, N.C. 27407

16 Working with a machining center

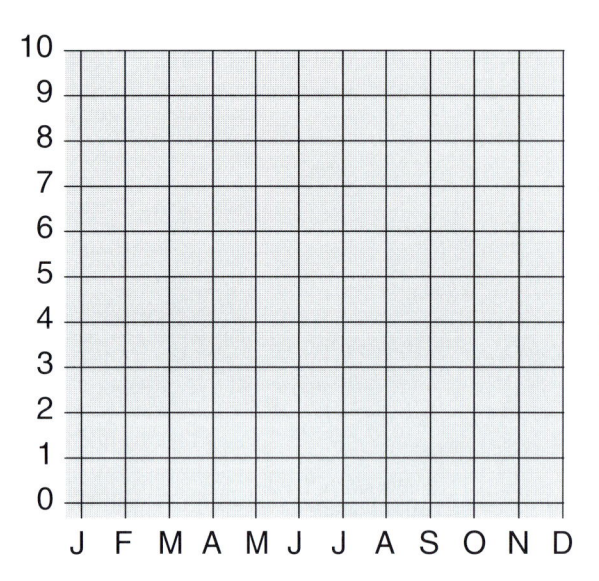

1
Listening comprehension.

Alice Sherwood, the sales engineer, still gets a lot of complaints from customers who are not satisfied with the CNC system. Use a graph like the one you can see here to show how many complaints the company had each month (1 to 10) from January (J) to December (D). In the recording, Alice is talking to Jerry Burton from the quality control department.

2
Optical illusions.

Have a look at the drawing.

Which of the two blue lines (A or B) is longer?

Discuss the drawing.

A LOOK AT GRAMMAR:

"As" / "because" / "since"

- She left the office early as she had to go to a meeting in Bristol.
- As he was tired, he sat down.
- As he has no car, he cannot get there easily.
- She stayed at home because she was ill.
- He left early yesterday because he had an urgent appointment.
- We did not stay outside long because it was too cold.
- Since you are leaving, I will type the rest of the letters and the report.
- Since she wasn't interested, I didn't tell her about it.
- She didn't call him since she didn't know his number.

NOTE: In the sentences above, either *as*, *since*, or *because* may be used with no difference in meaning (they answer the question "why?").

3

How can you connect the arguments? Put in *although* or *because* (*as* or *since* may also be used instead of *because*):

They bought the light rail transit system ...

a. ... it can be maintained easily and is cheaper to operate.

b. ... wheelchair-bound passengers can also use it.

c. ... there was strong opposition against the system at the beginning.

d. ... the vehicles are very comfortable.

'I'm afraid we're unable to show you the programme at the moment because the video recorder's been stolen.'

4

Questions on the text below and the technical drawings on the right.

a. What is the machining center built for?
b. In how many different versions can you buy the Milwaukee-Matic 1015?
c. Is this the only machining center they manufacture?
d. What do you think the coolant reservoir is for? What special unit is used for cooling the machining center?
e. Can the Milwaukee-Matic 1015 be used with industrial robots?
f. What is the total height of the machining center?
g. What does the text say about the price of the machining center?
h. What kind of services are offered by the manufacturer when you buy the Milwaukee-Matic 1015? Is this range of services also offered for other machines they produce?

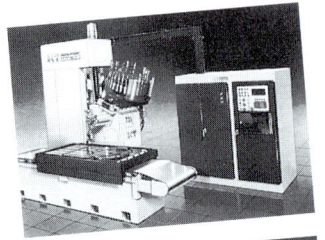

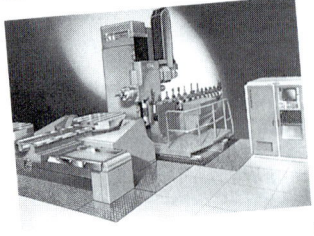

The new Kearney & Trecker MILWAUKEE-MATIC 1015 was engineered to deliver outstanding performance as a stand-alone machine —and to be integrated easily into manufacturing cells and Flexible Manufacturing Systems as needs arise in the future.

The 1015 is ruggedly built for superior machining accuracy, minimum maintenance requirements, and long life. To broaden its application possibilities, the 1015 is offered in two different versions: one with a Hi-Speed spindle that rotates at up to 10,000 rpm, and one with a Hi-Torque spindle offering speeds to 4000 rpm. In both versions, spindle drive is by a variable-speed AC motor developing 15 hp in continuous duty, and 20 hp machine tool duty.

The MILWAUKEE-MATIC 1015 machining center retains the rugged design characteristics of larger members of the MILWAUKEE-MATIC family. Its heavy, massive column provides rigid support for the spindle head. Ways are hardened and ground for precision, and replaceable to reduce long-term costs.

Standard equipment on the 1015 is the sophisticated KT-GEMINI-D computerized numerical control. This control, the most advanced in the industry, affords unexcelled data processing speed and capacity. And it gives the 1015 capabilities that up to now were offered only in far more costly machines.

The MILWAUKEE-MATIC 1015 itself and its GEMINI-D control can team up to meet a broad spectrum of requirements now and in the future. It is readily adaptable for operation in a manufacturing cell; it is well suited for use with robots; and it can be incorporated easily into Flexible Manufacturing Systems.

The affordably priced 1015 is backed by the same comprehensive factory support as any KT machine. A range of services from installation to operator training to emergency diagnosis and more, all contribute to peak performance and complete satisfaction... maximum return on your machine tool investment.

That's the Kearney & Trecker tradition.

16

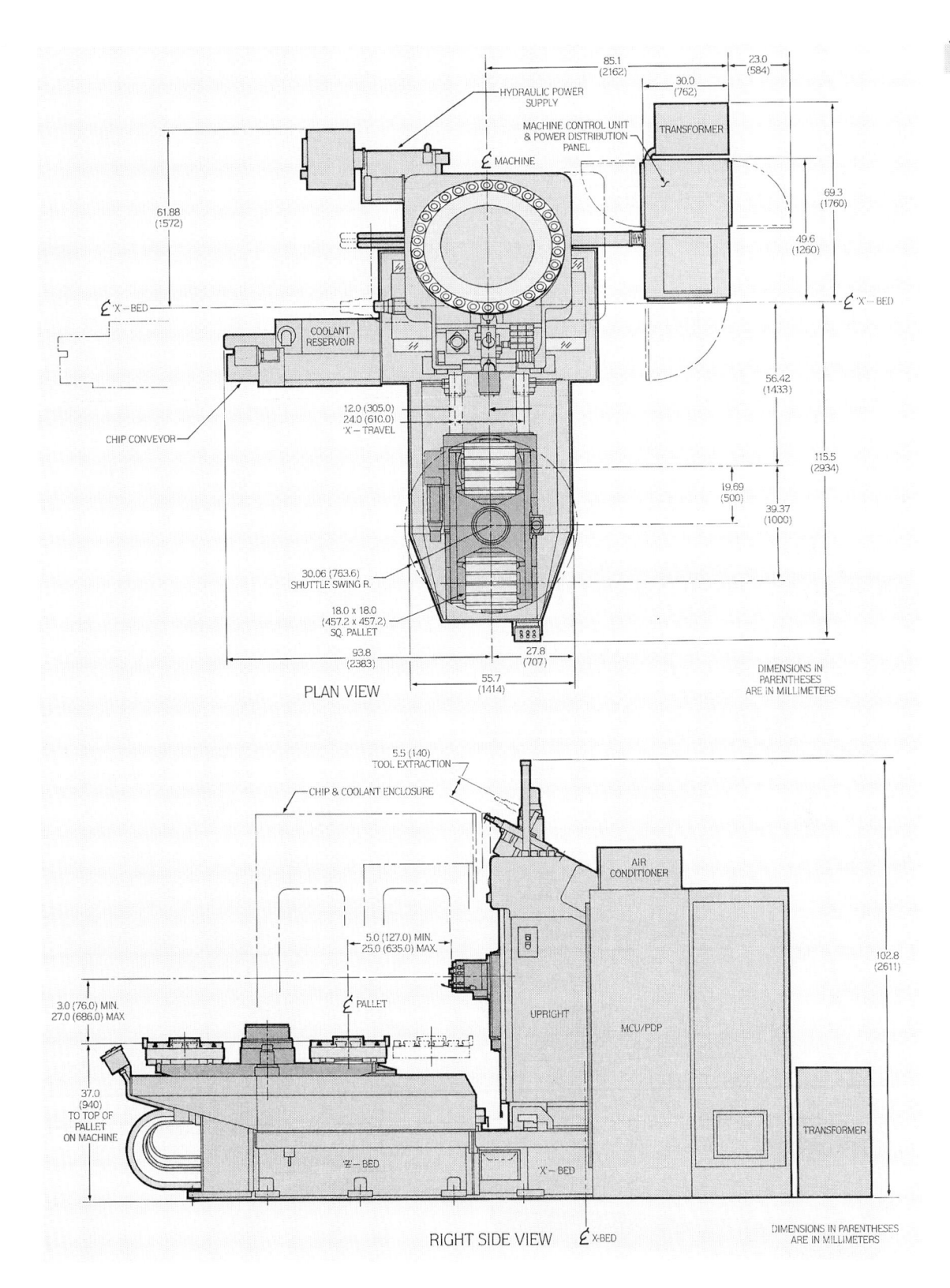

PLAN VIEW

- HYDRAULIC POWER SUPPLY
- MACHINE CONTROL UNIT & POWER DISTRIBUTION PANEL
- TRANSFORMER
- ℄ MACHINE
- ℄ 'X'–BED
- COOLANT RESERVOIR
- CHIP CONVEYOR
- 12.0 (305.0) / 24.0 (610.0) 'X'–TRAVEL
- 30.06 (763.6) SHUTTLE SWING R.
- 18.0 x 18.0 (457.2 x 457.2) SQ. PALLET

Dimensions:
- 85.1 (2162)
- 23.0 (584)
- 30.0 (762)
- 61.88 (1572)
- 69.3 (1760)
- 49.6 (1260)
- 56.42 (1433)
- 115.5 (2934)
- 19.69 (500)
- 39.37 (1000)
- 93.8 (2383)
- 27.8 (707)
- 55.7 (1414)

DIMENSIONS IN PARENTHESES ARE IN MILLIMETERS

RIGHT SIDE VIEW

- 5.5 (140) TOOL EXTRACTION
- CHIP & COOLANT ENCLOSURE
- AIR CONDITIONER
- 5.0 (127.0) MIN. / 25.0 (635.0) MAX.
- ℄ PALLET
- UPRIGHT
- MCU/PDP
- 3.0 (76.0) MIN. / 27.0 (686.0) MAX
- 37.0 (940) TO TOP OF PALLET ON MACHINE
- 'Z'–BED
- 'X'–BED
- TRANSFORMER
- 102.8 (2611)
- ℄ X-BED

DIMENSIONS IN PARENTHESES ARE IN MILLIMETERS

5

Listening comprehension and pair work.

Planning a trip to London (2)

Listen to the dialogue between Manfred and Peter and take notes of what the two people are saying. Play the situation – one student is Manfred, the other Peter.

While listening to the dialogue, pay attention to the following points:

– How do they want to travel to London?
– What do they say about the prices?
– Which airlines are mentioned in the dialogue?
– Who do they want to call?
– Which company will they choose?

LANGUAGE FUNCTIONS:

Satisfaction / dissatisfaction

We found the performance of the new turbine very satisfactory.

Most of the equipment in our plant is working to our full satisfaction.

We're satisfied with his work.

I'm afraid the fork lift trucks you sent us last week are not really adequate for our needs.

I know it's a different model but I'm quite sure they'll be quite satisfied when they see the excellent workmanship.

That's what we expected.

There's a short circuit in the control board? But that's terrible!

6

Have a look at the "Language Functions" on the left and put in *really* or *very*:

a. Is there … a short circuit in the control panel?
b. I'm not quite sure whether these machine tools are … suitable for our purposes.
c. This is a different model, but it's also … economical.
d. Did you … see the lift trucks they showed at the trade fair last month?
e. I don't … believe that the equipment in the machine shop is working to their full satisfaction.
f. That's … terrible!
g. Did she … find the performance of the machine satisfactory?
h. She likes music … much.
i. He's quite efficient, … .

7

Solving a puzzle.

Can you solve this number puzzle? How fast can you do it? The different symbols shown below have different values. If you add the values together, you will get the totals shown. What is the missing total for the left-hand column?

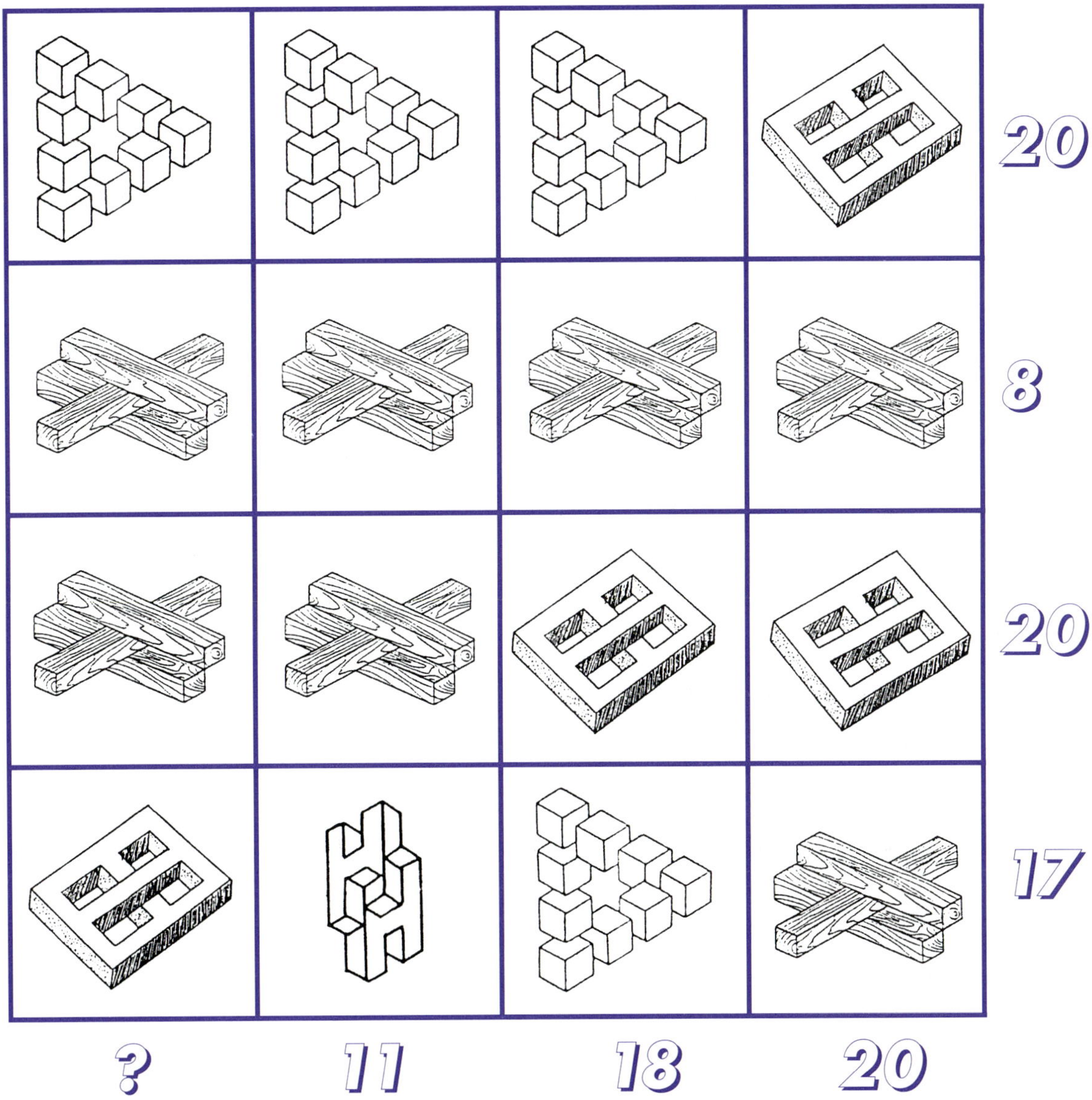

17 A helping hand (1)

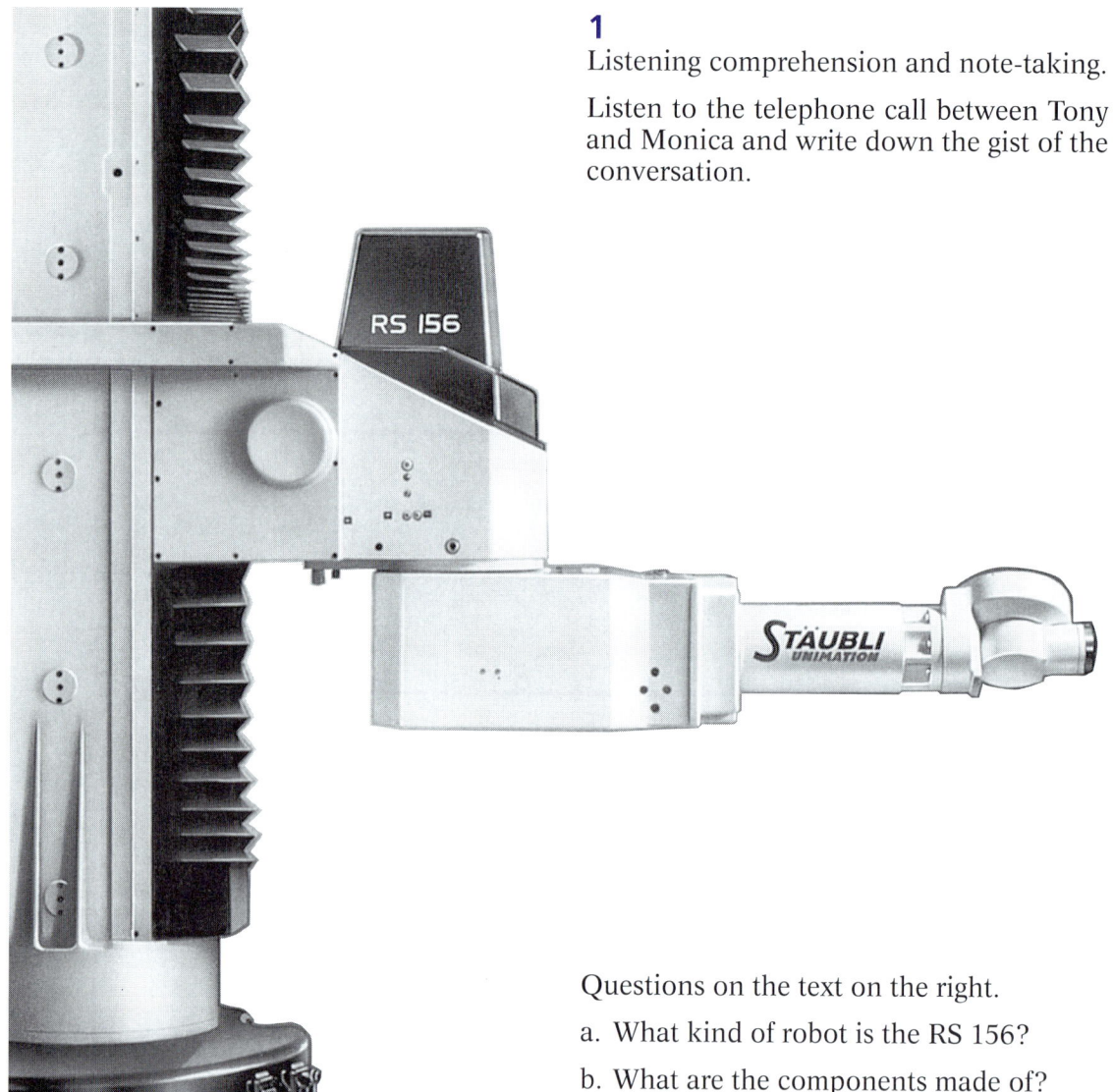

1

Listening comprehension and note-taking.

Listen to the telephone call between Tony and Monica and write down the gist of the conversation.

Questions on the text on the right.

a. What kind of robot is the RS 156?
b. What are the components made of?
c. What is special about the bearings?
d. How many axes does the robot have?

RS 156 Industrial Robot

The Industrial Robot RS 156 is a high payload robot. With six axes, a load carrying capacity of 30 kg and a reach of 1500 mm, it is part of the Stäubli-Unimation range of robots. The robot can easily be integrated into an existing manufacturing line. Cast aluminium components give great strength and rigidity. Axes 1 and 2 (movement of the arm on its base and movement of the forearm on the arm) are mounted on roller bearings of very high load capacity. These roller bearings require no adjustment and are easy to fit and remove. The vertical movement carriage is mounted on high load capacity roller bearings running in a hardened slideway. Very simple construction gives the system great reliability with easy access.

Axes 1, 2, 3, 4, 5 and 6 have an oil bath, guaranteeing long life and accuracy. Smooth lines and rounded edges give greater safety and allow easy cleaning. The servo motors require minimal maintenance and have very strong magnets.

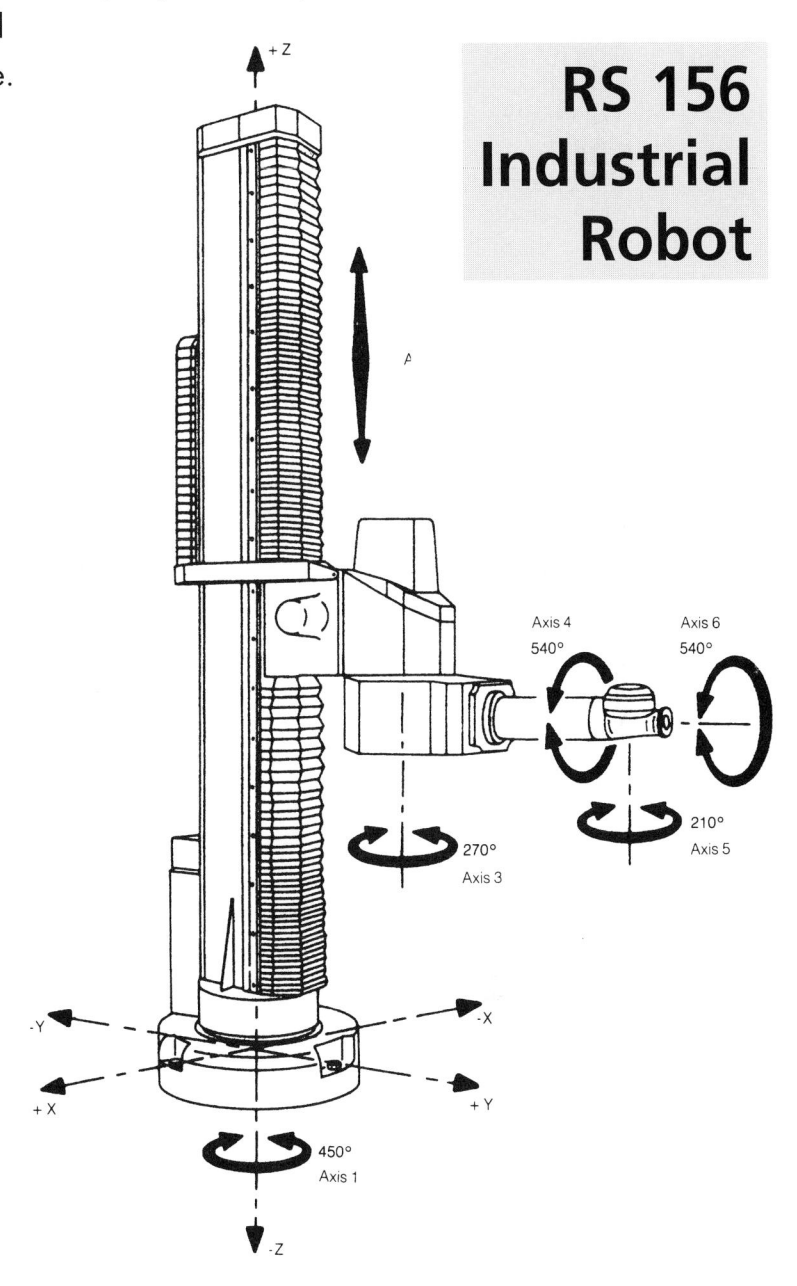

17 A LOOK AT GRAMMAR:

Expressions with "do" and "make"

DO How is your brother doing? – He's fine, I think.
Have you done the workshop? *(= cleaned the workshop)*
Has she done her homework?
We can't do a thing about it. *(= we can't change it at all)*
They do a lot of business with American companies.

MAKE You're making a lot of noise!
Could you make me a cup of coffee?
Will you be able to make it next Monday? *(= can you come …)*
I think we should make some plans for the coming conference.
A hundred cents make one dollar.
Don't make him do it. *(= don't force him to do it)*
What do you make of this letter? *(= what do you think this letter means?)*

NOTE: There is no rule for the use of *do* or *make* – it is necessary to learn the expressions.

LANGUAGE FUNCTIONS:

Requesting / ordering

Would you mind taking these drawings to the workshop, please? – No, not at all.

Could you watch the machine for a while?

There's no hurry – take your time!

Make sure you get the right tools.

Check the diagram, will you?

I wonder if I might ask you to have a look at these drawings.

Tell them we can't deliver the tubes before the middle of September.

2
Writing exercise.

Write a short article about the use of robots in industry and in households (in future?). Say what you think about the effects of automation (Jobs? Work satisfaction? Working hours? Quality of work?).

3

Have a look at the grammar explanations and the "Language Functions" on the left and decide which word is correct: *do*, *make* or *take*.

Our industrial robots are extremely accurate and … (a) use of the latest techniques. An industrial robot can be a very safe machine – or you as a user can … (b) it be a very dangerous one. So … (c) observe the following safety measures:

Please … (d) time to read the entire safety manual.

… (e) sure guards and shields are in place at all times.

… (f) not place your hands near a rotating machine part.

Never use wrenches, or other tools that … (g) not fit properly.

When you … (h) repairs, be sure to … (i) all necessary precautions to prevent accidents.

Always wear safety glasses when operating machines.

Clear vision helps you … (j) good work as well as avoid accidents.

… (k) certain all covers are closed before leaving any job.

4

Listening comprehension.

At Heathrow Airport

Listen to the dialogue between Manfred and Peter and answer these questions:

a. How was the flight?

b. How will they get to Richmond? Which underground lines do they have to take?

c. How long will the journey take?

5

Discussion / group work.

In groups of three or four students, discuss the role of industrial robots and similar automatic machines (Will they cause more unemployment? What other dangers are there?). One student takes notes of the group discussion.

18 A helping hand (2)

All Stäubli-Unimation electric robots series RS 156 are ... with the CS controller capable of operating in the most hostile industrial environments. This controller ... a heat-exchanger and air filtering equipment (protection class IP 54: 5° – 40°C). It is made up of the following components:

Industrial Visual Display Terminal
With integrated ... disk drive, printer output and lockable keyboard

Control Panel
Ergonomic design for easy ... to the control buttons and LED display of input and output ...

Teach ...
Protected with "deadman's" switch and ... stop button

Serial Communication
Five available ports, including one for the supervisor ... under DDCMP protocol, one for the ALTER protocol link for real time ... control and three others for auxiliary functions

1
Listening comprehension.

In the text on the left you can see nine gaps where words or figures are missing. Have a look at the text and try to guess the missing items. After that, listen to the recording – you will hear the complete text and can write down the missing items. Then listen again to the text.

LANGUAGE FUNCTIONS:

Requesting / giving permission

You don't mind if I make a few phone calls from here, do you? – No, not at all, go ahead.

Could I possibly borrow your dictionary for a few hours? There are some urgent faxes I have to translate. – Yes, by all means.

I wonder if I might use your terminal for half an hour or so. Mine's broken down, you know. – Yes, of course, go right ahead.

I don't suppose I could borrow your pen, could I? – Why not? Go right ahead.

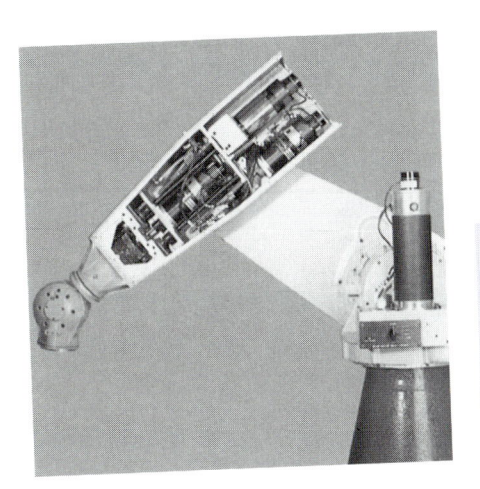

2
Listening comprehension.

Let's go to a museum

Listen to the conversation between Brian, Manfred and Jane. After listening, decide whether the sentences below are TRUE or FALSE:

	TRUE	FALSE
a. Brian, Manfred and Jane are having breakfast.	☐	☐
b. Jane and Brian always have a big breakfast.	☐	☐
c. On weekdays, Jane and Brian usually have muesli for breakfast.	☐	☐
d. Manfred would very much like to see the Science Museum today.	☐	☐
e. On the way they will have to change from one undergroud line to another.	☐	☐

ARM CONSTRUCTION

The arm consists of cast aluminium box sections giving it rigidity and lightness.

18 A LOOK AT GRAMMAR:

-ing form (1)

AS A SUBJECT OR OBJECT	Travelling makes people tired. Smoking in a laboratory may be dangerous. Her hobby is painting.	
AFTER CERTAIN WORDS	DO:	Have you done the cleaning?
	ENJOY:	I enjoy playing football.
	FINISH:	Just a moment – I'll have to finish writing this letter first.
	GO:	We usually go shopping on Saturdays.
	HATE:	I hate getting up early.
	NEED:	My hair needs cutting.
	LOOK FORWARD:	I look forward to spending some nice days in London.

NOTE: With some words or expressions, the -ing form is always used. There is, however, no rule for this, so the sentences will have to be learned.

3

Study the grammar above. Make sentences with the expression on the left:

keep	a.	he / make / mistakes all the time
enjoy	b.	she / work / with the new CAD software
look forward	c.	they / use / the new camcorder during their holiday in Canada
hate	d.	they / have to redesign / all the computer terminals
finish	e.	you / read / the specifications of the RS 156 Industrial Robot?
look forward	f.	she / meet / her English friend at the conference next week
hate	g.	the engineers / go / to that meeting every Monday
keep	h.	you / have to / try
need	i.	your car / wash
go	j.	he / usually / swim on Sundays
do	k.	you / do / check?
finish	l.	I / have to / write the accident report first
look forward	m.	she / spend / some time in Canada

4
Discussion / group work.

WHAT WILL THE FUTURE BRING ???

By the year 2030 …

1 =	will certainly happen
2 =	quite likely
3 =	possible
4 =	unlikely
5 =	impossible – will certainly not happen

1.	all factories will be fully automated.	1 2 3 4 5
2.	no more nuclear power stations will be built.	1 2 3 4 5
3.	people will be able to shop by computer.	1 2 3 4 5
4.	learning a foreign language will only take a week.	1 2 3 4 5
5.	most families will have a robot at home.	1 2 3 4 5
6.	people will be living in cities on the moon.	1 2 3 4 5
7.	smoking will be illegal.	1 2 3 4 5
8.	life expectancy in the industrialized countries will be 120.	1 2 3 4 5
9.	Europe will be one country with one parliament.	1 2 3 4 5
10.	English will be the world language.	1 2 3 4 5

AT THE SCIENCE MUSEUM

A special exhibition: Change and the chemical industry

The modern chemical industry began two hundred years ago when the processing of common salt to make raw materials for the manufacture of large quantities of soap and glass changed people's lives. Salt is also the source of chlorine, used in bleaching since the eighteenth century and today the starting point for a great range of chemicals with uses stretching from sterilised water to dry-cleaning fluids and PVC. After the Second World War giant plants were built to supply great quantities of the new plastics and synthetic fibres such as nylon, polyester and polythene. These characterised the whole chemical industry. Today the industry is changing – oil prices fluctuate dramatically and markets change. The chemical companies of Europe, Japan and America are spending hundreds of millions of pounds on research and development of products that will be profitable in small quantities. Most plastics and many other materials whose uses range from shampoo to shoelaces are based on the element carbon. For a hundred years carbon compounds were supplied mostly from tar, a by-product from the manufacture of coal gas, and from alcohol. But since the 1960s oil has been the principal source of carbon.

Petrochemical plants are often very large, not only because they involve many different stages, but also because their products are required in vast quantities. In contrast to the often noisy processes at a petrochemical works, biotechnology operates within the small quiet world of the living cell. This world is amazingly productive since many bacterial cells can double in number every twenty minutes.

5

Have a look at the text on the left and the "Language Functions" of this unit (p. 103). Decide which of the two forms in brackets is the correct one:

a. Could I perhaps (borrow/borrowing) your technical English dictionary? I'm not sure what "bleaching" (means/mean).

b. Today the chemical industry is (change/changing) very fast – I sometimes (wonder/wondering) what all this will lead to.

c. I don't mind what material you (use/using) as long as the process (works/working) properly.

d. I look forward to (see/seeing) you at the conference next week.

e. (Produce/Producing) large quantities of plastics and synthetic fibres (was/was being) very profitable for the chemical industry.

RULES FOR THE FACTORY

Rule 1

The BOSS is always RIGHT

Rule 2

When in doubt – refer to Rule 1.

19 Bits and bytes: PROCEDE for Windows

1

Introductory discussion – using CAD and CAM

On the next two pages, you will see the description of PROCEDE, an auxiliary program that can be used with CAD. Before you look at the text, talk about the following points:

a. What do CAD programs do? Do you use such programs in your job?

b. What are the advantages of the CAD/CAM combination?

c. What do you think about the increasing use of computers in offices and workshops?

2

Reading comprehension.

PROCEDE includes

FloSheet – for sketches and full-size engineering drawings
SpecSht – provides access to a library of specification sheets
SymGen – is used to maintain and edit the library
Exports – will send your drawings to other programs you are using

Read the next two pages and take notes of the most important points.

3

Listening comprehension and group work.

Listen to the recording and write down what the text says about CAD/CAM systems (What can they do? How do they do this? Who uses such systems? Why are they used?).

Go back to Exercise 1 and continue the discussion with the question "What will computers look like in the future?"

PROCEDE for Windows is a breakthrough in managing process design data. The name PROCEDE is derived from a project, the aim of which is to create a complete PROCess Engineer's Design Environment. With PROCEDE's sophisticated family of applications you can produce everything from high-quality drawings, reports and specification sheets to input for other programs such as simulators, word processors and rigorous design packages. One of the very best things about the PROCEDE programs is their simplicity. You do not need to be an experienced draughtsman or computer user to create professional looking drawings. Much of the simplicity comes from the fact that PROCEDE uses the facilities of Microsoft Windows to provide a common look and feel to all of its component programs. The user interface is consistent with other Windows applications, so that it is extremely easy to learn how to use PROCEDE. By using PROCEDE to produce drawings and data sheets, you save time and cut costs.

With PROCEDE you can produce a quality engineering drawing without a draughtsman or an expensive CAD system.

19 FLOSHEET

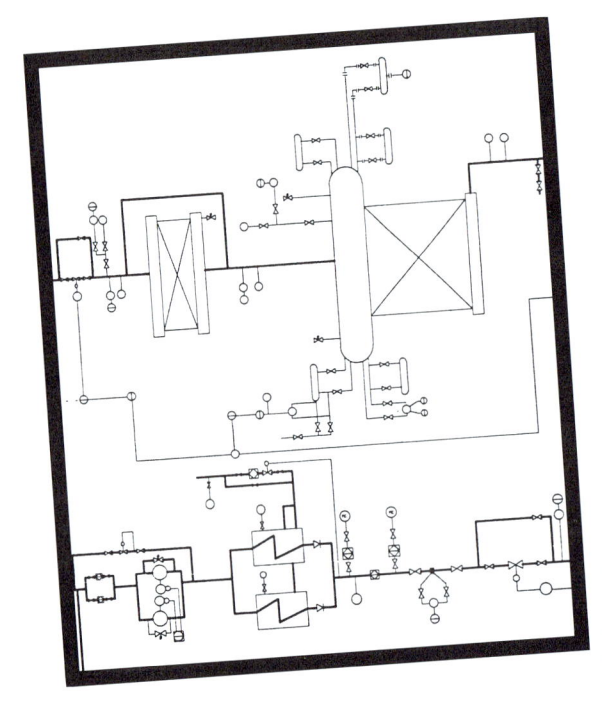

Make quick sketches and full-size engineering drawings simply by using the mouse to select pulldown menus and equipment icons.

With *FloSheet* you can create high-quality drawings such as:

- Process flowsheets
- Plant layouts
- Logic charts
- Control systems
- Circuit diagrams
- Engineering line diagrams

Produce anything from a small flowsheet sketch to be included in your report to a full scale industry standard drawing with all the necessary detail.

With *FloSheet 3.0* you can:

- Access the library of over 200 process engineering equipment symbols.
- Rotate, scale and drag symbols around the drawing.
- Connect symbols with lines representing process streams, pipe work, instrument lines etc.
- Create drawings on several different layers and combine to produce a large scale design.

PROCEDE and Windows act together to give you a quick start and a professional finish to your work.

- No training is required. Windows is easy to pick up. If you already use Windows, PROCEDE will be familiar to you the moment you start.
- Customize your own tools, and save them for future work.
- Use PROCEDE alongside your word processor or another application.
- PROCEDE can be used as an integrated system or the constituent parts *SpecSht*, *FloSheet* and *SymGen* can be used as separate programs.
- Use *SpecSht* as an independent program for managing process design data.
- High-quality laser output – no need to sketch or draw by hand any more!
- Use any printer or plotter connected to your Windows environment.
- Store your design data so that you can update drawings and specification data easily.
- Download your drawings to AutoCAD and carry them through to the next stage of development.

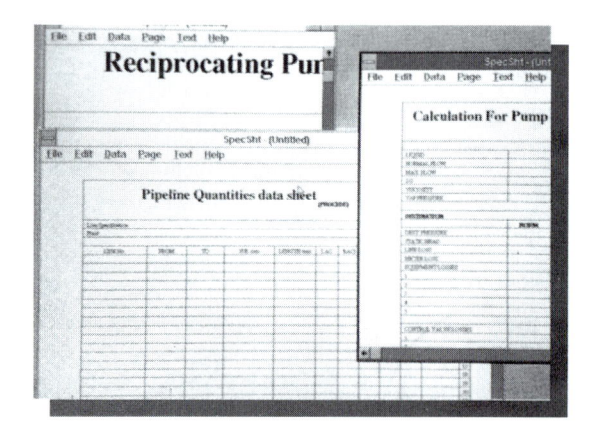

A LOOK AT GRAMMAR:

-ing form (2)

There is a small group of expressions with different meanings, depending on whether you use the -ing form or not:

- I'll never forget visiting them. *(= … my visit to them)*
- I certainly won't forget to visit them. *(= in the future!)*

- I regret telling her about the accident. *(= I'm sorry I told her)*
- I regret to tell you … *(= I am sorry I have to tell you)*

- Yes, I remember writing that letter. *(= I remember that I did it)*
- I must remember to write that letter. *(= I must not forget to do it)*

- She stopped talking *(= she was quiet)*
- She stopped to talk to him. *(= she stopped doing something in order to talk to him)*

4

Have a look at the grammar above and the "Language Functions" on the page 113. After that, try to find the correct form of the words in brackets (-ing or not?):

a. Remember (get) some detailed information about the properties of the new plastics.

b. You must remember (use) some sort of coating for these parts – iron is liable to rust.

c. We very much regret (send) you these faulty parts.

d. I can't hear what they're saying – stop (make) such an awful noise!

e. Don't forget (tell) them that we have developed new twin-track conveyors.

f. Do you remember (meet) her at the international plastics conference in Bristol?

g. We must not forget (inform) them that these materials are liable to corrosion.

Working with a modern user interface …

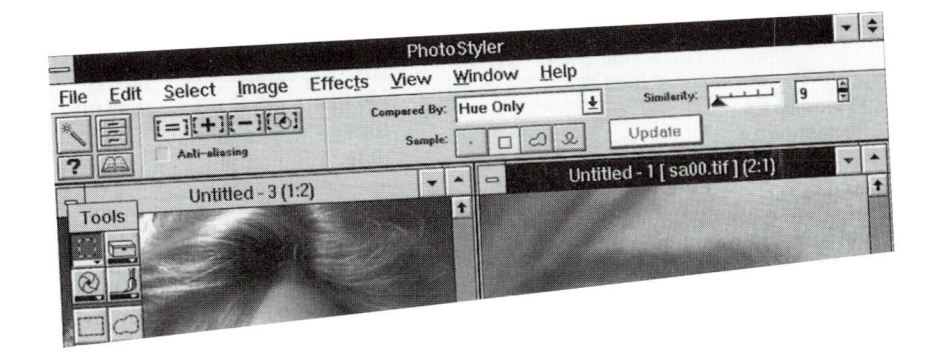

5
Have another look at the grammar explanations of this unit (p. 111) and try to rewrite the instructions below using *forget* and *remember*.
Where do you think such instructions can be found? What do you think about them?

Do you know how to use this buoy?

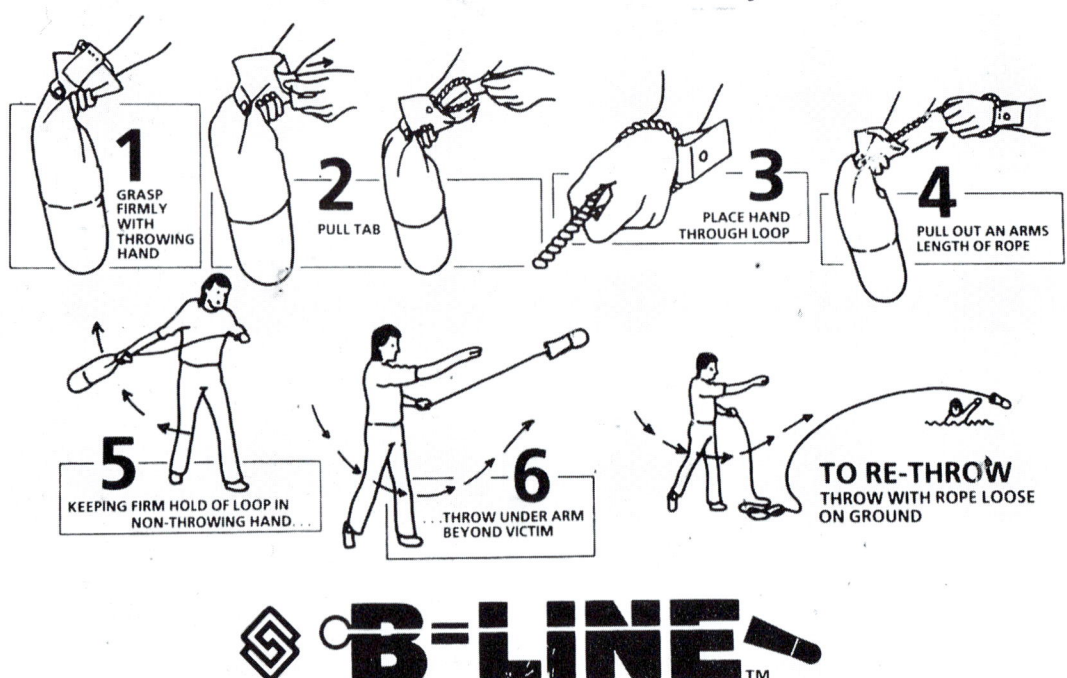

1. GRASP FIRMLY WITH THROWING HAND
2. PULL TAB
3. PLACE HAND THROUGH LOOP
4. PULL OUT AN ARMS LENGTH OF ROPE
5. KEEPING FIRM HOLD OF LOOP IN NON-THROWING HAND...
6. ...THROW UNDER ARM BEYOND VICTIM

TO RE-THROW
THROW WITH ROPE LOOSE ON GROUND

B-LINE™

Glasdon Limited, Blackpool, England. Tel: 0253 694811
Telex: 677288,

LANGUAGE FUNCTIONS:

What is it like?

What is their new plant like? – Very modern, you know – state-of-the-art, you might say.

It's essential to obtain some detailed information about the chemical properties of the compound.

Oil possesses the property of floating on water.

Components made of cast-iron are liable to rust.

Many of these components are used in their newly-developed twin-track conveyors.

This material is liable to corrosion.

6
Listening comprehension and pair work.

At the Science Museum (1)

Listen to the conversation between Peter and Manfred and write down the missing information of the following sentences.

a. They are in the Science Museum in the …

b. "Puffing Billy" was built … by … .

c. The museum has a special hall for … .

d. At the moment they are showing … .

Now listen to the conversation again and take notes – one of you writes down the part of Manfred, the other the part of Peter.

If necessary, listen to the dialogue a third time.

When you have finished the parts, play the situation.

I LOVE WORK

I could sit and look at it FOR HOURS

19

AT THE SCIENCE MUSEUM
"Puffing Billy" 1813 – oldest railway locomotive in existence

This is the oldest railway locomotive in existence and represents the first phase of successful steam working on railways. The locomotives built before 1829 were intended to replace horses, generally within the area of a private industrial railway. "Puffing Billy" worked on the railway between Wylam Colliery and the River Tyne five miles away, pulling loads of 50 tons at five miles per hour. The locomotive has two cylinders, to make it self starting in all positions, and the drive to the wheels is by an arrangement of beams, connecting rods, cranks, and gears. Driver and fireman stood at opposite ends of the boiler. Although it is a very primitive stage in the evolution of the locomotive, "Puffing Billy" had a useful life of nearly 50 years, and is today substantially in original condition.

Technology on the advance ...

In the cockpit of the Airbus A320, all information necessary for operating the aircraft is displayed on six colour monitors. The aircraft is controlled by electrical signals, and the conventional control columns have been replaced by sidestick controllers. These are installed to the left and right of the pilots in side consoles. The Airbus A320, which Lufthansa is operating on short and medium-range routes, is the first airliner in which "fly-by-wire" technology is being used.

7

Groupwork / Discussion. Read the text about "Puffing Billy" on the left. Technology has changed a lot since the days of this locomotive. In groups of three or four, make a list of all the new technologies you can think of. Discuss their advantages / disadvantages (Faster work? More stress? Better products? More free time? More safety? Unemployment problems? Effect on the environment? etc.)

NEW TECHNOLOGY	ADVANTAGES	DISADVANTAGES

20 Bits and bytes: Images and cyberspace

1

Listening comprehension and discussion.

Virtual reality (VR) – stepping into cyberspace – allows you to simulate human experience in 3-D. Listen to the text and say what you think about virtual reality. (What can it be used for? Are there any dangers?).

2

Have a look at the cartoon below and use one of the words shown there for each gap:

a. A digital … operates on data supplied and stored in digital form, i.e. based on a system in which information is represented in the form of changing electrical signals.

b. A … is a computer output device that produces hard copy.

c. A flat-bed … is used to scan texts and images; if it is a black-and-white appliance, it uses the so-called "grey scale", a series of shades of grey ranging from white to black.

d. In a … machine, graphic material is scanned and the image converted into electrical signals, for subsequent reconversion into a hard copy.

AT THE SCIENCE MUSEUM
The Boulton and Watt Rotative Beam Engine 1788

James Watt (1736-1819) was a scientific instrument maker who became interested in the steam engine when repairing a model of a Newcomen engine in 1765. He realised that heat was wasted by condensing the steam inside the cylinder, the substantial mass of which had to be heated and cooled for every double stroke of the engine. Watt's idea was to add a separate chamber in which a vacuum was maintained, and to open this to the cylinder when the steam was to be condensed. The steam passed into this "separate condenser" and was cooled, while the cylinder remained hot. Fuel consumption was reduced to less than one third that of a Newcomen type engine. With his partner, Matthew Boulton, Watt designed a rotative steam engine for driving machinery, of which this exhibit is an early example.

LANGUAGE FUNCTIONS:

Expressing belonging

The new plastic material for machine parts possesses a number of useful properties.

This tool kit is comprised of seven items.

The consignment consists of keyboard, monitor, mouse, disk drive, and printer.

The lift truck is our own design.

Ms Morgan is a member of our design team.

What department is John in? – Personnel Department.

3

Listening comprehension.

At the Science Museum (2)

Listen to the dialogue between Manfred and Peter and finish the sentences below:

a. At the moment, Peter and Manfred are looking at …

b. Many people think …

c. Actually, the first steam engine …

4

Ask questions and give appropriate answers according to this example:

open the window
Do you mind if I open the window?
Well, I'd rather you didn't.
No, not at all. / No, of course not.

a. program the computer

b. use your car for a day or two

c. explain this to you

d. ask you a question about a technical problem

e. have a look at your English book

f. give you a test

'And I bought this one to explain the manual of the first one.'

20 A LOOK AT GRAMMAR:

Expressions with "mind"

- Use your mind to solve this problem. (= *use your intelligence, your brain*)
- Sometimes, it's hard to keep your mind on your work. (= *it's hard to concentrate on your work*)
- She searched her mind for the man's name. (= *she tried to remember the man's name*)
- Did you change your mind about going to that conference? (= *did you change your plans?*)

- She really minds the rainy weather. (= *she really doesn't like …*)
- Never mind! (= *it doesn't matter*)
- Do you mind having to stay here alone? (= *do you have anything against …*)
- I don't mind the work, but I do mind the constant interruptions. (= *I have nothing against the work, but against the interruptions*)

NOTE: "Do" in the sentence above is a stronger form: I like it —> I do like it (= *I really like it very much*).

- Who will mind the machines when the technician is on holiday? (= *take care*)
- The best holiday, to my mind, is a month in the mountains. (= *in my opinion*)
- Mind your own business! (= *leave me alone – take care of your own problems*)
- Mind your head – that door is very low! (= *be careful or you might hit your head against the doorframe*)
- Do you mind if I open the window? (= *is it OK if I open the window?*)
- Do you mind opening the window? (= *could you open the window, please?*)
- Mind what you do! (= *be careful what you do, think about what you do*)
- Mind how you go! (= *be careful where / how you go*)
- Mind what the chief engineer tells you – it's important! (= *pay attention to what the chief engineer tells you*)
- They apologized later, mind you. (= *think of this fact*)
- You must bear in mind that stainless steel is a very expensive material. (= *you must remember / must not forget that …*)
- It has never crossed my mind. (= *I have never thought of it / about it*)

Other useful combinations with "mind"

- mindful (= *give thought and care or attention to something or somebody: mindful of one's duties*)
- mindless (= *something that does not require intelligence: "I'm afraid it's fairly mindless work."*)

5

Discussion. Listening to music and watching TV are the USA's favourite ways to spend free time – says a report published by a national institute. The report is based on a survey of nearly eight million households in over 200 metropolitan areas.

The figures show the percentage of households engaged in the activity:

Most frequent activities

Stereo/records/tapes	42.5%
Watching cable TV	40.9%
Walking for health	40.4%
VCR recording/viewing	39.5%
Working with computers	38.6%
Book reading	38%
Gardening	33.9%
Physical fitness/exercise	32.8%
Household pets	31.3%
Crafts	26.3%

At home activities

Book reading	38%
Gardening	33.9%
Household pets	31.3%
Crafts	26,3%
Catalog shopping	25.3%
Home workshop	22.9%
Crossword puzzles	21.6%
Needlework/knitting	20.8%
Sewing	20.4%
Caring for grandchildren	20.0%

Sporting activities

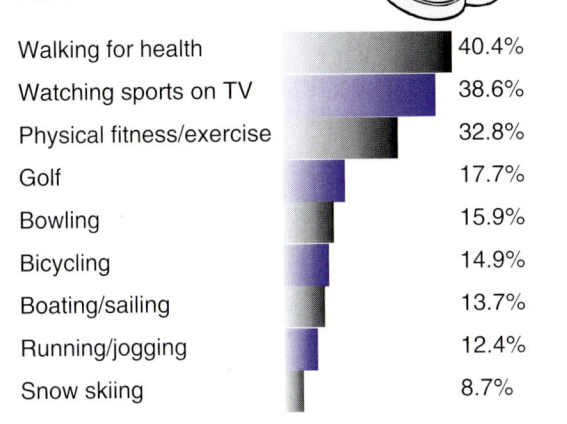

Walking for health	40.4%
Watching sports on TV	38.6%
Physical fitness/exercise	32.8%
Golf	17.7%
Bowling	15.9%
Bicycling	14.9%
Boating/sailing	13.7%
Running/jogging	12.4%
Snow skiing	8.7%

What do you think about these figures? What is the situation like in your country, do you think? Is it different? What are the most favourite activities in your country?

6

Change the sentences below using an expression with *mind*:

a. Could you open the window, please?

b. Please remember what I told you.

c. Is it all right with you if I open the window?

d. I have nothing against the rain.

e. You wanted to go to the conference, didn't you? Did you change your plans?

f. It's too late now, in my opinion.

g. Sometimes I find it quite hard to concentrate on my work.

h. She has nothing against working with computers, but she has something against bad monitors.

i. I'm still trying to remember her name.

7

Have a look at the text and the illustrations on the right and decide what is the correct word for each gap:

a. The word for a method or way of doing something difficult or complicated is … (distortion / image / source / technique).

b. A ruggedized computer is a … (big / new / old / tough) computer.

c. If a technical device is sophisticated, it is … (important / solid / technically advanced / very simple).

d. A module is a … (large monitor / precision instrument / standardized unit).

e. If something is unsurpassed, you cannot find anything that is … (better / newer / older / smaller).

f. The type of computer program that makes it possible to show figures in groups on a monitor screen is called … (calibration / capture / spreadsheet / subroutine).

g. Features are … (multiple measurements / special characteristics).

8

Have another look at the text and the illustrations on the right and try to answer these questions:

a. Can Image Analyst be used on a Macintosh computer?

b. Is Image Analyst useful for people who want to write their own programs?

c. Can multiple measurements be carried out with Image Analyst?

d. How can you customize the Image Analyst program?

e. Does Image Analyst have a library? (If yes, what kind of?)

'Would you mind if I plugged in my computer? I've made out my shopping list on it.'

FEATURES + FLEXIBILITY = POWER

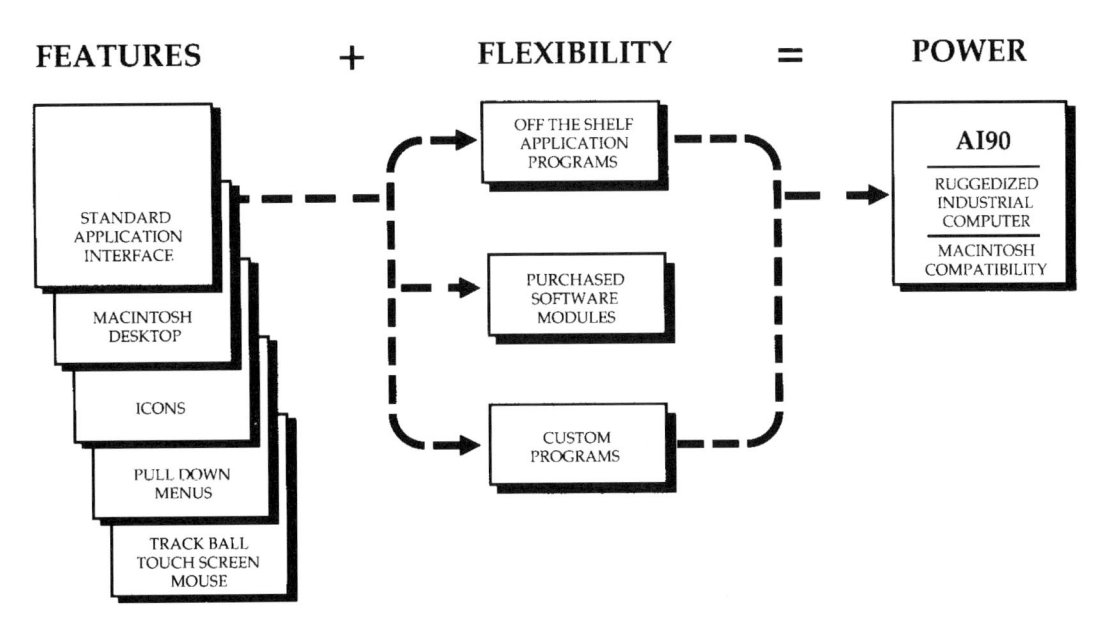

For users who don't want to write their own programs, Image Analyst is an easy-to-use applications software package designed to configure sophisticated imaging processing and measurement routines quickly. Unsurpassed in measurement, calibration, and sequencing functions, Image Analyst allows you to quickly capture, process, analyze, and display measurements and images.

A variety of image processing techniques are available, depending on what measurements are needed, the contrast between object and background, and the required accuracy.

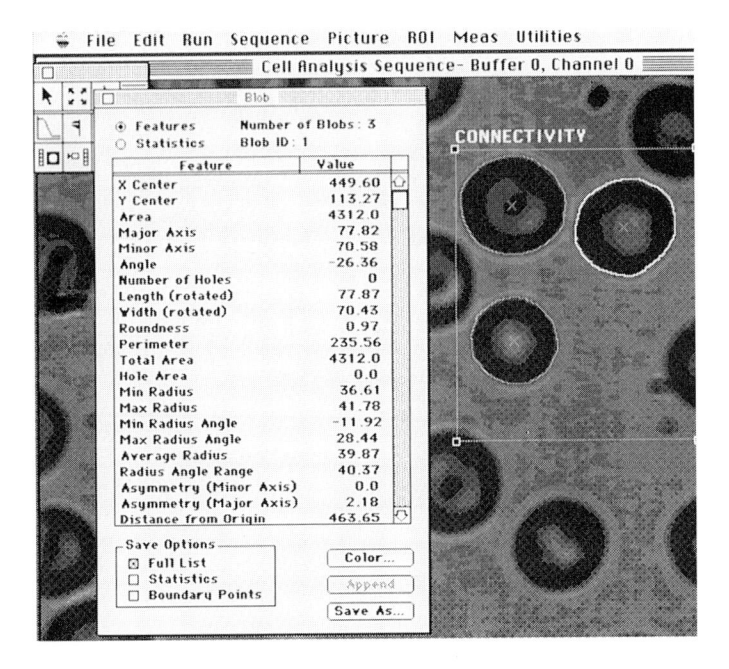

For repetitive applications, Image Analyst allows you to build sequences for implementing multiple measurements with a single command. As such, the software acts like an easy-to-use spreadsheet, as opposed to a macro routine.

Image Analyst uses a robust calibration technique for accurate, repeatable measurements. This technique removes the non-uniformity caused by optical and geometric distortions.

You can customize Image Analyst by developing your own processing and analysis algorithms. For these applications, Automatix offers the source code for Image Analyst, Image Analyst/Source, and its extensive image processing and robotic guidance subroutine library.

123

Testing Your Language — Part Two

A. Listening comprehension

43 You are going to hear a text with the title **What's going on with nuclear fusion?**.
Listen carefully to the text and decide if the statements below are TRUE or FALSE :

	Statement	TRUE	FALSE
1.	Hydrogen is located at the core of stars.	☐	☐
2.	The Princeton Plasma Physics Laboratory has the shape of a doughnut.	☐	☐
3.	Most of the visible universe is plasma.	☐	☐
4.	The plasma in the vacuum chamber is heated up by an electric current.	☐	☐
5.	The magnetic field is used to create a current.	☐	☐
6.	The power to energize the coils comes from electrical generators.	☐	☐
7.	Fusion energy is much cleaner than fission energy.	☐	☐
8.	A fusion reactor will not create any radioactive waste.	☐	☐
9.	A fusion reactor puts out dangerous neutrons, but they can be stopped.	☐	☐

deuterium-tritium fusion reaction

fusion reactor experiment

Testing

B. Listening comprehension

Below you can see the instruction for using the Cullmann "Clamp Magic", a special pocket clamp for cameras. Three of the instructions (B, C and G) are missing. You are going to hear the three missing items on the recording – decide which of them is B, C or G:

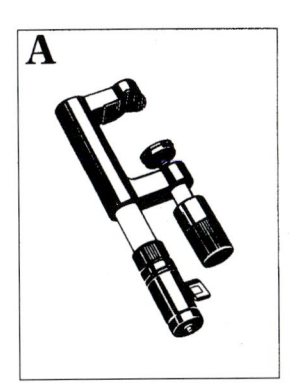

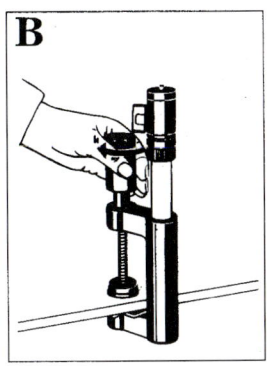

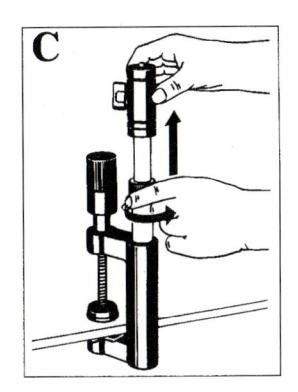

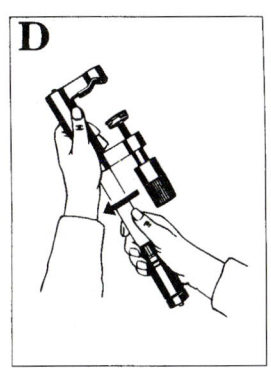

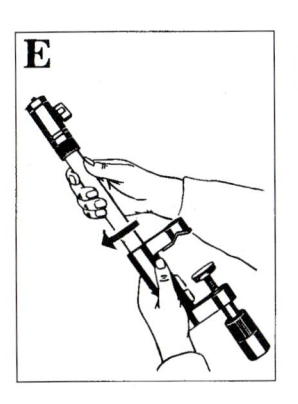

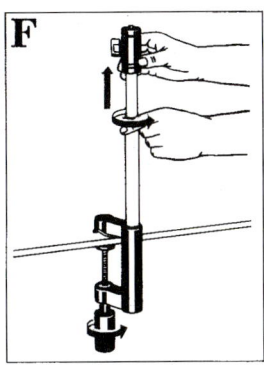

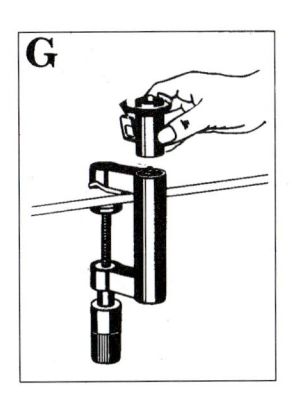

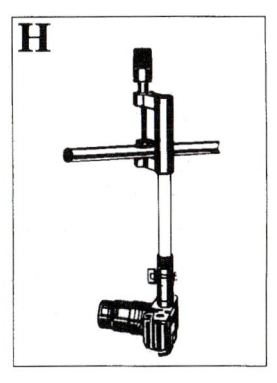

Ⓐ The CLAMP MAGIC (Item No. 2703) is supplied already assembled and is ready for use.
TIP:
The ballhead can be unscrewed when necessary. The lever on the ballhead serves to lock lateral motion!

Ⓑ ?

Ⓒ ?

Ⓓ For more convenient handling or when you wish to add extra height to the CLAMP MAGIC, simply unscrew the center column and reinsert it in the top socket (see illustration E).

Ⓔ Place the center column on the other side of the CLAMP MAGIC and screw into place.

Ⓕ The locking lever for the ballhead can now be more conveniently grasped. The height of the center column can be adjusted as shown under "C".

Ⓖ ?

Ⓗ The CLAMP MAGIC can be attached to many objects. Adjustments are possible vertically, horizontally and laterally.

125

Testing

A tire has ten lives

Aviation technology today is highly advanced, but each year inventors come up with new ideas on how to perfect aircraft. The landing gear, in particular, seems to offer the most scope for innovation.

Several inventors have suggested using motors to propel the aircraft's wheels. They have noticed that at every landing, the tires smoke and leave black stripes of abraded rubber on the runway, causing unnecessary wear and tear.

If the wheels were turning at the moment of making contact with the ground rather than having to instantly accelerate from zero to 150 miles per hour, their life could be extended many times. "Great idea!" say the aircraft designers, and they have been saying this for decades. But adding so many mechanical parts and so much weight to the landing gear would simply be impractical.

So things remain as they have always been: after about 150 landings, aircraft tires are worn down and have to be re-treaded. Once it has been ascertained that their basic structure is undamaged, a fresh tread is applied by means of rubber vulcanization. Unlike car tires, however, aircraft tires only have lengthwise grooves because once on the runway aircraft only travel in a straight direction. A tire can be retreaded as many as nine times, which means that a healthy aircraft tire can have ten lives.

Most car owners don't know much about their car wheels, except that they have a rim and a tire which has to be changed occasionally. At major airlines, changing tires is an everyday routine. The strict safety guidelines governing air traffic dictate that all wheels make regular trips to the workshop – before a defect turns up and not afterward. If you consider that the largest aircraft, the jumbo jet, has only two wings but no fewer than 18 wheels, you get some idea of just how much work this involves.

Each year, Lufthansa's wheel workshop at Frankfurt Airport checks 13,000 aircraft wheels, which come in 20 types and sizes. Automatic testing units use various methods to detect even the finest cracks in an aluminum rim. The "history" of each wheel is faithfully recorded: its origin and age, the number of breakdowns and repairs, tire changes, aircraft changes and everything else it has encountered during its lifetime of flying.

The cheapest part of a wheel is still the tire. A single jumbo tire sells for DM2,200 and can be retreaded for one-fourth of the price. Rims and brakes are, in comparison, much more expensive. A carbon disc brake costs as much as a complete automobile.

To reduce the fire hazard, the tubeless tires are filled with nitrogen rather than air. The pressure, which is checked daily, is between 12 and 14 bar, that is, six to eight times that of a car tire. If a tire has to be changed out on the apron, this high pressure comes in handy. Mechanics fill the aircraft jack with nitrogen from the tire, thus lifting the landing gear off the ground. However, as tires sometimes weigh in excess of 200 pounds, they don't remove them by hand.

Aircraft clock up considerable mileage – even while taxiing on the ground. Between each landing and takeoff they travel about five miles on average. In the course of a year, this can amount to over 6,000 miles. Each tire supports a weight of 15 to 25 tonnes and a far heavier force at the impact of landing.

What happens if the takeoff of a fully-loaded long-haul aircraft has to be aborted? It's the supreme test of any landing gear, with hot brakes and scraping, smoking, sometimes bursting tires. But as an aircraft has 18 tires, one of them can go flat without any risk whatsoever of skidding.❑

Testing

C. Reading comprehension

Have a look at the text on the left and mark the correct answer (a or b):

1. The aircraft's wheels
   a. are propelled by motors.
   b. make contact with the ground at 150 miles per hour.

2. Aircraft designers find some ideas
   a. impractical.
   b. too expensive.

3. Retreading aircraft tires is done after
   a. 150 miles.
   b. 150 landings.

4. The retreading process can be repeated if the tires
   a. are undamaged.
   b. have lengthwise grooves.

5. All aircraft wheels must be
   a. checked regularly.
   b. equipped with aluminium rims.

6. Lufthansa's wheel workshop at Frankfurt Airport
   a. checks 20 types of aircraft.
   b. has automatic testing units.

7. The aircraft's tubeless tires are filled with
   a. air.
   b. nitrogen.

8. Aircraft tires cannot be removed by hand because
   a. there's nitrogen in them.
   b. they are too heavy.

9. A jumbo jet has 18 wheels and
   a. needs them all for the landing process.
   b. could land on 17 only if necessary.

AUTOHOMES WORLD

Autohomes specifications

Base vehicle	Talbot Express					Ford Transit	
Model	CAMELOT 1000	CAMELOT 1400	HIGHWAYMAN	BEDOUIN	LANDLINER	FRONTIER	TRAVELHOME V
Type	High-top	High-top	Coachbuilt	Coachbuilt	Coachbuilt	High-top	Coachbuilt
Overall Length	4877mm 16′ 0″	4877mm 16′ 0″	5486mm 18′ 0″	5486mm 18′ 0″	6706mm 22′ 0″	4775mm 15′ 8″	5410mm 17′ 9″
Overall Width (ex mirrors)	1965mm 6′ 5⅜″	1965mm 6′ 5⅜″	2146mm 7′ 0½″	2146mm 7′ 0½″	2260mm 7′ 5″	1938mm 6′ 4¼″	2210mm 7′ 3″
Overall Height	2625mm 8′ 7⅜″	2625mm 8′ 7⅜″	2768mm 9′ 1″	2768mm 9′ 1″	2718mm 8′ 11″	2705mm 8′ 10½″	2826mm 9′ 3¼″
Gross Vehicle Weight	2450kg 2.41 tons	2900kg 2.85 tons	2900kg 2.85 tons	2900kg 2.85 tons	3100kg 3.05 tons	2440kg 2.40 tons	2570kg 2.52 tons
Kerb Weight	1867kg 1.84 tons	1882kg 1.85 tons	2047kg 2.01 tons	2160kg 2.12 tons	2305kg 2.27 tons	1812kg 1.78 tons	2104kg 2.07 tons
Load Capacity	583kg 0.57 ton	1018kg 1.00 ton	853kg 0.84 ton	740kg 0.73 ton	795kg 0.78 tons	628kg 0.62 ton	466kg 0.45 ton
Lower Double Bed	1880 x 1600mm* 6′ 2″ x 5′ 3″*	1880 x 1600mm* 6′ 2″ x 5′ 3″*	SEE	SEE	SEE	1981 x 1626mm 6′ 2″ x5′ 4″	1880 x 1270mm 6′ 2″ x 4′ 2″
OR Two Single Beds	1930 x 546mm* 6′4″x1′9½″*	1930 x 546mm* 6′4″x1′9½″*	FLOOR	FLOOR	FLOOR	1981 x 559mm* 6′6″x1′10″*	
Upper Double Bed	OPTIONAL 1829 x 1372mm 6′ 0″ x 4′ 6″	OPTIONAL 1829 x 1372mm 6′ 0″ x 4′ 6″	PLANS	PLANS	PLAN	OPTIONAL 1829 x 1372mm 6′ 0″ x 4′ 6″	1880 x 1220mm 6′ 2″ x 4′ 0″

* = maximum dimension. † = minimum dimension

Base vehicle	Vauxhall Rascal	Volkswagen Transporter			Nissan Urvan
Model	BAMBI	KAMPER	KAMEO	KOMET	NOMAD
Type	Mini Coachbuilt	Elevating Roof	High-top	High-top	High-top
Overall Length	3696mm 12′ 1½″	4570mm 15′ 0″	4570mm 15′ 0″	4570mm 15′ 0″	4860mm 15′ 11″
Overall Width (ex mirrors)	1733mm 5′ 8¼″	1850mm 6′ 0¾″	1850mm 6′ 0¾″	1850mm 6′ 0¾″	1690mm 5′ 6½″
Overall Height	2477mm 8′ 1½″	2293mm 7′ 6¼″ (roof closed)	2464mm 8′ 1″	2591mm 8′ 6″	2630mm 8′ 7½″
Gross Vehicle Weight	1410kg 1.39 tons	2390kg 2.35 tons	2390kg 2.35 tons	2390kg 2.35 tons	2750kg 2.70 tons
Kerb Weight	1013kg 1.00 ton	1706kg 1.68 tons	1747kg 1.72 tons	1752kg 1.72 tons	1813kg 1.78 tons
Load Capacity	397kg 0.39 ton	684kg 0.67 ton	643kg 0.63 ton	638kg 0.63 ton	937kg 0.92 ton
Lower Double Bed	1829 x 1588mm 6′ 0″ x 5′ 2½″	1855 x 1220mm 6′ 1″ x 4′ 0″	1854 x 1219mm 6′ 1″ x 4′ 0″	1854 x 1219mm 6′ 1″ x 4′ 0″	1829mm x 1219mm 6′0″ x 4′0″
OR Two Single Beds	1829 x 559mm 6′ 0″ x 1′ 10″				
Upper Double Bed		1829 x 1220mm 6′ 0″ x 4′ 0″		1829 x 1257mm 6′ 0″ x 4′ 1½″	1800 x 1140mm 5′ 11″ x 3′ 9″
Lower Single Bed	Opt. Extension 2362 x 534mm 7′ 9″ x 1′ 9″				
Optional Beds (single)	Overcab Child's Bed 1524 x 711mm 5′ 0″ x 2′ 4″	Rollaway Child's Cab Bunk 1422 x 1016mm 4′ 8″ x 3′ 4″	Rollaway Child's Cab Bunk 1422 x 1016mm 4′ 8″ x 3′ 4″	Rollaway Child's Cab Bunk 1422 x 1016mm 4′ 8″ x 3′ 4″	
	2nd Child's slide out Bed 1524 x 610mm 5′ 0″ x 2′ 0″ or				
Optional Rollaway Bunk	Adult 1829 x 559mm 6′ 0″ x 1′ 10″				

VAUXHALL BAMBI

DAY TIME

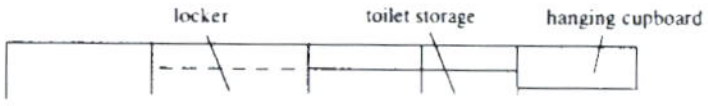

VOLKSWAGEN

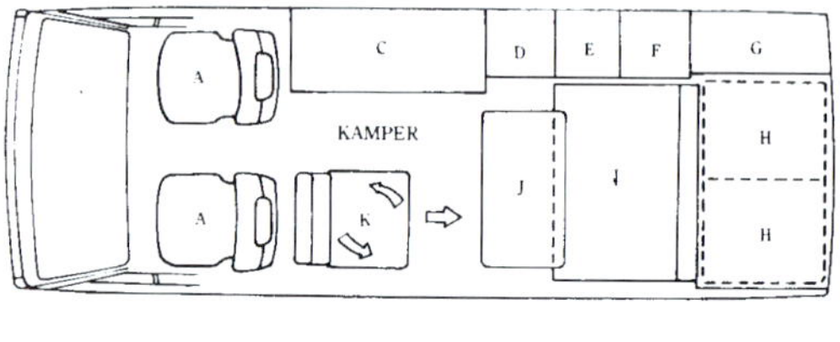

NISSAN NOMAD

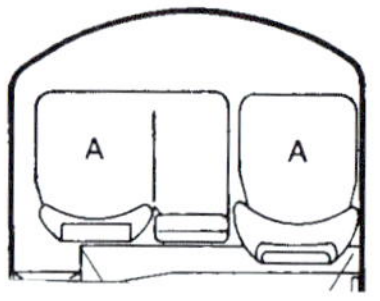

Testing

D. Reading comprehension

On the left you will find the specifications for several different motorhomes and campers ("Autohomes"). Read the questions below, then scan the specifications. Choose the vehicle which is most suitable, according to the information given. Mark the correct answer (a, b, c or d):

1. If you want a motorhome that is not higher than 2.30 m, you must take the
   a. Ford Transit Frontier.
   b. Nissan Urvan Nomad.
   c. Talbot Express Landliner.
   d. Volkswagen Transporter Kamper.

2. Most motorhomes shown here are
   a. 5.41 m long.
   b. 4.57 m long.
   c. longer than 6 m.
   d. shorter than 6 m.

3. If you want a double bed more than 1.30 m wide, you cannot take the
   a. Ford Transit Travelhome V.
   b. Ford Transit Frontier.
   c. Talbot Express Camelot 1400.
   d. Vauxhaul Rascal.

4. For people who want to put a lot of heavy things into their motorhome, the best choice would be the
   a. Ford Transit Frontier.
   b. Nissan Urvan Nomad.
   c. Talbot Express Camelot 1400.
   d. Volkswagen Transporter Komet.

... and finally: A Science Fiction Story

NOT YET THE END

By Fredric Brown

There was a greenish, hellish tinge to the light within the metal cube. It was a light that made the dead-white skin of the creature seated at the controls seem faintly green.
A single, faceted eye, front center in the head, watched the seven dials unwinkingly. Since they had left Xandor that eye had never once wavered from the dials. Sleep was unknown to the galactic race to which Kar-388Y belonged. Mercy, too, was unknown. A single glance at the sharp, cruel features below the faceted eye would have proved that.
The pointers on the fourth and seventh dials came to a stop. That meant the cube itself had stopped in space relative to its immediate objective. Kar reached forward with his upper right arm and drew the stabilizer switch. Then he rose and stretched his cramped muscles.
Kar turned to face his companion in the cube, a being like himself. 'We are here,' he said. 'The first stop, Star Z-5689. It has nine planets, but only the third is habitable. Let us hope we find creatures here who will make suitable slaves for Xandor.'
Lal-16B, who had sat in rigid immobility during the journey, rose and stretched also. 'Let us hope so, yes. Then we can return to Xandor and be honoured while the fleet comes to get them. But let's not hope too strongly. To meet with success at the first place we stop would be a miracle. We'll probably have to look a thousand places.'
Kar shrugged. 'Then we'll look a thousand places. With the Lounacs dying off, we must have slaves else our mines must close and our race will die.'
He sat down at the controls again and threw a switch that activated a visiplate that would show what was beneath them. He said, 'We are above the night side of the third planet. There is a cloud layer below us. I'll use the manuals from here.'
He began to press buttons. A few minutes later he said, 'Look, Lal, at the visiplate. Regularly spaced lights – a city! The planet is inhabited.'
Lal had taken his place at the other switchboard, the fighting controls. Now he too was examining dials. 'There is nothing for us to fear. There is not even the vestige of a force field around the city. The scientific knowledge of the race is crude. We can wipe the city out with one blast if we are attacked.'
'Good,' Kar said. 'But let me remind you that destruction is not our purpose – yet. We want specimens. If they prove satisfactory and the fleet comes and takes as many thousand slaves as we need, then will be time to destroy not a city but the whole planet. So that their civilization will never progress to the point where they'll be able to launch reprisal raids.'
Lal adjusted a knob. 'All right. I'll put on the megrafield and we'll be invisible to

them unless they see far into the ultraviolet, and, from the spectrum of their sun, I doubt that they do.'

As the cube descended the light within it changed from green to violet and beyond. It came to a gentle rest. Kar manipulated the mechanism that operated the airlock. He stepped outside, Lal just behind him.

'Look,' Kar said, 'two bipeds. Two arms, two eyes – not dissimilar to the Lounacs, although smaller. Well, here are our specimens.'

He raised his lower left arm, whose three-fingered hand held a thin rod wound with wire. He pointed it first at one of the creatures, then at the other. Nothing visible emanated from the end of the rod, but they both froze instantly into statuelike figures.

'They're not large, Kar,' Lal said. 'I'll carry one back, you carry the other. We can study them better inside the cube, after we're back in space.'

Kar looked about him in the dim light. 'All right, two is enough, and one seems to be male and the other female. Let's get going.'

A minute later the cube was ascending and as soon as they were well out of the atmosphere, Kar threw the stabilizer switch and joined Lal, who had been starting a study of the specimens during the brief ascent.

'Viviparous,' said Lal 'Five-fingered, with hands suited to reasonably delicate work. But – let's try the most important test, intelligence.'

Kar got the paired headsets. He handed one pair to Lal, who put one on his own head, one on the head of one of the specimens. Kar did the same with the other specimen.

After a few minutes, Kar and Lal stared at each other bleakly.

'Seven points below minimum,' Kar said. 'They could not be trained even for the crudest labor in the mines. Incapable of understanding the most simple instructions. Well, we'll take them back to the Xandor museum.'

'Shall I destroy the planet?'

'No,' Kar said. 'Maybe a million years from now – if our race lasts that long – they'll have evolved enough to become suitable for our purpose. Let us move on to the next star with planets.'

The make-up editor of the Milwaukee Star was in the composing room, supervising the closing of the local page. Jenkins, the head make-up compositor, was pushing in leads to tighten the second last column. 'Room for one more story in the eighth column, Pete,' he said. 'About thirty-six picas. There are two there in the overset that will fit. Which one shall I use?'

The make-up editor glanced at the type in the galleys lying on the stone beside the chase. Long practice enabled him to read the headlines upside down at a glance. 'The convention story and the zoo story, huh? Oh, hell, run the convention story. Who cares if the zoo director thinks two monkeys disappeared off Monkey Island last night?'

Fredric Brown (1906–1972): American writer of science fiction, novels, short stories and thrillers; he was born in Cincinnati and worked for many years in an office and as a proofreader for the Milwaukee Journal; his stories show a special sense of humour, and very often they have a surprise ending – something that the reader has not expected.

Questions on the text

1. How does the story begin? (Where does it begin?)
2. What do we learn about the "people" living on Xandor?
3. What do the beings from Xandor want to do on earth?
4. What is happening to the race called "Lounacs"?
5. Why is it easy for the beings from Xandor to land on earth without being seen?
6. How many specimens did they take? Why?
7. What was the result of the "intelligence test" they did with their specimens?
8. Can you describe the surprise ending of the story?

Group work / General discussion

1. The story assumes that there are planets other than earth with intelligent beings on them. What do you think about this idea?
2. What do you think about such things as "UFOs" (= unidentified flying objects)?
3. Are you interested in science fiction? (Why? / Why not?)
   What do you think about science fiction films such as "Star Trek"?
4. Some people say we should wait until all our problems on earth are solved before we spend money on space research. Do you agree?
   (Give reasons.)

For vocabulary see pages 164/165.

Appendix

A technical dictionary – words and phrases

GB = der Ausdruck kommt hauptsächlich im britischen Englisch vor
US = der Ausdruck kommt hauptsächlich im amerikanischen Englisch vor
A = Arbeitsbuch
T = Test

Die Zahlen verweisen auf die Lektionen, in denen der Ausdruck in einer bestimmten Bedeutung zum ersten Mal vorkommt.

A

abnormal [æb'nɔːml] 2 ungewöhnlich; abnorm

abort [ə'bɔːt] T2 *the flight had to be aborted* der Flug mußte abgebrochen werden

abraded rubber [ə'breɪdɪd] T2 abgeschürfter Gummi

ABS (= anti-lock brake system) A2/A12 Antiblockiersystem

absorb [əb'sɔːb] 2/7 absorbieren; aufnehmen; schlucken (z. B. Geräusche oder Lärm)

accelerate [ək'seləreɪt] 14 beschleunigen; *accelerate to 60 km/h* auf 60 km/h beschleunigen

accommodate [ə'kɒmədeɪt] 6/A6 *it accommodates a broad range of needs* (etwa:) es kann für eine breite Palette von Aufgaben eingesetzt werden; *the office building can accommodate a large number of people* das Bürogebäude hat Platz für eine ganze Reihe von Leuten

accommodation [ə'kɒmə'deɪʃn] 14 Unterbringung; Versorgung

account [ə'kaʊnt] 5/8 Konto

accounting [ə'kaʊntɪŋ] 5 Buchführung, Rechnungswesen; *the accounting process* der Buchführungsvorgang

accumulator [ə'kjuːmjuleɪtə] A9 Akku

accuracy ['ækjʊrəsɪ] 16/17/20 Genauigkeit *a much greater degree of accuracy* ein viel höherer Genauigkeitsgrad; *superior machining accuracy* überlegene Bearbeitungsgenauigkeit

accurate ['ækjʊrət] 12/A16/A19/20 genau; zuverlässig

acquire something [ə'kwaɪə] A20 etwas erwerben

acquisition [ækwɪ'zɪʃn] 14/A20 Erfassung; Erwerbung; *image acquisition* Bilderfassung; *data acquisition* Datenerfassung

adapt [ə'dæpt] A20 anpassen; angleichen; adaptieren; *adapt something to your needs* etwas auf Ihre Bedürfnisse ausrichten

adaptable [ə'dæptəbl] 16 anpassungsfähig; adaptierbar; *it is readily adaptable for operation in a manufacturing cell* es läßt sich leicht auf den Betrieb in einer Fabrikationszelle umstellen

adapter [ə'dæptə] A13/13 Adapter; Zwischenstecker

addition [ə'dɪʃn] A6 *in addition* zusätzlich

additive ['ædɪtɪv] 13 Zusatzstoff; Additiv; *petroleum additives* Erdölzusätze

adequate ['ædɪkwət] 16 angemessen; ausreichend; *the fork lift trucks are not adequate for our needs* die Gabelstapler reichen für unsere Bedürfnisse nicht aus

adjust [ə'dʒʌst] 2/4/A10 justieren; einstellen

adjustable [ə'dʒʌstəbl] 2 einstellbar; verstellbar

administrative functions [əd'mɪnɪstrətɪv] 14 Verwaltungsaufgaben

ads [ædz] → advertisements

advanced [əd'vɑ:nst] 8/A12/A15/16 fortschrittlich; modern; *advanced technology* Hochleistungstechnik; *the most advanced control in the industry* die modernste Steuerung in der Industrie; *advanced material systems* fortschrittliche Materialsysteme

advantage [əd'vɑ:ntɪdʒ] 2/3/A8 Vorteil; *take advantage of something* sich etwas zunutze machen

advertisements [əd'vɜ:tɪsmənts] 10 Annoncen; Anzeigen

advise [əd'vaɪz] A6 *advise on something* bei etwas beraten

aerospace ['eərəʊspeɪs] 1/8 Luft- und Raumfahrt

afford [ə'fɔ:d] 16 *I can't afford it* ich kann es mir nicht leisten; *affordably priced* erschwinglich im Preis; *it affords excellent data processing speed* es bietet eine ausgezeichnete Datenverarbeitungsgeschwindigkeit

aftercooler ['ɑ:ftəku:lə] 15 Nachkühler

agenda [ə'dʒendə] A11 Tagesordnung; *what's on the agenda?* was steht auf der Tagesordnung?

aid [eɪd] A7/20 Hilfe; *the latest manufacturing aids* die neuesten Produktionshilfsmittel

air compressor ['eə kəm'presə] 15 Luftkompressor

air conditioner ['eə kən'dɪʃənə] 15 Klimaanlage

air traffic controller 1 Fluglotse

airfreight ['eəfreɪt] 15 Luftfracht; *airfreight something* etwas mit (als) Luftfracht befördern; *send something by airfreight* etwas per Luftfracht versenden

alcohol ['ælkəhɒl] 18 Alkohol

algorithm ['ælgərɪðəm] 20 Algorithmus

alignment [ə'laɪnmənt] 2 Justierung; (Auto:) Spur

alkaline ['ælkəlaɪn] 7/A11 alkalisch; Alkali-

allocate ['æləʊkeɪt] 14 zuweisen; bestimmen; *allocated to heavy maintenance* für gründliche Überholungen bestimmt

allotment garden [ə'lɒtmənt] 5 Schrebergarten

allowance [ə'laʊəns] 11 Toleranz; Spiel; *make allowance for* bedenken, berücksichtigen

alternating ['ɔ:ltəneɪtɪŋ] A15/A18 wechselnd; alternierend; *alternating current* Wechselstrom

alumina [ə'lu:mɪnə] 7 Aluminiumoxid

amazed [ə'meɪzd] 10 verblüfft; verwundert

amazing [ə'meɪzɪŋ] 18 verblüffend; *amazingly productive* unglaublich produktiv

ambulance ['æmbjʊləns] 14 Krankenwagen

ammonia [ə'məʊnjə] A18 Ammoniak

ammonium chloride [ə'məʊnjəm 'klɔ:raɪd] A18 Ammoniumchlorid

amount to [ə'maʊnt] T2 sich belaufen auf; hinauslaufen auf; *it amounts to the same thing* es läuft auf dasselbe hinaus

analyse ['ænəlaɪz] 19/20 analysieren

analysis [ə'næləsɪs] (Mehrzahl: analyses [ə'næləsi:z]) 12/20 Analyse

analytical [ænə'lɪtɪkəl] A20 analytisch

angle ['æŋgl] 2 Winkel; *the lower portion is angled* der untere Teil ist winkelförmig

annual ['ænjʊəl] 10 jährlich; Jahres-

anode ['ænəʊd] 7/A15 Anode

anodize ['ænəʊdaɪz] (auch:) anodise 4/8 eloxieren; anodisieren

antenna [æn'tenə] T1 (Mehrzahl: antennas; bei Insekten: antennae [æn'teni:] Antenne; (Insekten:) Fühler

anti-knock ['æntɪ'nɒk] A4 Antiklopf-; klopffest

anti-lock brake system (ABS) A2 Antiblokkiersystem

anti-submarining protection (submarine ['sʌbməri:n] = Unterseeboot) 2 (etwa:) Schutz vor dem Runterrutschen/dem „Abtauchen"

APM (= automatic payment machine) A5/5 Zahlautomat

apparatus [æpə'reɪtəs] A10 Apparat

apparently [əˈpærəntlɪ] A20 offensichtlich; anscheinend

appearance [əˈpɪərəns] A12 Aussehen; äußere Erscheinung

applicant [ˈæplɪkənt] 1/3/10 Bewerber/in

apply [əˈplaɪ] 10 sich bewerben; *apply for a job* sich um eine Stelle bewerben

appointment [əˈpɔɪntmənt] 1/2/16 Verabredung; Termin; *make an appointment* einen Termin vereinbaren; *an urgent appointment* ein dringender Termin; *an appointment at ten* ein Termin um zehn (Uhr)

apprenticeship [əˈprentɪsʃɪp] 1/10 Ausbildung; Lehre, Lehrstelle

approach [əˈprəʊtʃ] A4/A18 *develop new approaches* neue Ansätze (Methoden) entwickeln; *the energy efficient approach* (etwa:) der energiesparende Weg

approval [əˈpruːvl] 8 Zustimmung; Genehmigung

apron [ˈeɪprən] T2 (hier:) betoniertes Vorfeld (des Flugplatzes)

arc [ɑːk] 9 Lichtbogen

architecture [ˈɑːkɪtektʃə] A19 Architektur

area code (US) 10 Vorwahlnummer

arise [əˈraɪz] (arose [əˈrəʊz] – have arisen [əˈrɪzn]) 16 *as needs arise in future* je nach dem zukünftigen Bedarf

arrangement [əˈreɪndʒmənt] 19 Anordnung; *by an arrangement of beams* durch eine Anordnung von Balken

array [əˈreɪ] A20 Reihe; Menge

arrest [əˈrest] 2 *arrest collision* den Aufprall auffangen

articulated vehicles [ɑːˈtɪkjʊleɪtɪd] 14 Gelenkfahrzeuge

artist [ˈɑːtɪst] 19 Künstler, Künstlerin

ascertain [æsəˈteɪn] T2 feststellen; ermitteln

aseptic [eɪˈseptɪk] 8 aseptisch; keimfrei

assign [əˈsaɪn] A19 zuordnen; zuteilen

associate [əˈsəʊʃɪeɪt] A19 *we only associate ourselves with the very best hardware* wir arbeiten nur mit der allerbesten Hardware; *an associated company* eine Schwestergesellschaft

asymmetry [eɪˈsɪmətrɪ] 20 Asymmetrie

atmospheric [ætməsˈferɪk] A9/A18 atmosphärisch; *atmospheric pressure* Luftdruck; *atmospheric nitrogen* Luftstickstoff

ATO system (= automatic train operation system) A16 automatische Zugsteuerung

atomizer [ˈætəʊmaɪzə] 15 Zerstäuber

audible [ˈɔːdəbl] 5 hörbar; *an audible click* ein hörbares Klicken

authorize [ˈɔːθəraɪz] 2/10 authorisieren; genehmigen; *I hereby authorize the above work* ich erteile Ihnen hiermit den festen Auftrag für die obige Arbeit

auto [ˈɔːtəʊ] 19 Auto-; automatisch; selbsttätig

automate [ˈɔːtəʊmeɪt] 5/18/19 automatisieren; *all factories will be fully automated* alle Fabriken werden vollautomatisiert sein

automation [ɔːtəˈmeɪʃn] 1/10 Automatisierung

auxiliary [ɔːgˈzɪljərɪ] 18/19 Hilfs-; Neben-; *auxiliary program* Hilfsprogramm; *for auxiliary functions* für zusätzliche Funktionen

availability [əveɪləˈbɪlətɪ] 10 Verfügbarkeit; Einsatzfähigkeit

aviation [eɪvɪˈeɪʃn] 8 Flugwesen; *aviation industry* Luftfahrtindustrie

award [əˈwɔːd] 10 *she was awarded the prize* der Preis wurde ihr verliehen; *award somebody a diploma* jemandem ein Diplom zuerkennen (geben); *certificates and diplomas awarded* Zeugnisse und Diplome, die man erhalten hat

axis [ˈæksɪs] (Mehrzahl: axes [ˈæksiːz] A16 Achse

B

back A6/A9/16 unterstützen; *back-up service* Kundendienst (zur Unterstützung); *back-up clearance* Sicherheitsabstand; Sicherheitsspielraum

bacterial [bækˈtɪərɪəl] 18 bakteriell; Bakterien-

balance [ˈbæləns] 2 *tyre balance* Reifenauswuchtung

ball bearing [ˈbɔːl ˈbeərɪŋ] 11 Kugellager
ballhead T2 Kugelkopf (auf einem Stativ)
bankrupt [ˈbæŋkrʌpt] 15 zahlungsunfähig; bankrott; *go bankrupt* in Konkurs gehen, Bankrott machen
bar [bɑː] A14 Balken; Querstreifen, Querstrich
barber [ˈbɑːbə] 1 Friseur (Herrenfriseur)
barrel [ˈbærəl] 11 Faß; Tonne; Trommel
barrier [ˈbærɪə] A19 Barriere; Hindernis; *without the language barrier* ohne die Sprachbarriere
base [beɪs] A5/A6/10/13/19 Basis; Fundament; *a London-based firm* eine Firma mit Sitz in London; *baseplate* Grundplatte; *PC-based CAD systems* CAD-Systeme auf PC-Basis; *it is based on facts* es stützt sich auf Tatsachen
batch [bætʃ] 13 Stapel; Stoß; *in batches* schubweise
bauxite [ˈbɔːksaɪt] 7 Bauxit
bearing [ˈbeərɪŋ] 1/17 Lager; *ball bearing* Kugellager
bed 16 Unterlage; Auflage; Untergestell
bellows [ˈbeləʊz] 2 Blasebalg; Gebläse
belt [belt] A9 Band; Riemen; Gurt
bench [bentʃ] A11 Bank; Werkbank
beneath [bɪˈniːθ] 10 unterhalb; unter; *the boxes beneath* die Kästchen darunter; *beneath a tree* unter einem Baum
benefit [ˈbenɪfɪt] A4/8/12 Vorteil; Nutzen; *for the benefit of* zugunsten von
beverage [ˈbevərɪdʒ] A8/8 Getränk; *beverage can* Getränkedose; *beverage container* Getränkebehälter
billet [ˈbɪlɪt] 8 (hier:) Walzblock; Barren
biotechnology [baɪəʊtekˈnɒlədʒɪ] 18 Biotechnologie
BIW (= body in white) A12 Rohkarosserie
blast furnace [ˈblɑːst ˈfɜːnɪs] A9 Hochofen
blind [blaɪnd] 11 *blind rivets* Blindnieten; *blind holes* Sacklöcher
blow [bləʊ] 9 Schlag; *by a hammer blow* durch einen Hammerschlag
body 2 (Auto:) Karosserie

bogie [ˈbəʊgɪ] 14 (Eisenbahnwaggon:) Drehgestell; Bogie
bonnet [ˈbɒnɪt] A2 Motorhaube (hauptsächlich GB; US: hood (hʊd])
bonus [ˈbəʊnəs] 10 Bonus; Prämie
bottleneck [ˈbɒtlnek] A20 Engpaß
boundary [ˈbaʊndərɪ] 20 *boundary point* Grenzpunkt
brain-storming session 3 Brainstorming (= Sitzung, bei der die Anwesenden versuchen, spontane Einfälle zu entwickeln und sammeln)
brake circuit A2 Bremskreislauf
brake pedal [pedl] A2 Bremspedal
brand goods [brænd] 1 Markenartikel
breakage [ˈbreɪkɪdʒ] A13 Bruch; Bruchschaden; Bruchstelle
breakthrough 19 Durchbruch (= Erfolg)
brittle [ˈbrɪtl] 11 spröde; brüchig; *become brittle* spröde werden, brüchig werden
broaden [ˈbrɔːdn] 16 erweitern; verbreitern; *to broaden its application possibilities* um die Anwendungsmöglichkeiten zu erweitern
bucket [ˈbʌkɪt] A9 Eimer; (Bagger:) Löffel; *bucket wheel excavator* Schaufelradbagger
buckle [ˈbʌkl] A11 knicken; einknicken; krumm werden
buffer store [ˈbʌfə] 6 Pufferspeicher
bug [bʌg] 16 "Wanze" (= Miniabhörgerät); Fehler (in einem System)
building construction 1 Hochbau
bulk handling [bʌlk] A9 Abfertigung von Massengut
bullet [ˈbʊlɪt] 3 Geschoß; Kugel
bump [bʌmp] 13 (heftig) stoßen; anprallen; Stoß; Beule; *I bumped my head against the door* ich stieß mit dem Kopf gegen die Tür; *bump a car* auf ein Auto auffahren; *to protect fruits from bumps* das Obst vor Druckstellen bewahren
bundle [ˈbʌndl] A19 Bündel; Paket; *at a special bundle price* zu einem speziellen Pauschalpreis
buoy [bɔɪ] 19 (Rettungs-)Boje

burst [bɜːst] (burst – have burst) T2 platzen; zerplatzen; bersten; *burst open* aufplatzen; *burst up* zerbrechen

by the way 8 übrigens

by-pass [ˈbaɪpɑːs] 6 Umleitung; *by-pass the paint line conveyor* den Spritzbereichsförderer umgehen; *by-pass valve* Drucküberlaufventil

C

cabinet [ˈkæbɪnɪt] 15 Büroschrank; Karteischrank; Gehäuse

cable car [ˈkeɪbl kɑː] A10 Seilbahn

cage [keɪdʒ] 2 Gehäuse; Käfig

calcium hydroxide [ˈkælsɪəm haɪˈdrɒksaɪd] A18 Kalziumhydroxid

calibration [kælɪˈbreɪʃn] 20 Kalibrierung; Eichung

camshaft [ˈkæmʃɑːft] A4 Nockenwelle

capability [keɪpəˈbɪləti] 15 Fähigkeit; Befähigung

capable [ˈkeɪpəbl] A20 fähig; tüchtig; *the best graphics your computer is capable of running* die besten Grafikprogramme, die Ihr Computer bewältigen kann; *capable of doing something* fähig, etwas zu tun

capture [ˈkæptʃə] 20 (hier:) Erfassung (von Daten etc.); (Daten) erfassen

carburettor (auch: carburetter) [kɑːbəˈretə] 8 Vergaser

care [keə] 20 *care for children* sich um Kinder kümmern

career [kəˈrɪə] 1 berufliche Laufbahn; Karriere; *career opportunities* berufliche Aussichten

carriage [ˈkærɪdʒ] 3/17 *(Eisenbahn:)* Wagen; Laufwerk; Fahrgestell; Schlitten (einer Werkzeugmaschine)

carrier [ˈkærɪə] 6 Träger; Trägerelement; Förderbehälter

carrying capacity A6 Förderkapazität

Cartesian [kɑːˈtiːzjən] A18 kartesisch; kartesianisch

case [keɪs] 12 (hier:) Umhüllung; Ummantelung

cast aluminium 17 Aluminiumguß

catch up with the timetable 14 wieder im Fahrplan sein

cathode [ˈkæθəʊd] A15 Kathode

caustic soda [ˈkɔːstɪk ˈsəʊdə] 7 Ätznatron

cavity [ˈkævəti] A2 Hohlraum; Loch (z. B. im Zahn)

celebrate [ˈselɪbreɪt] 13 feiern

centre column T2 Mittelsäule

centrifugal [senˈtrɪfjʊgl] A9/A19 zentrifugal; Zentrifugal-; *centrifugal pump* Zentrifugalpumpe; *centrifugal compressor* Kreiselverdichter; Turbokompressor

certificate [səˈtɪfɪkeɪt] 10 Zeugnis; Zertifikat; Urkunde

certify [ˈsɜːtɪfaɪ] 10 beglaubigen; beurkunden; bescheinigen

challenge [ˈtʃælɪndʒ] 1/3/A10 Herausforderung; herausfordern; *in challenging environments* in schwierigen Verhältnissen

chamber [ˈtʃeɪmbə] 20 Kammer

character [ˈkærəktə] 5/A20 *characters of information* Informationssymbole, Informationszeichen; *large characters* große Buchstaben

characteristic [kærəktəˈrɪstɪk] 19/20 charakteristisch; Kennzeichen; Eigenart

charge [tʃɑːdʒ] 5/12 Charge; Gebühr; berechnen; *she charged me two pounds for it* sie berechnete mir zwei Pfund dafür; *charge too much* zuviel berechnen; *free of charge* kostenlos

charitable [ˈtʃærətəbl] A8 wohltätig

charity [ˈtʃærəti] A8 Wohltätigkeitseinrichtung

chart [tʃɑːt] 19 Diagramm; Grafik; grafische Darstellung

check off (US) 2 *check off services needed* kreuzen Sie die benötigten Serviceleistungen an

chemical engineering 1 chemische Verfahrenstechnik

chemistry [ˈkemɪstri] 2/19 Chemie

chill [tʃɪl] 15 kühlen; (Metall:) abschrecken

chip conveyor 16 Späneförderer

chisel [ˈtʃɪzl] 1 Meißel; Beitel

chromate [ˈkrəʊmeɪt] A9 Chromat (chromsaures Salz)

chuck [tʃʌk] 1 Spannfutter

chute [ʃuːt] 2 Rutsche; Schacht; *put envelope into chute* (etwa:) stecken Sie den Umschlag in den Schlitz

circuit breaker 14 Ausschalter; Stromkreisunterbrecher

circuitry [ˈsɜːkɪtrɪ] 12 Schaltungen; Schaltsystem

circular [ˈsɜːkjʊlə] A8 rund; kreisförmig

circumstances [ˈsɜːkəmstənsɪz] A10 Umstände; Verhältnisse; *under the circumstances* unter diesen Umständen; *in some circumstances* unter gewissen Umständen; *under no circumstances* unter keinen Umständen

civil engineering [ˈsɪvl] 1 Bauwesen; Bauingenieurwesen

clinch [klɪntʃ] 9 pressen; clinchen; zusammenpressen

clock up considerable mileage T2 (etwa:) eine beträchtliche Meilenzahl auf dem Tacho haben

closeness [ˈkləʊsnɪs] 1 (hier:) Genauigkeit; Strenge; *closeness of supervision* Striktheit der Überwachung

CNC (= computer numerical control) 16 programmierbare numerische Steuerung

coal gas 18 Steinkohlengas

coating [ˈkəʊtɪŋ] A2/9 Schicht; Beschichtung; Belag; *zinc coating* Verzinkung; Zinküberzug

cockpit [ˈkɒkpɪt] 20 Cockpit

code [kəʊd] A20 Code; *application code* Anwendercode

coil [kɔɪl] Wicklung; Spule; *coiler* Wickelmaschine

collapse [kəˈlæps] 2 zusammenbrechen; einknicken; einfallen

collapsible [kəˈlæpsəbl] 2 *collapsible steering column* abknickbare Lenksäule

collar [ˈkɒlə] T2 Kragen; Manschette; Muffe; *locking collar* (hier:) Verschraubung

collision [kəˈlɪʒn] 2 Zusammenstoß; Kollision; *collision forces* beim Zusammenstoß auftretende Kräfte

comb [kəʊm] 1 Kamm

come true 20 *when your dreams come true* wenn Ihre Träume wahr werden

command [kəˈmɑːnd] 20 Steuerbefehl; Befehl; Anweisung

commence [kəˈmens] 8 beginnen; anfangen

commercial [kəˈmɜːʃl] 10/A15/A17 kaufmännisch; geschäftlich; kommerziell; *commercial illustrator* Gebrauchsgraphiker; *they do commercial air conditioning* sie machen Klimaanlagen für Büros und Betriebe; *commercial vehicle* Nutzfahrzeug

commitment [kəˈmɪtmənt] A7 Verpflichtung; Engagement

common [ˈkɒmən] 8/18 häufig; normal; allgemein verbreitet; *common salt* gewöhnliches Kochsalz; *they are pretty common now* sie sind derzeit ziemlich gebräuchlich

communicate [kəˈmjuːnɪkeɪt] A14 kommunizieren; sich verständigen

community [kəˈmjuːnətɪ] 5 Gemeinschaft; Gemeinde

comparatively [kəmˈpærətɪvlɪ] 19 *at a comparatively low cost* zu einem verhältnismäßig niedrigen Preis

comparison [kəmˈpærɪsn] A20 Vergleich

compatibility [kəmpætəˈbɪlətɪ] 20 Kompatibilität

competitive [kəmˈpetətɪv] A11 konkurrenzfähig; wettbewerbsfähig

completion [kəmˈpliːʃn] A19 Fertigstellung; Vollendung; *we can take the project to completion* (etwa:) wir können das Projekt bis zur Fertigstellung betreuen

compound [ˈkɒmpaʊnd] 18/A18 *chemical compound* chemische Verbindung; *carbon compounds* Kohlenstoffverbindungen

comprehensive [kɒmprɪˈhensɪv] 10/16 umfassend; *comprehensive school* Gesamtschule

compress [kəmˈpres] A18 verdichten; zusammendrücken; komprimieren; *compressed air* Druckluft; *compressed air motor* Druckluftmotor

compression [kəm'preʃn] A11 Druck; Kompression

compressive [kəm'presɪv] 9 Druck-; Kompressions-

compressor [kəm'presə] A9 Kompressor; Verdichter; Verdichtungseinheit

comprise [kəm'praɪz] 6 umfassen; sich zusammensetzen aus; *it is comprised of ten parts* es besteht aus zehn Teilen

concentric [kən'sentrɪk] 1 konzentrisch; *a concentric chuck* ein selbstzentrierendes Spannfutter

concertina [kɒnsə'tiːnə] 2 Ziehharmonika; *the mounting will concertina...* die Befestigung wird sich zusammenschieben...

conclusion [kən'kluːʒn] 6 Schlußfolgerung; Schluß; *draw a conclusion* einen Schluß (aus etwas) ziehen; *come to a conclusion* zu einem Schluß kommen

condensation [kɒnden'seɪʃn] A11 Kondensation; Verdichtung

condense [kən'dens] 20 kondensieren; verdichten

condenser [kən'densə] 15 Kondensator

conditioned air 15 klimatisierte Luft

confidence ['kɒnfɪdəns] A6/A18 Vertrauen; Zutrauen; Zuversicht *a feeling of confidence* ein Gefühl des Vertrauens

configuration [kənfɪgə'reɪʃn] A19 Konfiguration *(= Ausstattung der EDV-Anlage mit den erforderlichen Einheiten)*

configure [kən'fɪgə] 19/20 *(auch:)* configurate; *configure a system* ein System konfigurieren

confirm [kən'fɜːm] 1 bestätigen

connectivity [kənek'tɪvətɪ] 20 Anschlußfähigkeit

connector [kə'nektə] A13 Verbindungsstück; Anschlußteil

consequently ['kɒnsɪkwəntlɪ] 3 folglich; infolgedessen

consider [kən'sɪdə] 1 in Betracht ziehen; *we must consider the consequences* wir müssen die Konsequenzen in Betracht ziehen

consideration [kənsɪdə'reɪʃn] 11/A13/19 *take into consideration* in Betracht ziehen, berücksichtigen; *the matter is under consideration* die Sache wird gerade geprüft; *other quality considerations* weitere Dinge, die bezüglich der Qualität berücksichtigt werden müssen; *design considerations* Erwägungen bezüglich des Designs

consignment [kən'saɪnmənt] 20 Warensendung; Sendung

consistent [kən'sɪstənt] A7/A19 konsequent; folgerichtig; logisch

consortium [kən'sɔːtjəm] A17 Konsortium; Vereinigung; Gruppe

constituent part [kən'stɪtjuənt] 19 Bestandteil

consultancy [kən'sʌltənsɪ] A12 Beratungsfirma

continuous [kən'tɪnjuəs] A9/12/16 fortlaufend; fortwährend; *in continuous duty* im Dauerbetrieb; *continuous strip heating* Bandheizung; *continuous caster* Stranggußmaschine

contractor [kən'træktə] A10/A15 Zulieferer; Lieferant; (auch:) Bauunternehmer

contribute [kən'trɪbjuːt] 16 beitragen; beisteuern; *all contribute to peak performance* alle tragen zur Spitzenleistung bei

contribution [kɒntrɪ'bjuːʃn] A17 *make an important contribution* einen wichtigen Beitrag leisten

control valve 15 Steuerventil; Regulierventil

controller 17/18 Steuergerät; Regler

conventional [kən'venʃənl] 3 konventionell; herkömmlich

convert [kən'vɜːt] A20 umwandeln

conveyor [kən'veɪə] A5/A6/6/8/19 Förderanlage; Förderer

convince [kən'vɪns] 3 überzeugen

coolant ['kuːlənt] 16 Kühlmittel; Kühlflüssigkeit

co-ordinates [kəʊ'ɔːdɪneɪts] A18 Koordinaten

core [kɔː] 15 Kern; *core memory* Kernspeicher; *core diameter* Kerndurchmesser; *reactor core* Reaktorkern; *core drill* Kernbohrer; *core sample* Bohrkernprobe

corrode [kəˈrəʊd] A9/10 korrodieren; *zinc corrodes much more slowly than steel* Zink korrodiert viel langsamer als Stahl

corrosion [kəˈrəʊʒn] 8/11 Korrosion; *corrosion-resistant* korrosionsbeständig; *corrosion resistance* Korrosionsbeständigkeit

corrosive [kəˈrəʊsɪv] A9 korrosiv; korrodierend

council house [ˈkaʊnsl] 5 Haus des sozialen Wohnungsbaus

count [kaʊnt] 6/A16 zählen; *count up* vorwärtszählen; *count down* rückwärtszählen

couple [ˈkʌpl] 6 verbinden; koppeln

crack [kræk] 4 *cracks in the ceiling* Risse in der Decke

cracking [ˈkrækɪŋ] A18 Kracken (= Spaltverfahren)

crafts [krɑːfts] 20 (Kunst-)Handwerk

craftsman [ˈkrɑːftsmən] A12 Handwerker; Kunsthandwerker

craftsmanship [ˈkrɑːftsmənʃɪp] A2 handwerkliche Qualität; Verarbeitungsqualität

craftsperson [ˈkrɑːftspɜːsn] 1 Handwerker; Kunsthandwerker (männliche und weibliche Form)

cramp [kræmp] A11 Klammer; Zwinge

crank [kræŋk] 12/19 Kurbel; *crankshaft* Kurbelwelle

crash [kræʃ] 16 Zusammenstoß; Sturz; (Computer:) Absturz

critical [ˈkrɪtɪkl] A20 kritisch

crossword puzzle [ˈkrɒswɜːd ˈpʌzl] 20 Kreuzworträtsel

crumple [ˈkrʌmpl] 2 (zer)knautschen; zerknittern; *crumple zone* Knautschzone (beim Auto)

crush [krʌʃ] 7 zerdrücken; zerkleinern; zerstoßen

crust [krʌst] A8 Rinde; Kruste; *the earth's crust* die Erdkruste

cryolite [ˈkraɪəlaɪt] 7 Kryolith (Natriumfluoroaluminat)

cubicle [ˈkjuːbɪkl] 4 Kabine; Zelle

culminate [ˈkʌlmɪneɪt] A10 kulminieren; den Höhepunkt bilden

current [ˈkʌrənt] 8/10/A12/15 *your current employer* Ihr jetziger Arbeitgeber; *current events* Tagesereignisse; *not in current use* nicht allgemein üblich; *current price* Tagespreis; *currently* derzeitig; gegenwärtig

curriculum vitae (CV) [kərɪkjələm ˈviːtaɪ] 10 Lebenslauf

custom [ˈkʌstəm] A15/20/A20 *custom-made* nach Kundenangaben angefertigt; *custom programs* auf den Kunden zugeschnittene Programme; *custom designed* nach Kundenwünschen konstruiert

customize (auch:) customise [ˈkʌstəmaɪz] 19/20 auf den Kundenbedarf zuschneiden

cut costs 19 Kosten senken

cut edge A9 Schnittkante

cutting tool A16 Schneidwerkzeug

CV → curriculum vitae

cyberspace [ˈsaɪbəspeɪs] 20 Cyberspace

cylindrical [sɪˈlɪndrɪkl] 1 zylindrisch; Zylinder-

D

damper [ˈdæmpə] 15 Dämpfer; Regelklappe (eines Luftfilters); *relief damper* Ausgleichsklappe; Druckausgleichsklappe

data processing 1/16 Datenverarbeitung

DDCMP protocol 18 (= direct digital control microprocessor) Protokoll der direkten digitalen Steuerung

deadline [ˈdedlaɪn] 14 Termin; *meet the deadline* den Termin einhalten

deadman switch 18 „Totmannschalter" (= Sicherheitsschaltvorrichtung)

deal [diːl] 1/A4/A14 sich befassen (mit); *deal with a problem* sich mit einem Problem befassen

debug [diːˈbʌg] A20 debuggen; „entwanzen" (= Fehler aus einem System beseitigen); *debugging* Debugging; Fehlersuche und -beseitigung

decompose [diːkəmˈpəʊz] 7 zerfallen; sich zersetzen; abbauen

decrease [diːˈkriːs] 6 *output will decrease* die Produktion wird zurückgehen

dedicated ['dedɪkeɪtɪd] 6/13 *they are dedicated to this proposition* sie widmen sich dieser Sache; *dedicated manufacturing cells* spezielle (zweckorientierte) Fertigungsbereiche; *dedicated circuit* Schaltung, die auf ein bestimmtes Problem zugeschnitten ist; *dedicated computer* Spezialrechner

defence industry [dɪˈfens] 1 Wehrtechnik

definitely ['defɪnɪtlɪ] 1/7 bestimmt; eindeutig

deflect [dɪˈflekt] A11 ablenken; auslenken

deflection [dɪˈflekʃn] A11 Ablenkung; Durchbiegung; *deflection curve* elastische Linie, Biegelinie

deliver [dɪˈlɪvə] 4 liefern; *deliver outstanding performance* hervorragende Leistung bieten

demonstrate ['demənstreɪt] 2 etwas demonstrieren (= vorführen, zeigen)

denote [dɪˈnəʊt] 7 anzeigen; andeuten; kennzeichnen

density ['densətɪ] A9 Dichte; Densität

dent [dent] A11 Delle; Einbeulung; Beule

department [dɪˈpɑːtmənt] 2 Abteilung

dependability [dɪpendəˈbɪlətɪ] 6 Zuverläßlichkeit; Verläßlichkeit

deposit [dɪˈpɒzɪt] 5/13 *the cheques deposited* die eingezahlten Schecks; *deposit trash in landfills* Abfall in Müllgruben lagern

derive [dɪˈraɪv] 19 *the name is derived from a project* der Name stammt von einem Projekt

desert ['dezət] A15 Wüste

desire [dɪˈzaɪə] T2 wünschen; verlangen; *the desired height* die gewünschte Höhe

detect [dɪˈtekt] T2 entdecken; herausfinden; feststellen

detection [dɪˈtekʃn] A16/A20 Feststellung; Erkennung; *broken tool detection* Erkennung defekter Werkzeuge

determine [dɪˈtɜːmɪn] A16/18 entscheiden; bestimmen; beschließen *beyond pre-determined parameters* über die vorherbestimmten Parameter hinaus; *diameter measurements can be determined* die Durchmesser können festgelegt werden (bestimmt werden); *determine if tools are worn* Stellen Sie fest, ob Werkzeuge abgenutzt sind

deuterium [djuːˈtɪərɪəm] T2 Deuterium (= schwerer Wasserstoff)

dewpoint ['djuːpɔɪnt] 15 Taupunkt

diagnosis [daɪəgˈnəʊsɪs] 16 Diagnose

dialog box ['daɪəlɒg] A20 Dialogfeld (= Feld in Dialogfenstern von Anwenderprogrammen, über das man mit dem Programm oder System kommunizieren kann)

die [daɪ] 8 Matrize (in der Strangpresse)

dim [dɪm] 15 abblenden; *dim lights* abgeblendetes Licht

diploma [dɪˈpləʊmə] 10 Diplom; Urkunde

direct [dɪˈrekt] 20 leiten; richten; *direct the radiation beams towards the tumours* die Bestrahlung auf die Tumore richten

direct current [dɪˈrekt] 14 Gleichstrom

directory [dɪˈrektərɪ] A20 Verzeichnis; Adreßbuch; Telefonbuch

disc brake [dɪsk] T2 Scheibenbremse

discount ['dɪskaʊnt] 4/16 Rabatt; *a good discount rate* (etwa:) ein guter Preisnachlaß

dispatch [dɪˈspætʃ] 6 *finished goods dispatch area* Versandbereich für Fertigprodukte

dissolve [dɪˈsɒlv] 7 auflösen; sich auflösen; *the alumina dissolves in the liquid* das Aluminiumoxid löst sich in der Flüssigkeit auf; *dissolved substance* gelöster Stoff

distortion [dɪˈstɔːʃn] 20 Verzerrung; Verzeichnung; Verformung

divorce [dɪˈvɔːs] 10 trennen; scheiden; sich scheiden lassen; *divorced* geschieden

documentation [dɒkjʊmenˈteɪʃn] 1 Dokumentation

double glazing ['gleɪzɪŋ] 4 Doppelverglasung

download ['daʊnləʊd] 19 Download (= 1. Datenübertragung von einem Großrechner auf einen PC oder Datenfernübertragung vom entfernten zum lokalen Computer; 2. Laden von Zeichen oder Zeichensätzen in den Speicher eines Druckers)

draft [drɑːft] 19 Entwurf; *the drafting process* der Vorgang des Entwerfens

drag [dræg] 19 Drag (= Verschieben von Bildschirmsymbolen in grafischen Benutzeroberflächen mit gedrückter Maustaste)

drain [dreɪn] A2/11 entwässern; drainieren; trockenlegen; dränieren; *drain off water* Wasser abfließen lassen; *it drains off into the river* es läuft in den Fluß ab; *drain holes* Abflußlöcher

draining ['dreɪnɪŋ] 11 Dränage; Entwässerung; Trockenlegung; *draining ditch* Drängraben

drainpipe ['dreɪnpaɪp] A11 Abflußrohr; Abfallrohr

draught (US: draft) [drɑːft] 4 Zugluft; Zug

draughtproof (US: draftproof) ['drɑːftpruːf] 4 *draughtproof doors* gegen Zugluft abgedichtete Türen

draughtsman (US: draftsman) ['drɑːftsmən] A12/19 technischer Zeichner

draw on something A12 auf etwas zurückgreifen; von etwas Gebrauch machen; *we can draw on an extensive library of special furnace designs* wir können auf eine umfangreiche Bibliothek von Ofensonderanfertigungen zurückgreifen

drift [drɪft] 20 treiben; *the boat drifted on the river* das Boot trieb auf dem Fluß

drip [drɪp] 15 tropfen; tröpfeln; *a dripping water tap* ein tropfender Wasserhahn

drive off 7 (hier:) vertreiben; austreiben; *drive off the chemically combined water content* das chemisch gebundene Wasser entfernen

driving licence (hauptsächlich GB; US: driver's license) 10 Führerschein

drop 15 Leistungsverlust; Rückgang; *a drop in your available voltage* ein Rückgang (Abfall) der Ihnen zur Verfügung stehenden Spannung

dry-cleaning 18 (Kleidung:) chemische Reinigung

duct [dʌkt] 4/A10 Kanal; Strömungskanal; Dukt

dummy ['dʌmɪ] 2 Dummy (= Puppe bei Crashtests)

duplicate ['djuːplɪkeɪt] A2/2 vervielfältigen; (ver)doppeln; *the electronics is duplicated* die Elektronik ist zweimal vorhanden

durable ['djʊərəbl] 8 haltbar; strapazierfähig

duration [djʊəˈreɪʃn] 10 Dauer

duty ['djuːtɪ] 16/20 (hier:) Betrieb; Betriebsart; *machine tool duty* Werkzeugmaschinenbetrieb

E

ease [iːz] 13 lindern; erleichtern; *to ease landfill shortages* um dem Mangel an Mülldeponien entgegenzuwirken

ease of use [iːz] A20 Benutzerfreundlichkeit

eccentric [ɪkˈsentrɪk] A15 exzentrisch; außermittig; *eccentric wheel* Exzenterscheibe

economics [iːkəˈnɒmɪks] 12 Volkswirtschaftslehre; wirtschaftlicher Aspekt; *the economics of it* die wirtschaftliche Seite der Sache

edit ['edɪt] 19/A20 bearbeiten; redigieren; aufbereiten; *edit the library* die Bibliothek bearbeiten

editor ['edɪtə] 1/A12 Redakteur/-in; Schriftleiter/-in *(einer Zeitschrift)*

electrocoating [ɪˈlektrəʊˈkəʊtɪŋ] A2 elektrophoretische Beschichtung; Elektrophorese-Verfahren

electroless nickel plating [ɪˈlektrəʊles] 11 außenstromlose Nickelbeschichtung

electrolysis [ˈɪlekˈtrɒləsɪs] A7 Elektrolyse

electrolytic bath [ɪlektrəʊˈlɪtɪk] A2 galvanisches Bad

electrometallurgical plant [ɪˈlektrəʊmetəˈlɜːdʒɪkl] A9 Elektrometallurgie-Anlage

electrophoretic [ɪlektrəʊfəˈretɪk] A8 elektrophoretisch; *electrophoretic technique* Elektrophoreseverfahren; *electrophoretic paint plant* Elektrophorese-Lackieranlage

electroplating [ɪˈlektrəʊpleɪtɪŋ] 11 Galvanisieren

electrostatic [ɪˈlektrəʊˈstætɪk] A8 elektrostatisch; *electrostatically sprayed* elektrostatisch gespritzt

embrace [ɪmˈbreɪs] A6 *it embraces all aspects*

of conveying es umfaßt alles, was mit Förderanlagen zu tun hat

emission fumes [ɪˈmɪʃn ˈfjuːmz] 3 Emissionsabgase

emphasis [ˈemfəsɪs] A18 Betonung; Schwerpunkt; *lay emphasis on something* etwas betonen

employ [ɪmˈplɔɪ] 10/18 beschäftigen; einsetzen; *employer* Arbeitgeber/-in

employment [ɪmˈplɔɪmənt] 10 Beschäftigung; Arbeit; *employment in Indonesia* Beschäftigung (Arbeit) in Indonesien; *employment office* Arbeitsamt

enclose [ɪnˈkləʊz] A13 umhüllen; einkapseln; *enclosed self-cooled machine* geschlossene selbstkühlende Maschine

enclosure [ɪnˈkləʊʒə] 16 *chip and coolant enclosure* Gehäuse für Späneförderer und Kühlmittelanlage

encounter [ɪnˈkaʊntə] T2 (einer Sache) begegnen; (auf etwas) treffen; *encounter difficulties* auf Schwierigkeiten stoßen

energy-absorbing properties [əbˈsɔːbɪŋ] 2 energie-absorbierende Eigenschaften

engineer something [endʒɪˈnɪə] 16 etwas konstruieren; etwas entwickeln

engineering [endʒɪˈnɪərɪŋ] 1/2/6/17 Technik; Ingenieurwesen

enhance [ɪnˈhɑːns] 13 erweitern; steigern; vergrößern; *enhance the value* den Wert erhöhen

enhancement [ɪnˈhɑːnsmənt] A20 Erweiterung; Steigerung; Erhöhung; *image enhancement* Bilderweiterung; Bildverstärkung

ensure [ɪnˈʃʊə] A2/5/12/14/16/A19 (etwas) sicherstellen; (etwas) garantieren; Gewähr leisten (für etwas); *it ensures excellent all-round rust protection* es bietet einen ausgezeichneten Gesamtschutz gegen Rost; *ensure maximum reliability* äußerste Zuverlässigkeit sicherstellen; *ensure that the trains observe speed limits* sichergehen, daß die Züge die Geschwindigkeitsbegrenzungen einhalten

enter [ˈentə] T1 eingeben; *enter data* Daten eingeben

entertainment [entəˈteɪnmənt] 1 Unterhaltung

enviable [ˈenviəbl] 6 beneidenswert; *an enviable reputation* beneidenswert guter Ruf

epoxy primer [ɪˈpɒksɪ ˈpraɪmə] A2 Epoxidharz-Grundlackierung

equal [ˈiːkwəl] 10/A13 gleich; *equally important considerations* genauso wichtige Erwägungen

ergonomic [ɜːgəʊˈnɒmɪk] 18 ergonomisch

escape [ɪˈskeɪp] 4 entweichen; entkommen; ausströmen

estate agency [ɪˈsteɪt eɪdʒənsɪ] 9 Immobilienagentur

estimate [ˈestɪmeɪt] A15 Voranschlag; Schätzung; Kostenvoranschlag; *free estimates* kostenlose Voranschläge

evaluation [ɪvæljuˈeɪʃn] A12/15 Auswertung; Beurteilung; Bewertung

excavator [ˈekskəveɪtə] A9 Bagger; *bucket wheel excavator* Schaufelradbagger

excess [ɪkˈses] T2/15 *in excess of five million dollars* über fünf Millionen Dollar

excitement [ɪkˈsaɪtmənt] 1 Aufregung; Erregung

exclude [ɪkˈskluːd] 4 ausschließen; *draught excluder* Gerät zum Fernhalten der Zugluft

exclusive [ɪkˈskluːsɪv] 10 1. exklusiv; 2. ausschließlich, abgesehen von; *exclusive of bonus* ohne den Bonus (= Prämie)

execution [eksɪˈkjuːʃn] A20 Ausführung; Durchführung

exhaust air [ɪgˈzɔːst] 15 Abluft

exhibit [ɪgˈzɪbɪt] 20 Ausstellungsstück; Exponat

expense [ɪkˈspens] A3 *at owner's expense* auf Kosten des Besitzers

expertise [ekspɜːˈtiːz] A6/A10 Sachkenntnis

exploration [ekspləˈreɪʃn] 10 Untersuchung; Erforschung; Exploration; (Erdöl etc.:) Aufsuchen und Erforschen neuer Lagerstätten

extend [ɪkˈstend] A19 ausdehnen; erweitern; *extended maintenance service* erweiterter Wartungsdienst

extension [ɪk'stenʃn] A12 Erweiterung; Ausdehnung; Verlängerung; *extension cord* Verlängerungsschnur, Verlängerungskabel

extensive [ɪk'stensɪv] 20 umfassend; extensiv

external [ɪk'stɜ:nl] 4 außen; Außen-; extern

extraction [ɪk'strækʃn] 7 Extraktion; Förderung; Gewinnung; *aluminium extraction* Gewinnung von Aluminium

extrude [ɪk'stru:d] 8 extrudieren (= strangpressen)

extruded [ɪk'stru:dɪd] 4/8 *extruded frames* stranggepreßte Rahmen; *extruded components* stranggepreßte Teile

extrusion [ɪk'stru:ʒn] 4/6/8 Extrusion; Strangpreßverfahren

F

fabricate ['fæbrɪkeɪt] A13 herstellen; fertigen; *fabricated from plastic* aus Kunststoff hergestellt

fabrication [fæbrɪ'keɪʃn] 6/9 Herstellung; Fertigung; *large steel fabrications* große Stahlkonstruktionen

face 3/7 *they have to face a lot of competition* sie stehen sehr viel Konkurrenz gegenüber; *before they face each other again* bevor sie sich wieder gegenüberstehen

facia ['feɪʃə] A2 (Auto:) Armaturenbrett

facilitate [fə'sɪlɪteɪt] 14 erleichtern; fördern

fail [feɪl] A1/3/19 *fail a test* einen Test nicht bestehen; *he failed to come* er kam nicht; *the plan failed* der Plan scheiterte; *if everything else fails* wenn alles andere nicht funktioniert; *fail-safe* pannensicher, absolut zuverlässig

familiar [fə'mɪljə] 5/19 *I'm familiar with this kind of work* ich bin mit dieser Art von Arbeit vertraut

fan [fæn] 15 Ventilator; Lüfter

fastener ['fɑ:snə] 9 Befestigungselement; Verbindungselement; *compressive fastener* Druckverbinder

favour (GB; US: favor) ['feɪvə] 9 *the most favoured technique* die beliebteste Technik

feasible ['fi:zəbl] 19 durchführbar; machbar

feed back 20 rückkoppeln; *the glove allows the sense of touch to be fed back to the person wearing it* der Handschuh macht es möglich, die Tastwahrnehmung zu der Person zurückzuführen, die ihn trägt

feed line A18 Zufuhrsystem

fence [fens] T2 Zaun; Einzäunung

field [fi:ld] 1/A6 Bereich; Anwendungsbereich; Gebiet; *in the field of engineering* auf dem Gebiet der Technik; *in-the-field dependability* (etwa:) Zuverlässigkeit im praktischen Einsatz; *field effect* Feldeffekt; *field of force* Kraftfeld; *field-work* Außenarbeit, Arbeit im Gelände, Außendienst; *field worker* Außendienstmitarbeiter

file [faɪl] 6/19/A20 (Computer:) Datei; *have something on file* etwas in der Datei haben; *we must file it* wir müssen es in der Datei speichern; *file maintenance* Dateipflege; *source file* Ursprungsdatei (von der Kopien gemacht werden)

fill out (US; GB: fill in) 2 *fill out a form* ein Formular ausfüllen

filtration [fɪl'treɪʃn] 15 Filterung; Filtration

fin [fɪn] 11 Rippe; Kühllamelle; Wulst

finish 4/6/8 *attractive finishes* attraktive Oberflächen; *finishing* Endbearbeitung; *finishing coat* Deckanstrich; *finishing plant* Weiterverarbeitungsbetrieb

fir tree [fɜ:] 20 Tanne

fire brigade [brɪ'geɪd] A14 Feuerwehr

fire extinguisher [ɪk'stɪŋgwɪʃə] A14 Feuerlöscher

firefighter 1 Feuerwehrmann

fire hose [həʊz] A17 Feuerlöschschlauch

fireman 19 Heizer

fit 2/12/17 *all furnaces are fitted with an outer mesh* alle Brennöfen sind mit einem Außengitter versehen; *the roller bearings are easy to fit* die Rollenlager sind leicht einzubauen; *it fits well* es paßt gut

fix [fɪks] A5/20 befestigen; festmachen; festsetzen; festlegen; fixieren; *I fixed my eyes on the church* ich richtete meine Augen auf die Kirche; *fixing* Befestigung; Halterung; *fixing bolt* Befestigungsschraube

flame-resistant [ˈfleɪmrɪˈzɪstənt] 2 flammfest

flat-bed scanner 20 Flachbettscanner

flexibility [fleksəˈbɪlətɪ] 6 Flexibilität

float [fləʊt] 19 schwimmen; treiben (z. B. auf dem Wasser)

floor pan [pæn] A2/9 Bodenblech

flow sheet [fləʊ] 19 Fließbild; Fließschema; Ablaufschema

fluctuate [ˈflʌktʃʊeɪt] 18 fluktuieren; schwanken

foam [fəʊm] 2/13 Schaum; Schaumstoff; *foam packing crates* Schaumstoffverpackungen; *soft foam padding* weiche Schaumstoffpolsterung

focus [ˈfəʊkəs] A15 fokussieren; scharf einstellen (auf); *a finely focused beam of light* ein genau fokussierter Lichtstrahl

foil [fɔɪl] 4/7 Folie

forefront 1 *at the forefront* in der vordersten Reihe; ganz vorne

forest ranger (US) 1 Förster

form A6 gründen; bilden

forward 2 *forward of the rear axle* vor der Hinterachse gelegen

foundation [faʊnˈdeɪʃn] A6 Fundament; Grundlage; Unterbau

fraction [ˈfrækʃn] A18 Fraktion; Bruchteil; Bruch(zahl)

frame [freɪm] 2 Rahmen

friction [ˈfrɪkʃn] 3 Reibung

front wheel [ˈfrʌnt] A2 Vorderrad

frontal collision [ˈfrʌntl kəˈlɪʒn] 2 Frontalzusammenstoß

fumes [fjuːmz] 3 Abgas; Rauchgas; Dämpfe

furnace [ˈfɜːnɪs] A15 Brennofen; Feuerungsanlage; *gas furnace* Gasofen; *heat treatment furnace* Wärmebehandlungsofen; *furnace lining* Ofenauskleidung

furniture [ˈfɜːnɪtʃə] 1 Möbel

fusion [ˈfjuːʒn] 9 Fusion

fusion welding [ˈfjuːʒn] A10 Schmelzschweißen

G

gageline (US; GB: gaugeline) [ˈgeɪdʒlaɪn] A16 Nullinie

galvanic [gælˈvænɪk] A9 galvanisch

galvanneal [gælvəˈniːl] A9 wärmebehandeln nach dem Verzinken

gang [gæŋ] 8 Truppe; *welcome to the gang* (umgangssprachlich:) willkommen bei unserer „Truppe"

gangway [ˈgæŋweɪ] 6 Gang; Mittelgang; Arbeitsgang

garment [ˈgɑːmənt] 6 Kleidung(sstück)

gasket [ˈgæskɪt] 4 Dichtungsscheibe; Flachdichtung

geometric [dʒɪəʊˈmetrɪk] 20 geometrisch

geometry [dʒɪˈɒmətrɪ] A20 Geometrie

giant [ˈdʒaɪənt] 18 riesig; gigantisch

gist [dʒɪst] 17 *the gist of the conversation* die wesentlichen Punkte der Unterhaltung

given A10 *over a given period* während einer bestimmten, festgelegten Zeit

global communication [ˈgləʊbl] 20 weltweite Kommunikation

goggles [ˈgɒglz] A11 Schutzbrille; *wear goggles* eine Schutzbrille tragen

grade [greɪd] A9 Grad; Härtegrad; Güteklasse

graduate [ˈgrædjʊeɪt] 10 *I graduated from university* ich habe ein Studium an der Universität abgeschlossen; *graduate engineer* (etwa:) Diplom-Ingenieur

grandchild [ˈgræntʃaɪld] 20 Enkel/-in; Enkelkind

graphic designer 19 Grafikdesigner/-in

graphic material 20 grafisches Material

graphics-oriented software 19 grafikorientierte Software

grasp [grɑːsp] T2/19 packen; fassen; ergreifen; *grasp something firmly* etwas fest packen

gravity [ˈgrævətɪ] 15 Gravitation; Schwerkraft; *gravity feed* Schwerkraftzuführung; *gravity feed tank* Falltank

grease gun [ˈgriːs gʌn] 13 Fettpresse; Schmierpresse

grey (GB; US: gray) [greɪ] 20 grau

grid [grɪd] A19 Raster; Gitter; Rasternetz

grille [grɪl] 15 (Auto:) Kühlerschutzgitter, Kühlergrill; Gitter

grind [graɪnd] (ground [graʊnd] – have ground) 16 schärfen; schleifen

groove [gruːv] T2 Rinne; Furche; Nut; Rille

ground → grind

guidance ['gaɪdəns] A9/20 Führung; Lenkung; Führungsschiene; *for guidance only* nur für die Spurführung; *robotic guidance* Lenkung durch Roboter

guide [gaɪd] A11 führen; leiten; lenken

guide wheel ['gaɪd wiːl] 3 Führungsrad; Lenkrad

guideway ['gaɪdweɪ] 3 Gleitbahn; Führungsbahn

H

hairdressing industry 1 Friseurhandwerk

hand [hænd] A10 *when replacement parts are not to hand* wenn Ersatzteile nicht zur Hand sind

handling ['hændlɪŋ] 6/A7/A9 *automatic machines for handling and processing* automatische Maschinen für Beförderung und Verarbeitung; *the trickiest handling problems* die schwierigsten Handhabungsprobleme; *handling and distribution systems* Beförderungs- und Verteilungssysteme

handy ['hændɪ] T2/15 *it comes handy* es ist sehr nützlich; *are you handy with tools?* können Sie gut mit Werkzeugen umgehen?

hard copy 20 Computerausdruck

hard disk 20 Festplatte

hardwood ['hɑːdwʊd] A11 Hartholz

hazard ['hæzəd] T2/A18 Gefahr; Risiko

head 2/A17 *a German consortium headed by...* ein deutsches Konsortium angeführt von...; *head restraint* (Auto:) Kopfstütze

headset ['hedset] 20 Kopfhörer (hier auch mit Sichtgerät)

heat exchanger 18/A19 Wärmetauscher

heat treatment ['triːtmənt] A9 Wärmebehandlung

heavy current A1 Starkstrom

heavy duty A6 Hochleistungs-; *heavy duty oil* Hochleistungsöl

high current A9 Hochstrom; Starkstrom

histogram ['hɪstəgræm] A20 Histogramm (= grafische Darstellung einer Häufigkeitsverteilung)

hit 12/A20 *if a lightning hits a telephone line* wenn ein Blitz in eine Telefonleitung einschlägt; *a near hit* ein Beinaheeinschlag

hold 10/A20 (held – have held) *hold a driving licence* einen Führerschein haben; *CDs can hold an enormous amount of information* CDs können eine enorme Menge von Informationen speichern; *hold furnace* Warmhalteofen (auch: holding furnace)

hose reel ['həʊz 'riːl] A17 Schlauchhaspel

hostile ['hɒstaɪl] 18 feindlich; aggressiv

hot-dip zinc coating A9 Verzinken im Schmelzbad

hot testing A12 heiße Prüfung

household pets 20 Haustiere

housewarming party 10 Einzugsparty (beim Beziehen einer neuen Wohnung)

housing A2 Gehäuse; Ummantelung

hover ['hɒvə] A3 schweben; gleiten; *hover above a special track* schweben über einem Spezialschienensystem

hue [hjuː] 19 Farbe; Farbtönung; Farbton

human ['hjuːmən] A3 menschlich

humble ['hʌmbl] 15 *we are humbled by the faith which you have placed in us* (etwa:) das Vertrauen, das Sie in uns gesetzt haben, berührt uns zutiefst

humidity [hjuːˈmɪdətɪ] A9/15/A18 Feuchtigkeit

hybrid ['haɪbrɪd] 13 Hybrid; *hybrid resins* Hybridharze

hydraulic [haɪˈdrɔːlɪk] 16 hydraulisch; Wasser-

I

illusion [ɪˈluːʒn] 16 *optical illusion* optische Täuschung

image ['ɪmɪdʒ] 19/20 1. Image; Vorstellung;

2. Bild; Abbildung; *image processing* Bildbearbeitung; *image enhancement* Bilderweiterung; *image library* Bildbibliothek; *image quality* Bildqualität

imagination [ɪmædʒɪ'neɪʃn] 10 Phantasie; Vorstellungskraft

imaging ['ɪmɪdʒɪŋ] 20 Bildverarbeitung

immerse [ɪ'mɜːs] A2 eintauchen; untertauchen

immersion [ɪ'mɜːʃn] 11 Eintauchen; Untertauchen; *immersion heater* Tauchsieder

impact ['ɪmpækt] 2/T2/A13 *the impact of landing* das Aufsetzen beim Landen; *impact strength* Schlagfestigkeit; *impact-absorbent* stoßdämpfend; *high impact forces* große Schlagkräfte; *impact printer* Anschlagdrucker (mechanischer Drucker)

implement ['ɪmplɪmənt] 20 einführen; implementieren

implementation [ɪmplɪmen'teɪʃn] 10 *the implementation of your automation programme* die Durchführung ihres Automatisierungsprogramms

import [ɪm'pɔːt] A19 1. importieren; 2. (hier:) importieren; übertragen (von Daten)

improper [ɪm'prɔpə] A16 ungeeignet; unkorrekt; unrichtig

improve [ɪm'pruːv] 2/A13 verbessern

improvement [ɪm'pruːvmənt] 20 Verbesserung

impulse ['ɪmpʌls] A1 Impuls

incinerate [ɪn'sɪnəreɪt] 13 verbrennen

incoming clothes T1 (die) hereinkommenden Kleidungsstücke

in-company training 1 innerbetriebliche Ausbildung/Weiterbildung

incorporate [ɪn'kɔːpəreɪt] T1/16 *they incorporate computer control* sie verfügen über Computersteuerung; *it can be incorporated easily* es kann leicht eingebaut werden (integriert werden)

indestructible [ɪndɪ'strʌktəbl] A20 unzerstörbar

indication [ɪndɪ'keɪʃn] 14 Angabe; Anzeichen; Anzeige; *indication error* Anzeigefehler; *alarm and trip indications* Alarm- und Fahrtenangaben

individual [ɪndə'vɪdʒʊəl] 1 Individuum; Einzelperson

inexperienced 2 unerfahren

inflight personnel T1 fliegendes Personal

influence ['ɪnfluəns] 1 beeinflussen

initiative [ɪ'nɪʃɪətɪv] 1 Initiative

injection [ɪn'dʒekʃn] A9 Injektion; Einspritzung; *injection moulding* Spritzgießverfahren; *injection pump* Einspritzpumpe

injure ['ɪndʒə] 14 verletzen

injury ['ɪndʒərɪ] 14/A20 Verletzung

innovation [ɪnəʊ'veɪʃn] A10 Neuheit; Innovation

innovator ['ɪnəʊveɪtə] 3 Neuerer (= jemand, der Neuerungen einführt oder entwickelt)

input 18 Eingabe; Eingangsleistung; *input and output status* Eingabe- und Ausgabestatus

insert [ɪn'sɜːt] 5 einfügen; *insert key* (Computer:) Einfügungstaste; *insert mode* (Computer:) Einfügemodus

instruct [ɪn'strʌkt] 14 instruieren; beauftragen; *it is instructed to switch to the faster program* es wird angewiesen, auf das schnellere Programm umzuschalten

integral ['ɪntɪgrəl] 8/9 *an integral part* ein integraler Bestandteil; *integral calculus* Integralrechnung

integration [ɪntɪ'greɪʃn] 19 Integration; Verknüpfung (z. B. von Computern)

intend [ɪn'tend] 19 beabsichtigen; vorhaben; planen; *they were intended to replace horses* sie waren dazu bestimmt, die Pferde zu ersetzen

interact [ɪntər'ækt] 3 aufeinander wirken; sich gegenseitig beeinflussen

interaction [ɪntər'ækʃn] 20 Wechselwirkung

intermediate [ɪntə'miːdjət] A2 dazwischenliegend; Zwischen-; Mittel-

interpreter [ɪn'tɜːprɪtə] A20 1. Dolmetscher; 2. (Computer:) Interpretierer (= übersetzt ein Quellprogramm Anweisung für Anweisung in den ausführbaren Objektcode)

interpretive [ɪnˈtɜːprɪtɪv] A20 (Computer:) interpretierend
interruption [ɪntəˈrʌpʃn] A1 Unterbrechung; Störung
intersect [ɪntəˈsekt] A18 sich überschneiden; sich kreuzen
intervals [ˈɪntəvəlz] A10 *at regular intervals* in regelmäßigen Abständen
intervention [ɪntəˈvenʃn] A16 Eingriff; Intervention; *without operator intervention* ohne daß die Bedienungsperson eingreift
interview 10 *job interview* Vorstellungsgespräch
invoice [ˈɪnvɔɪs] 2 Rechnung
involve [ɪnˈvɒlv] 1/6/8 umfassen; einschließen; involvieren; *jobs which involve hard work* Berufe, in denen man schwer arbeiten muß; *the manufacturing cells involved* die daran beteiligten Fertigungszellen; *are you involved in this?* haben Sie damit zu tun? *involved in an accident* in einen Unfall verwickelt
ISO (= International Standard Organization) A12 Internationale Normungsinstitution (vergibt unter anderem Gütezertifikate)

J

jam [dʒæm] A20 *if it jams…* wenn es festklemmt…
jaw [dʒɔː] 1 Backe; Klemmbacke; Spannbacke
job history 10 beruflicher Werdegang
joint [dʒɔɪnt] 2/9 Verbindung; Verbindungselement; *welded joints* verschweißte Verbindungen; *joint robot* Drehgelenkroboter

K

key pad [ˈkiː pæd] 5 Tastatur
knitting [ˈnɪtɪŋ] 20 Stricken
knob [nɒb] A3 Knopf

L

lab [læb] (= laboratory) A7/10/18 Labor
lack [læk] 3 Fehlen; Mangel; Knappheit; *lack of noise* kein Lärm; *lack of emission fumes* keine Emissionsabgase

ladder [ˈlædə] 1 Leiter
laminate [ˈlæmɪneɪt] 7 Schichtstoff; laminieren; beschichten; *laminated foil* kaschierte Folie
landfill (hauptsächlich US) 13 Mülldeponie
landing gear T2 Fahrgestell (eines Flugzeuges)
landscape [ˈlændskeɪp] 19 Landschaft
large-scale 6 großangelegt; umfangreich; Groß-; *large-scale garment storage* Großraumlagerhaltung von Textilien; *large-scale experiment* Großversuch; *large-scale manufacture* Serienherstellung
laser inspection [ɪnˈspekʃn] A9 Laserkontrolle
laser output 19 *high quality laser output* (hier:) hochwertige Laserprintouts
lateral [ˈlætərəl] T2 seitlich; Seiten-; Quer-
lathe [leɪð] 4 Drehmaschine; *lathe-chuck* Drehmaschinenfutter
law [lɔː] 15 *sister-in-law* Schwägerin
layout 6 Übersichtsplan; Plan; Layout; Anordnung
leading 6 *they are the leading force in the world of overhead handling* im Bereich der Gehängeförderer haben sie eine führende Position inne
lead [led] 14 Blei; *lead-weighted* mit Blei beschwert
leak [liːk] 4 tropfen; lecken; *unwanted draughts leak through gaps* (etwa:) unerwünschte Zugluft strömt durch die Lücken
leakage [ˈliːkɪdʒ] 4 Auslaufen; Lecken; Leckage; *leakage current* Reststrom; Kriechstrom; Streustrom; *leakage path* Kriechweg
leave 19 *where CAD leaves off* wo CAD aufhört
lecture [ˈlektʃə] 10 Vorlesung
legal dependants [ˈliːgl dɪˈpendənts] 10 (etwa:) Angehörige, für die man laut Gesetz verantwortlich ist (z. B. Kinder)
legally separated [ˈliːgəli ˈsepəreɪtɪd] 10 rechtsgültig getrennt
leisure [GB: ˈleʒə; US: ˈliːʒə] 10 Freizeit
lengthy [ˈleŋθɪ] A10 *a lengthy breakdown* eine langanhaltende Panne

leveller [ˈlevələ] A9 *tension leveller* Spannungsnivellierer

liable [ˈlaɪəbl] 19 *liable to corrosion* korrosionsanfällig

library [ˈlaɪbrərɪ] 19/20 Bücherei; Bibliothek (auch im Computerbereich)

life A16 Haltbarkeit; Lebensdauer

life-span [ˈlaɪfspæn] A20 *the computer's lifespan* die Lebensdauer des Computers

lift 9/14/20 heben; anheben; hochheben

lift truck (= fork lift truck) 20 Gabelstapler

lifting appliances A9 Hebezeug; Hebevorrichtungen

lifting jack 14 Winde; Hebebock

light duty A6 für geringe Beanspruchung

lighting fixtures [ˈlaɪtɪŋ ˈfɪkstʃəz] A13 Beleuchtungskörper

lightning [ˈlaɪtnɪŋ] A20 Blitz

lightweight [ˈlaɪtweɪt] 3/8 *the material is lightweight* es handelt sich um leichtes Material; *lightweight construction* Leichtbauweise

line 2/15/17/19 *line voltage* Netzspannung; Betriebsspannung; *manufacturing line* Fertigungsprogramm; *line of sight* Blickrichtung; *along these lines* nach diesen Grundsätzen; *line of business* Branche, Geschäftszweig; *that's not in my line* das schlägt nicht in mein Fach; *the line is engaged* die Leitung ist besetzt; *line drawing* Strichzeichnung; *line printer* Zeilendrucker; *line space* Zeilenabstand; *line width* Zeilenbreite; *in line with the steering column* auf gleicher Höhe wie das Lenkrad

linear motor [ˈlɪnɪə] 3 Linearmotor

lining [ˈlaɪnɪŋ] 2 Verkleidung

link [lɪŋk] 6/20 verbinden; Verbindung; *linked* verbunden, verknüpft; *link chain* Gliederkette

live [laɪv] A17 stromführend; *live electrical equipment* unter Strom stehende Elektrogeräte (= spannungsführende Elektrogeräte); *live rail* Stromschiene

load [ləʊd] 4/6/11/15/17 *load a truck* (US; GB: lorry) einen Lastwagen beladen; *high load capacity* hohe Belastbarkeit *load carrying capacity* Lastaufnahmefähigkeit; *load source file* laden Sie die Ursprungskartei; *at full load* bei voller Auslastung; *loader* Ladeprogramm

local authority [ˈləʊkl ɔːˈθʊrətɪ] 5 örtliche Behörde

lockable [ˈlɒkəbl] 18 verriegelbar; abschließbar

locking collar [ˈkɒlə] T2 (hier:) Verschraubung

locomotive [ˈləʊkəməʊtɪv] 19 Lokomotive

log [lɒg] 14 aufzeichnen; protokollieren; Aufzeichnung; Protokoll; *all events are logged* alle Vorkommnisse (Ereignisse) werden aufgezeichnet

logic [ˈlɒdʒɪk] 19 logisch; Logik

long-haul aircraft [ˈlɒŋhɔːl] T2 Langstreckenflugzeuge

long-term [ˈlɒŋtɜːm] A9/16 langfristig; Langzeit-

loop [luːp] A8/19 Schleife; Schlinge; Schlaufe; Kreislauf

loss [lɒs] 2/4 Verlust

loudness [ˈlaʊdnɪs] A4 Lautstärke

louver [ˈluːvə] 15 Belüftungsklappe

lube [luːb] 2 (auch: lube oil) US: Schmieröl (von: *lubricant*)

lubricant [ˈluːbrɪkənt] 1 Schmiermittel

lung [lʌŋ] 10 Lunge

M

machine A1/19 maschinell bearbeiten; spanabhebend bearbeiten

machine tool A1 Werkzeugmaschine

macro routine [ˈmækrəʊ ruːˈtiːn] 20 Makroroutine (Makro = Computerbefehl, der sich aus vielen Einzelbefehlen zusammensetzt)

MAG (= metal active-gas welding) A15 MAG-Schweißen

Maglev trains [ˈmæglev] (auch: [maglev]) 3 Magnetschwebezüge

magnetic [mægˈnetɪk] 3 *magnetic field* Magnetfeld; *magnetic force* magnetische Feld-

stärke; *magnetic levitation* Magnetschwebetechnik
magnificent [mæg'nıfısənt] A5 fabelhaft; herrlich
magnitude ['mægnıtju:d] 18/A18 Größe; Größenordnung; Ausmaß; Magnitude
mains 1 Leitungsnetz; Hauptleitung (z. B. Wasser oder Strom)
major ['meıdʒə] 20 bedeutend; Haupt-
make 2/A15 Fabrikat; Marke; *our own make* unser eigenes Fabrikat
make-up 7/15 Zusammensetzung; *simple make-up units* Einheiten in einfacher Ausführung; *make up for something* etwas ausgleichen
manage ['mænıdʒ] 5/19 *manage process design data* mit Verfahrensentwicklungsdaten umgehen; *can you manage?* kommen Sie zurecht? *I'll manage* ich komme schon zurecht; *I'm afraid I can't manage it* ich fürchte, es ist mir leider nicht möglich
manipulation [mənıpju'leıʃn] A20 Bearbeitung; Manipulation
manpower A10 *experienced manpower* erfahrene Arbeitskräfte
manual ['mænjʋəl] A17 manuell; handbetrieben
mark [ma:k] A20 kennzeichnen; markieren
market share ['ʃeə] 14 Marktanteil
mask [ma:sk] 11 abdecken; maskieren; Abdeckung; Maske
mass produce [mæs] 11 in Massenfertigung herstellen, serienmäßig herstellen
materials-handling A6/A9 Fördertechnik; Materialtransport
matrix ['meıtrıks] A20 Matrix; Matrize; *matrix display* Matrixbildschirm
MCU (= machine control unit) 16 Steuereinheit der Maschine (bei numerisch gesteuerten Maschinen)
mechanical engineering [mı'kænıkl] 1 Maschinenbau
mechanics [mı'kænıks] 10 Mechanik
mechanism ['mekənızəm] 6 Mechanismus; Mechanik (= mechanische Teile)

menu ['menju:] 5/20 (Computer etc.:) Menü
mess [mes] 13 Unordnung; Durcheinander; „Schlamassel"
metallic [mı'tælık] 7 metallisch
metallurgical plant [metə'lɜ:dʒıkl] A9 Hütte; Hüttenwerk
metallurgy [me'tælədʒı] 1 Metallurgie
microelectronics ['maıkrəʋılek'trɒnıks] 6 Mikroelektronik
microprocessor ['maıkrəʋ'prəʋsesə] 2/12 Mikroprozessor
mind [maınd] 5 *I don't mind* ich habe nichts dagegen
mineral ['mınərəl] 4 mineralisch; Mineral-
minor ['maınə] A5 *minor axis* Nebenachse; *minor faults* kleinere Fehler
mobile ['məʋbaıl; US: 'məʋbəl] A9/A1 *mobile crane* Mobilkran; *mobile home* US: Wohnwagen (fest auf einem Platz abgestellt)
mobilize ['məʋbılaız] A10 *mobilized with the required equipment* mobil ausgestattet mit der erforderlichen Ausrüstung
modem ['məʋdem] 1/20 Modem
modify ['mɒdıfaı] A2 modifizieren; verändern
modular ['mɒdjʋlə] A6 modular; Modul-; *modular design* Modulbauweise
moist [mɔıst] A11 feucht
moisture ['mɔıstʃə] A2 Feuchtigkeit; *moisture-resistant* feuchtigkeitsbeständig; *moisture-sensitive* feuchtigkeitsempfindlich
moldability [məʋldə'bılətı] A13 Formbarkeit (GB auch: mouldability)
monorail ['mɒnəʋreıl] 3 Einschienen-
mortgage ['mɔ:gıdʒ] 5 Hypothek
motherboard A20 Mutterplatine; Hauptplatine
motor mechanic 10 Kfz-Mechaniker/-in
motorized ['məʋtəraızd] A4 motorisiert
mould [məʋld] 2 formen; Formen bauen (US auch: mold)
mountainous ['maʋntınəs] A7 gebirgig; Berg-
mounting ['maʋntıŋ] 2 Montierung; Montage; Aufhängung
movement ['mu:vmənt] 1 Bewegung

multiple [ˈmʌltɪpl] 20 mehrfach; multipel; Vielfach-; Mehrfach-

N

narrow [ˈnærəʊ] A4/15 eng; schmal; verengen
natural scientist [ˈnætʃrəl] 1 Naturwissenschaftler/-in
nature [ˈneɪtʃə] A18 Natur; Charakter; Eigenart; *the nature of work in the chemical industry* die Art der Arbeit in der Chemieindustrie
neck vertebrae [ˈnek ˈvɜːtɪbrə] 2 Halswirbelsäule
needlework [ˈniːdlwɜːk] 20 Näherei (Handarbeit)
neglect [nɪˈglekt] 13 vernachlässigen; versäumen; mißachten
neon [ˈniːɒn] A4 Neon
neoprene gasket [ˈniːəʊpriːn ˈgæskɪt] 4 Neoprendichtung
net A4 netto; Netto-
networking A19 Vernetzung
non-porous [nɒnˈpɔːrəs] 11 porenfrei; porenlos
non-uniformity [nɒnjuːnɪˈfɔːmətɪ] 20 Ungleichmäßigkeit
notch [nɒtʃ] A11 einkerben; kerben; ritzen; *notched test piece* Kerbstab
notice period 10 Kündigungsfrist
novelty [ˈnɒvəltɪ] 8 Neuheit; *they were a novelty* sie waren etwas Neues
nuclear [ˈnjuːklɪə] 1/18 nuklear; Nuklear-; *nuclear engineering* Kerntechnik, Nukleartechnik; *nuclear power station* Kernkraftwerk
number plate A3 (Auto:) Nummernschild
numerous [ˈnjuːmərəs] A14 zahlreich
nylon [ˈnaɪlɒn] 18 Nylon

O

objective [əbˈdʒektɪv] A12 Ziel
observe [əbˈsɜːv] 14 *observe speed limits* Geschwindigkeitsbeschränkungen einhalten
obtain [əbˈteɪn] A7/10 erlangen; bekommen; erhalten; gewinnen; *obtain aluminium* Aluminium gewinnen; *the qualifications obtained* die erreichten Qualifikationen
occupants [ˈɒkjʊpənts] 2 Insassen (z. B. eines Autos)
occur [əˈkɜː] 19 geschehen; sich ergeben; *it occurred to me that…* es kam mir der Gedanke, daß …
off the shelf [ʃelf] 20 *off the shelf application programs* Standard-Anwenderprogramme
off-load 6 [ˈɒfləʊd] abladen
oil rig [rɪg] 1 Bohrinsel
on request 10 auf Anfrage
on-site A19 an Ort und Stelle; auf der Baustelle
open-cast mining A6 Tagebau
opportunity [ɒpəˈtjuːnətɪ] 1/A4/9/12 (günstige) Gelegenheit
optimize [ˈɒptɪmaɪz] A20 optimieren
option [ˈɒpʃn] 5 Wahlmöglichkeit; Option
ore [ɔː] A7 Erz
origin [ˈɒrɪdʒɪn] A18 Ursprung; Herkunft; Anfang; *certificate of origin* Herkunftszeugnis; *country of origin* Ursprungsland
otherwise [ˈʌðəwaɪz] 4 sonst; andernfalls
outer [ˈaʊtə] 2 äußere; außen; Außen-
outlet [ˈaʊtlet] A13 (hier:) Steckdose
outpatients department 14 Ambulanz (eines Krankenhauses)
outstanding 13 hervorragend; überragend
oval [ˈəʊvəl] A8 oval
overhead camshaft [ˈəʊvəhed ˈkæmʃɑːft] A4 obenliegende Nockenwelle
overhead conveyor [ˈəʊvəhed kənˈveɪə] 6 Gehängeförderer
overleaf [əʊvəˈliːf] A19 *use the order form overleaf* verwenden Sie das Auftragsformular auf der anderen Seite/Rückseite
override [əʊvəˈraɪd] A4 eingreifen (in einen automatischen Vorgang) *…so that they override the boiler thermostat* (etwa:) so daß sie in die Funktion des Boiler-Thermostaten eingreifen können
overview A14/14 Überblick; Übersicht
own goal 1 Eigentor
oxide [ˈɒksaɪd] 7 Oxid

P

package ['pækɪdʒ] 19 Packen; Paket; Packung
packing charge [tʃɑːdʒ] 12 Verpackungsgebühren
padding ['pædɪŋ] 2 Polsterung; *heavy padding throughout the interior* dicke Polsterung überall im Innern; *foam padding* Schaumstoffpolsterung
paint plant 6 Lackiererei
paint tank [tæŋk] 6 Farbbehälter
paintwork A2 Lackierung
pallet ['pælɪt] 16 Palette
paperboard ['peɪpəbɔːd] 13 Karton; Pappe
parameter [pə'ræmɪtə] A16 Parameter
parenthesis [pə'renθɪsɪs] (Mehrzahl: parentheses [pə'renθɪsiːz]) 16 runde Klammer
parking site 15 Parkplatz
part specifications 19 (etwa:) Teileliste
pass A13 *pass a test* einen Test bestehen
patent ['peɪtənt/'pætənt] 2 Patent; patentieren; *patented* patentiert
path control [pɑːθ] 18 Steuerung des Weges (der Bahn); *path time diagram* Weg-Zeit-Diagramm
pavement ['peɪvmənt] 14 GB: Pflasterung; Straßenpflaster; (auch:) Bürgersteig; US: (nur:) Pflasterung; Straßenpflaster; *wet concrete pavement* (hier:) nasser Beton-Straßenbelag
paving ['peɪvɪŋ] A9 Straßenpflaster; *paving width* Pflasterbreite
payload 17/A18 Nutzlast
pay-off reel [riːl] A9 Abwickelspule
PDP (= power distribution panel) 16 Stromverteiler-Konsole
penicillin [penɪ'sɪlɪn] 2 Penicillin
performance products 13 (etwa:) Hochleistungsprodukte
periodic [pɪərɪ'ɒdɪk] 7/A18 periodisch; regelmäßig wiederkehrend
peripherals [pə'rɪfərəlz] A19 Peripheriegeräte
permanent magnet ['pɜːmənənt] 3 Dauermagnet
permission [pə'mɪʃn] A3 Erlaubnis; Genehmigung; *special permission* Sondererlaubnis

personnel department [pɜːsə'nel] 14/20 Personalabteilung
pesticide ['pestɪsaɪd] A18 Pestizid
petrochemical ['petrəʊ'kemɪkl] 18 *petrochemical plants* Petrochemiewerke
PFD (= process flow diagram) A19 Verfahrens-Flußdiagramm
pharmaceuticals [fɑːmə'sjuːtɪkəlz] A18 Pharmazeutika
phase [feɪz] A18/19 Phase
pH-value A9 pH-Wert (reines Wasser = pH-Wert 7; saure Lösungen haben einen kleineren, alkalische einen größeren pH-Wert als 7)
philosophy [fɪ'lɒsəfɪ] A6 Philosophie
physical ['fɪzɪkl] 1/A9/20 *a physical barrier* eine physische Barriere; *physical exercise* körperliche Bewegung; *physical fitness* körperliche Fitness
physicist ['fɪzɪsɪst] A20 Physiker
piano tuner [pɪ'ænəʊ] 1 Klavierstimmer
pick up 19 *Windows is easy to pick up* Windows ist leicht zu lernen
pile up 13 sich stapeln; sich auftürmen; *the waste problem is quickly piling up into a great mess* das Abfallproblem entwickelt sich schnell zu einem richtigen Chaos/zu einem richtigen Durcheinander
pipe fitting A19 Rohrformstück
pixel ['pɪksl] A20 Pixel; Bildelement; Rasterpunkt
plasma ['plæzmə] T2 Plasma
plaster ['plɑːstə] A11 1. Gips; Verputz; 2. Heftpflaster
plate [pleɪt] 11 beschichten
platform ['plætfɔːm] A14 Plattform; GB auch: Bahnsteig; *yellow platforms* (hier:) gelbe Bahnsteige (= gelb angezeigte Bahnsteige auf dem Computerdisplay)
plating ['pleɪtɪŋ] 11 Beschichtung
PLC (= programmable logic controller) 6 speicherprogrammierte Steuerung
plotter ['plɒtə] 19 Plotter (= Planzeichner)
pneumatic [njuː'mætɪk] A9/20 pneumatisch; Druckluft-

polyarylate [pɒlɪˈærɪleɪt] A13 Polyarylat

polychloroprene [pɒlɪˈklɒrəpriːn] 4 Polychloropren

polyester [pɒlɪˈestə] A2/18 Polyester; *polyester-based* auf Polyesterbasis

polythene [ˈpɒlɪθiːn] 18 Polyethylen (auch: Polyäthylen)

pop-up dialog box [ˈpɒpʌp] A19 Dialogfeld, das dort erscheint, wo sich der Mauszeiger gerade befindet

port [pɔːt] 18 (Computer:) Port (= Anschlußstelle)

portion [ˈpɔːʃn] 2 Teil; Portion; Teilstück

position A19 positionieren; an den richtigen Platz bringen

positive [ˈpɒzətɪv] A9/A16 (allgemein:) positiv; *the axis moves in a positive direction* die Achse bewegt sich entgegen dem Uhrzeigersinn (= positive Bewegung); *positive displacement machine* Kolbenverdichter

post graduate study [ɡrædʒʊət] 10 weiterführendes Studium

post pot overage [ˈəʊvəreɪdʒ] A9 (etwa:) zusätzliches Vergüten mit höherer Temperatur

postage [ˈpəʊstɪdʒ] 12 Porto; *postage charge* Portogebühren

potential [pəʊˈtenʃl] 4/13/20 Potential; potentiell; *they are potentially dangerous* sie könnten möglicherweise gefährlich sein; *a potential market* ein potentieller Markt; *potential air leakage* möglicher Luftaustritt

powder-coated 8 pulverbeschichtet

powdered-metal 1 Sintermetall

power transistor [trænˈsɪstə] A16 Leistungstransistor

power transmission A17 Energieübertragung

power unit A12 Antriebsaggregat

power up A20 *the very short period during which the circuit is powering up* die sehr kurze Zeit, in der der Schaltkreis die Spannung aufbaut

power-and-free conveyor 6 Schleppkreisförderer; Power-and-Free-Förderer

precaution [prɪˈkɔːʃn] 15 Vorsichtsmaßnahme

precise [prɪˈsaɪs] 12/19 präzise; genau; klar; *precise temperature control* präzise Temperaturführung

precision [prɪˈsɪʒn] 6 Präzision; Genauigkeit; Klarheit

pre-code 6 vorkodieren

prefer [prɪˈfɜː] 1 vorziehen; bevorzugen; lieber haben

preference [ˈprefərəns] 11 Vorzug; Bevorzugung; Präferenz

preliminary [prɪˈlɪmɪnərɪ] 14 Vor-; einleitend; vorläufig; *preliminary accident report* vorläufiger Unfallbericht

presentation [prezənˈteɪʃn] A20 Darstellung; Präsentation

preserve [prɪˈzɜːv] 8 erhalten; konservieren; präservieren

press [pres] 6/A9 Presse

pretreatment 6 Vorbehandlung

pride [praɪd] 6 Stolz; *the department prides itself on finding cost effective solutions* die Abteilung ist stolz darauf, kostengünstige Lösungen zu finden

principal [ˈprɪnsəpl] 11/A12/18 hauptsächlich; Haupt-; *our principal objectives* unsere Hauptziele; *two principal methods* zwei wesentliche Methoden; *the principal source of carbon* die Hauptkohlenstoffquelle

printout T2/A3/14 Ausdruck

prior to [ˈpraɪə] A16 vor; bevor; *prior to performing any maintenance adjustments* bevor man irgendwelche Wartungseinstellungen vornimmt

process [ˈprəʊses] 1/15/19/20 Verfahren; Verarbeitung; verarbeiten; *process engineering* Verfahrenstechnik; *process design* Verfahrensplanung; *process engineer* Verfahrensingenieur; *process flowsheet* Verfahrensfließbild; *process streams* (etwa:) Verfahrensabläufe; *process piping* Rohrleitungen

processing [ˈprəʊsesɪŋ] A7/18/20 Bearbeitung; Verarbeitung; *the processing of common salt* die Verarbeitung von gewöhnlichem Salz

production engineer A1 Fertigungsingenieur
production line A9 Fertigungsstraße; Fertigungslinie
productive [prəˈdʌktɪv] 18 produktiv; rentabel; ertragreich
profile [ˈprəʊfaɪl] 8 Profil
profitable [ˈprɒfɪtəbl] 18 gewinnbringend
projecting [prəˈdʒektɪŋ] 2 hervorstehend; vorspringend
projection [prəˈdʒekʃn] 9 Projektion; Darstellung; Ansichtszeichnung; *projection welding* Buckelschweißen
promote [prəˈməʊt] 12 fördern; unterstützen
promotion [prəˈməʊʃn] 1/19 Beförderung; Aufstieg; Unterstützung
propel [prəˈpel] 3 antreiben; vorwärts treiben
proper [ˈprɒpə] 15/19 richtig; korrekt; *operate properly* richtig arbeiten
properties [ˈprɒpətɪz] 2 Eigenschaften
proposition [prɒpəˈzɪʃn] 13 *they are dedicated to this proposition* sie widmen sich dieser Sache
prospects [ˈprɒspekts] 1 Aussichten; Möglichkeiten
protect [prəˈtekt] 2 schützen
protection [prəˈtekʃn] 1/18 Schutz
protocol [ˈprəʊtəkɒl] 18 Protokoll; protokollieren
proven [ˈpruːvn] A6/A20 *proven knowledge* nachgewiesene Kenntnisse; *proven subroutines* bewährte Unterprogramme
provide [prəˈvaɪd] 9/T1 *provided that...* vorausgesetzt, daß...
public [ˈpʌblɪk] 1 Öffentlichkeit
puff [pʌf] 19 „schnaufen"
pull-down menu 19/20 Balkenmenü (wird von oben nach unten aufgerollt)
pull test A13 Test auf Zugbelastung
pulsation [pʌlˈseɪʃn] A2 Pulsieren; Pulsation
puncture [ˈpʌŋktʃə] 15 US: Reifenpanne
purchase [ˈpɜːtʃəs] A19/20 kaufen; *purchasing department* Einkaufsabteilung
pure [pjʊə] 7 rein; unvermischt; pur
puzzle [ˈpʌzl] 16 Rätsel
PVC (= polyvinyl chloride) 18 PVC

pyramid [ˈpɪrəmɪd] 10 Pyramide

Q

qualifications [kwɒlɪfɪˈkeɪʃns] 5/10 Qualifikationen; *she has the necessary qualifications* sie hat die nötigen Voraussetzungen

R

radiator [ˈreɪdɪeɪtə] 4 1. Heizkörper; 2. (Auto:) Kühler
radical [ˈrædɪkəl] A18 radikal; Grund-; Radikand (= Zahl, aus der eine Wurzel gezogen wird); *radical sign* Wurzelzeichen
radio A15 (hier:) Funk-
raise [reɪz] (rose – have risen) A3 heben; hochheben; emporheben; *raise a wall* eine Mauer errichten; *raise money* Geld beschaffen
raise cutter head [reɪz] A9 Raise-Bohrkopf
ram [ræm] 8 Kolben; Stempel; Rammsporn
rapid transit system 3/A10 (etwa:) Stadtschnellverkehr
rate [reɪt] 4 Grad; Rate
reach [riːtʃ] 17 reichen; erreichen; Reichweite
readily 16 leicht; ohne weiteres
reading [ˈriːdɪŋ] A16 Anzeige (z. B. auf einem Instrument)
real time A16/18 Echtzeit; Realzeit
rearrange [riːəˈreɪndʒ] A11 umstellen; neu arrangieren
reasonable [ˈriːzənəbl] 10 vernünftig; angemessen; *at a reasonable price* zu einem vernünftigen Preis
reassure [riːəˈʃɔː] 5 *I reassure you that...* ich versichere Ihnen, daß...
receipt [rɪˈsiːt] 12/13 1. Empfang; Eingang; *on receipt of the spare parts* bei Erhalt der Ersatzteile; 2. Quittung; *sales receipt* Verkaufsquittung
receiver 15 (hier:) Behälter; Kessel
recent [ˈriːsnt] 10 vor kurzem; neulich; *a recent development* eine Entwicklung neueren Datums
reciprocating pump [rɪˈsɪprəkeɪtɪŋ] 19 Rückförderpumpe; Kolbenpumpe

reclaimer [rɪˈkleɪmə] A9 Rückladebagger

reconversion [ri:kənˈvɜ:ʃn] 20 *reconversion into a hard copy* Wiederumwandlung in einen Computerausdruck

record [rɪˈkɔ:d] A11/14/A16/A17 aufzeichnen; registrieren; erfassen; *record results* Ergebnisse erfassen; *record operation data* Betriebsdaten aufzeichnen; *record an increase in the volume of business* einen Anstieg im Umsatzvolumen verzeichnen; *all events are recorded on a printer* alle Vorkommnisse werden auf dem Drucker gespeichert

recording [rɪˈkɔ:dɪŋ] 5/12/20 Aufzeichnung; Aufnahme; Erfassung; *the recording process* das Aufzeichnungsverfahren; *recording head* Aufnahmekopf

records [ˈrekɔ:dz] A10 Unterlagen; Aufzeichnungen; *keep records* Aufzeichnungen aufbewahren

recruit [rɪˈkru:t] A12 einstellen; rekrutieren

recruitment consultancy [rɪˈkru:tmənt kənˈsʌltənsɪ] A12 Personalberatungsfirma

recyclable [ri:ˈsaɪkləbl] 13 wiederverwertbar

REF (= reference) A5 Bezug

refer [rɪˈfɜ:] 10 *it refers to* es bezieht sich auf

reflect [rɪˈflekt] 4 reflektieren; zurückwerfen; *this reflects heat back into the room* das reflektiert die Wärme zurück ins Zimmer

reflective [rɪˈflektɪv] 4 *reflective foil* reflektierende Folie

refuse collection [ˈrefju:s] 5 Müllabfuhr

Reg. No. (= registration number) 2 *(Auto:)* amtliches Kennzeichen

register [ˈredʒɪstə] 5 registrieren; erfassen

reinforce [ri:ɪnˈfɔ:s] 2 verstärken

reinsert [ri:ɪnˈsɜ:t] T2 wieder einfügen; wieder einsetzen

relation [rɪˈleɪʃn] A16 *in relation to...* in Bezug auf...

relationship [rɪˈleɪʃnʃɪp] A16 Relation; Verhältnis; Beziehung

reliability [rɪlaɪəˈbɪlətɪ] 12/A19 Zuverlässigkeit

relocate [ri:ləʊˈkeɪt] A13 versetzen; verlagern

relocation [ri:ləʊˈkeɪʃn] A13 Umsetzung; Verlagerung; Verschiebung

rely [rɪˈlaɪ] A19 *a service they can rely on* ein Kundendienst, auf den sie sich verlassen können

renovate [ˈrenəʊveɪt] 4 renovieren

renovation [renəʊˈveɪʃn] A4/8/10 Renovierung

rent [rent] 5/10 Miete; Pacht

repeatable [rɪˈpi:təbl] 20 wiederholbar

repetitive [rɪˈpetətɪv] 20 *for repetitive applications* für sich wiederholende Anwendungen

replaceable [rɪˈpleɪsəbl] 16 austauschbar; auswechselbar

replacement [rɪˈpleɪsmənt] 4 Austausch; Ersatz; Auswechseln

representative [reprɪˈzentətɪv] 15 Vertreter; Repräsentant

reproduce [ri:prəˈdju:s] A15 reproduzieren

reproducible [ri:prəˈdju:səbl] 12 reproduzierbar

reputation [repjʊˈteɪʃn] 6 (guter) Ruf; Name

resin [ˈrezɪn] 13 Harz

resist [rɪˈzɪst] 11 *resist corrosion* der Korrosion widerstehen

resistance [rɪˈzɪstəns] A11 Widerstand; *resistance to impact* Schlagfestigkeit; *corrosion resistance* Korrosionsbeständigkeit

resistant [rɪˈzɪstənt] 13 resistent; widerstandsfähig; *resistant to stains* schmutzabweisend; *corrosion-resistant* korrosionsbeständig

resources [rɪˈsɔ:sɪz] 13/A18/A19 Ressourcen; *natural resources* Bodenschätze; *financial resources* Finanzmittel; *our engineers have the resources* unsere Ingenieure haben die nötigen Mittel

respond [rɪˈspɒnd] A2 reagieren; antworten

retail [ˈri:teɪl] A8 Einzelhandel; Einzelhandels-

retain [rɪˈteɪn] 16 beibehalten; halten; *retaining screw* Halteschraube

retread [ˈri:tred] T2 neubereifen

return 10/16 *return the form* schicken Sie das

Formular zurück; *maximum return on your investment* maximale Rendite für Ihre Investitionen

reverse [rɪ'vɜːs] 2 Rückseite; Kehrseite; *(Auto:)* Rückwärtsgang; *reverse order* umgekehrte Reihenfolge; *reverse current* Gegenstrom

revolute ['revəluːt] A18 *revolute coordinates* Werkzeugkoordinaten

revolution [revə'luːʃn] A11 Umdrehung

rework ['riːwɜːk] A16 Nachbehandlung; Nacharbeiten

rib [rɪb] 11 Rippe

ridiculous [rɪ'dɪkjʊləs] 12 lächerlich; *it does sound ridiculous* es klingt wirklich lächerlich

rigid ['rɪdʒɪd] 16 starr; steif; fest; *it provides rigid support* es sorgt für eine feste Unterlage

rigidity [rɪ'dʒɪdətɪ] A13/17 Starre; Steife; Steifigkeit

rigorous ['rɪgərəs] 19 streng; exakt; genau

rim [rɪm] 2/T2 *steering-wheel rim* Lenkradkranz

rinse [rɪns] 6 *after rinse* nach dem Ausspülen

rivet ['rɪvɪt] 9 nieten; Niet; *blind rivet* Blindniet; *full tubular rivet* Hohlniet

road finisher A9 Straßendecken-Fertiger

robotic [rəʊ'bɒtɪk] 20 Roboter-

robotics [rəʊ'bɒtɪks] 17 Robotik; Robotertechnik

robust [rəʊ'bʌst] 20 robust; widerstandsfähig

roller bearing 17 Rollenlager

rolling edge [edʒ] 11 Walzkante

rolling mill A9 Walzwerk

roof [ruːf] 4 Dach; *roof hatch* Dachluke

rotary ['rəʊtərɪ] 7 Dreh-; *rotary kiln* Drehofen

rotation [rəʊ'teɪʃn] A18 Rotation; Drehung; Umdrehung

rotative ['rəʊtətɪv] 20 rotierend; Dreh-; *rotative beam engine* rotierende Balancierdampfmaschine

rotor ['rəʊtə] A16 Rotor

roughness ['rʌfnɪs] 11 Rauheit; Rauhigkeit

rounded ['raʊndɪd] 17 abgerundet

rugged ['rʌgɪd] 16 unempfindlich; robust; widerstandsfähig; *it is ruggedly built* es ist robust gebaut

ruggedize ['rʌgɪdaɪz] 20 unempfindlich machen gegen rauhe Behandlung

ruler ['ruːlə] A11 Lineal

runout A16 Auslauf; *runout time* Auslaufzeit (eines Werkzeugs)

S

sailboard ['seɪlbɔːd] 13 US: Surfbrett (zum Windsurfen)

sailing ['seɪlɪŋ] 20 Segeln

salary ['sælərɪ] 3/10/A12 Gehalt

sanding machine 1 Sandpapier-Schleifmaschine

satisfaction [sætɪs'fækʃn] 1 Zufriedenheit; *job satisfaction* Zufriedenheit mit dem Beruf

satisfy ['sætɪsfaɪ] 1 zufriedenstellen

satisfying ['sætɪsfaɪɪŋ] 1 zufriedenstellend

scale [skeɪl] A5/A11/19 1. Skala; 2. Maßstab; maßstäblich; 3. skalieren; *scale drawing* maßstäbliche Zeichnung; *Richter scale* Richter-Skala; *you can scale symbols* Sie können Symbole skalieren

scan [skæn] 20 scannen; abtasten

scanner ['skænə] 20 Scanner

scare [skeə] 7 *that does not scare me* das macht mir keine Angst

schematic [skɪ'mætɪk] 6 schematisch

scientific [saɪən'tɪfɪk] 20 wissenschaftlich

scope [skəʊp] T2 Bereich; Anwendungsbereich; *scope for innovation* Möglichkeiten für Innovationen; *within the scope of…* im Rahmen von…

score a goal [skɔː] 1 ein Tor schießen

scrap [skræp] A16 Schrott; Abfall; Ausschuß; verschrotten

scrape [skreɪp] T2 kratzen; schaben.

scratch [skrætʃ] 8/A9 Kratzer; Schramme; *scratch-proof* kratzfest

screw thread [θred] 11 Schraubengewinde

script [skrɪpt] A20 *they can be saved as a script* sie können als Makroprogramm gespeichert werden

seal [siːl] 4 abdichten; versiegeln; *gaps can be sealed* (die) Lücken können abgedichtet werden

seamless [ˈsiːmlɪs] A9 nahtlos

search [sɜːtʃ] A20 Suche; *the search for space on your hard drive* die Suche nach Platz auf Ihrer Festplatte

seat back 2 Stuhllehne

secondary education [ˈsekəndərɪ] 10 höheres Schulwesen

secure [sɪˈkjʊə] 1 sicher; *a secure job* ein sicherer Arbeitsplatz

security [sɪˈkjʊərətɪ] 1 Sicherheit

seek time A20 Positionierungszeit; (auch:) Suchzeit

select [sɪˈlekt] 5/12/A13/15/19 wählen; auswählen; selektieren; *carefully selected* sorgfältig ausgewählt; *select payment options* den gewünschten Zahlungsmodus wählen

self-centring 1 selbstzentrierend

self-contained [ˈselfkənˈteɪnd] 1 in sich abgeschlossen; unabhängig; autonom; *self-contained unit* in sich abgeschlossene Einheit

self-employed 10 selbständig; freiberuflich

self-lubricating 1 selbstschmierend

self-tapping screw [ˈtæpɪŋ] 9 Blechschraube; Schneidschraube

sense of touch [sens] 20 Tastgefühl

sensitive [ˈsensɪtɪv] A20 empfindlich

separator [ˈsepəreɪtə] 15 Separator; Trenner; Abscheider

serial [ˈsɪərɪəl] A9 Serien-; seriell; Reihen-; *serial lifting equipment* Mehrfach-Hebeanlage

servo motor [ˈsɜːvəʊ] 17 Servomotor

set A4/9 *set hot water temperature* stellen Sie die Warmwassertemperatur ein; *pre-set temperature* (die) vorher eingestellte Temperatur; *set rivets* Nieten setzen

setting [ˈsetɪŋ] 9 Einstellung (einer Maschine)

settle [ˈsetl] 9/11 *have you settled down?* (etwa:) haben Sie sich eingelebt? *particles may settle on some surfaces* auf einigen Oberflächen könnten sich Partikel absetzen

sequence [ˈsiːkwəns] 20 Folge; Reihenfolge

sequencing [ˈsiːkwənsɪŋ] 20 Sequentialisieren (= in eine Reihenfolge bringen)

sewing [ˈsəʊɪŋ] 20 Nähen; Näharbeiten

shade [ʃeɪd] 15/20 Schatten; Schattierung; *shades of grey* Grauschattierungen; *a parking site where your RV will be shaded* ein Parkplatz, wo Ihr Wohnmobil im Schatten steht

shaft [ˈʃɑːft] A9 (Bergbau:) Schacht; (sonst auch:) Welle

shallow [ˈʃæləʊ] 11 flach; mit geringer Tiefe

shampoo [ʃæmˈpuː] 18 Shampoo; Haarwaschmittel

share [ʃeə] A19 gemeinsam benutzen; sich teilen; *all kinds of data can be easily shared* alle Arten von Daten können gemeinsam benutzt werden

shareware [ˈʃeəweə] A5 Shareware (= Software, die man erst nach einer kostenlosen Prüfung bezahlen muß)

shears [ˈʃɪəz] A9 Führung; Bettführung

sheet metal 2 Blech

sheet mills A9 Blechwalzwerke

sheet steel 2 Stahlblech

shield [ˈʃiːld] 2 *well-shielded* gut abgeschirmt

shiploader A9 Schiffsbelader

shoelace [ˈʃuːleɪs] 18 Schnürsenkel

short circuit 16 Kurzschluß

shortage [ˈʃɔːtɪdʒ] 13 Mangel; Engpaß

shorthand A13 Stenografie; Kurzschrift

shuttle swing radius [ˈʃʌtl] 16 Schwenkbereich des Werkzeugschlittens

side-effect A18 Nebenwirkung

signalling system [ˈsɪgnəlɪŋ] A14 Signalsystem

signature [ˈsɪgnətʃə] 2 Unterschrift

sill [sɪl] 4 (hier:) Türschwelle

simplicity [sɪmˈplɪsətɪ] 19 Einfachheit; Unkompliziertheit

simulate [ˈsɪmjʊleɪt] 19/20 simulieren; *simulated stress* Belastungssimulation

simulator [ˈsɪmjʊleɪtə] T1/20 Simulator

single glazed windows [gleɪzd] 4 Fenster mit einfacher Verglasung

siphon off [ˈsaɪfn] 7 hebern; mit Hilfe eines Siphons entleeren; leerhebern

situate ['sɪtjʊeɪt] 14 *the building is situated close to Poplar Station* das Gebäude befindet sich in der Nähe des Bahnhofs Poplar

skid [skɪd] T2 rutschen; schleudern; *go into a skid* ins Schleudern geraten; *skid mark* Bremsspur

skills 10 Fertigkeiten; Können; *language skills* Fremdsprachenkenntnisse

sleeping bag 13 Schlafsack

slide [slaɪd] 6 *slide component* Gleiter-Komponenten (= für die Herstellung von Autositzen)

slideway ['slaɪdweɪ] 17 Gleitbahn; Führungsbahn

slip [slɪp] 14 *he slipped on the wet concrete* er rutschte auf dem nassen Beton aus

slot [slɒt] 11 Spalt; Schlitz; Rille

smelt [smelt] A7/A8 schmelzen; einschmelzen; *smelting plant* Metallhütte; Schmelzhütte

smelter ['smeltə] A7 Schmelzofen

smooth [smu:ð] A5/11/17 glatt; eben; glätten; *edges should be smoothed out* Kanten sollten abgerundet werden

snap-in [snæp] A13 *snap-in cable sets* Snap-In-Kabelsätze (= mit Schnapp- oder Federverschluß)

soap [səʊp] 18 Seife

soda ['səʊdə] A8/A18 1. Soda (= Natriumkarbonat); Natriumhydrogenkarbonat; 2. Sodawasser (= Sprudelwasser); *a can of soda* eine Dose mit Sprudelwasser

sodium aluminate ['səʊdɪəm ə'lu:mɪneɪt] 7 Natriumaluminat

soil [sɔɪl] A10 Erde; *soil chemistry* Bodenchemie

solid waste ['sɒlɪd] 13 feste Abfälle

sound 6 einwandfrei; fehlerfrei; gesund; *sound advice* ein vernünftiger Ratschlag

space 11 *space them as widely as possible* ordnen Sie sie mit möglichst großem Abstand an

spare ['speə] 12/14 *a spare room* (etwa:) ein Gästezimmer; *spares* (= *spare parts*) Ersatzteile

special purpose vehicle A12 Spezialfahrzeug

specialisation [speʃəlaɪ'zeɪʃn] 10 Spezialisierung

specialty tools [speʃltɪ] A10 Spezialwerkzeuge

specify ['spesɪfaɪ] A9 spezifizieren; Soll-; *specified yield stress* Soll-Streckspannung

spectrum ['spektrəm] A6 Spektrum

spindle ['spɪndl] 16 Spindel; Zapfen; *hi-speed spindle* Hochgeschwindigkeitsspindel; *spindle drive* Spindelantrieb; *spindle head* Spindelkopf

split [splɪt] (split – have split) 7 aufspalten; trennen; sich spalten; *this causes the alumina to split into aluminium and oxygen* dies bewirkt, daß sich das Aluminiumoxid in Aluminium und Sauerstoff aufspaltet

spread [spred] A2 ausbreiten; streuen; verbreiten

spreadsheet ['spredʃi:t] 2/A3 Bildschirmtabelle, elektronisches Arbeitsblatt

square [skweə] 10 Quadrat; Viereck; *square bracket* eckige Klammer; *square root* Quadratwurzel

stacker ['stækə] A9 Stapler

staging ['steɪdʒɪŋ] 1 Arbeitsbühne; Arbeitsgerüst

stain [steɪn] 13 Schmutzfleck

stairwell ['steəwel] 4 Treppenhaus

starving ['stɑ:vɪŋ] A7 (umgangssprachlich:) *I'm starving* ich komme bald um vor Hunger

state-of-the-art T1/13 auf dem neuesten Stand der Technik; *state-of-the-art technology* Technik nach dem neuesten Stand

statement ['steɪtmənt] 10/A20 Anweisung; (amtliche) Erklärung; Aussage; *input and output statements* Eingabe- und Ausgabeanweisungen; *program control statements* Anweisungen für die Programmsteuerung

stationary ['steɪʃənərɪ] A12 stationär

steam [sti:m] 19/20 Wasserdampf; Dampf

steel mill A9 Stahlwerk

steering column ['kɒləm] 2 (Auto:) Lenksäule

steering gear 2 Lenkgetriebe

steering wheel 2 (Auto:) Lenkrad
sterilised ['sterəlaɪzd] 18 sterilisiert
stiff [stɪf] A11 starr; steif; unbiegsam
stiffness ['stɪfnɪs] A11/13 Steifigkeit; Steifheit
stone chippings ['stəʊn 'tʃɪpɪŋz] A2 Steinsplitter
storage ['stɔːrɪdʒ] 4 Lagerung; Speicherung; Speicher; *storage battery* Akku; *electric storage radiators* Elektrospeicherheizung
storehouse of knowledge ['stɔːhaʊs] 19 (etwa:) ein Speicher für Informationen
stoving oven ['stəʊvɪŋ 'ʌvn] 6 Einbrennofen
strain [streɪn] A11 Belastung; Beanspruchung; Verformung (unter Last)
strategy ['strætɪdʒɪ] 4 Strategie; Taktik
stream [striːm] 19 strömen; Strom; Datenstrom
streamer ['striːmə] 19 Magnetbandstation
streamline ['striːmlaɪn] 6 modernisieren; straffen; *streamline production* die Produktion modernisieren
stress [stres] 2/A11 Beanspruchung; Spannung; Stress; *under abnormal stress* bei ungewöhnlich starker Belastung
strike A20 *a direct strike* (Blitz etc.:) ein direkter Einschlag
string [strɪŋ] A20 (Computer:) Zeichenfolge; Kette; (allgemein:) Faden; Kordel; Schnur
strip mill A9 Bandstahlwalzwerk
strive [straɪv] A19 *we strive for quality* wir streben nach Qualität
stroke [strəʊk] 20 *for every double stroke of the engine* für jeden Doppeltakt des Motors; *four-stroke engine* Viertaktmotor
stud [stʌd] 9 Bolzen; (hier:) Nietansatz (= hervorstehendes Teil)
sturdy ['stɜːdɪ] 13 robust; kräftig; stabil
submarine ['sʌbməˈriːn] 14 Unterseeboot
subroutine ['sʌbruːtiːn] 20 (Computer:) Unterprogramm
subsequent ['sʌbsɪkwənt] 20 nachfolgend; später; nachgestellt; Nach-; *subsequent research has produced good results* die folgenden Forschungen haben gute Ergebnisse hervorgebracht

substantial [səbˈstænʃl] A7/19 beträchtlich; erheblich
substation ['sʌbsteɪʃn] 14 Nebenstelle; Außenstelle
suit [suːt; auch: sjuːt] 16/A19 passen; sich eignen; zusagen; *well suited for use with robots* gut geeignet für den Einsatz mit Robotern; *a machine that suits you* eine Maschine, die für Sie geeignet ist
superior [suːˈpɪərɪə] 16 hochwertig; Qualitäts-
supervision [suːpəˈvɪʒn] 1 Überwachung; Beaufsichtigung; Aufsicht
supervisor ['suːpəvaɪzə] 1/18 Aufsichtsführende/-r; Kontrolleur/-in; (Computer:) Supervisor (= Steuerroutine mit bestimmten Aufgaben)
supreme [sʊˈpriːm] T2 höchst; oberst; Ober-
surgeon ['sɜːdʒən] 20 Chirurg/-in
surplus capacity ['sɜːpləs] T1 überschüssige Kapazität
surround [səˈraʊnd] 2 umgeben; umschließen
suspend [səˈspend] 11 *articles are suspended on wires* (die) Artikel hängen an Drähten
suspension [səˈspenʃn] A9/A12 Aufhängung; (Auto:) Radaufhängung
switching diagram 14 Schaltdiagramm
system integration [ɪntɪˈgreɪʃn] 10 Systemintegration
systems engineering A9 Systemtechnik

T

tab [tæb] 19 *pull tab* ziehen Sie die Lasche heraus
tackle ['tækl] A6 *tackle a problem* ein Problem in Angriff nehmen
tailor ['teɪlə] A12 auf bestimmte Bedürfnisse zuschneiden; *a furnace tailored to your requirements* ein Ofen, der auf Ihre Bedürfnisse zugeschnitten ist
take 1/A14/A16 *take measurements* Messungen durchführen; *take risks* Risiken eingehen; *take place* stattfinden
tap [tæp] 15/A20 *water tap* Wasserhahn; *tap into subroutines* in Unterprogramme gehen („anzapfen")

tax [tæks] 5/12 Steuer
teach pendant ['pendənt] 18 Handprogrammiergerät
team [tiːm] 16 *they can team up* sie können sich zusammenschließen
telescopic [telɪˈskɒpɪk] 2 *the upper section is telescopic* der obere Teil läßt sich zusammenschieben
teletext 10 Videotext; Bildschirmtext
temper mill ['tempə] A9 Dressierwalzwerk; Nachwalzwerk
tensile strength ['tensaɪl 'streŋθ] A9/A11 Zugfestigkeit
tension ['tenʃn] A9 Spannung; *tension leveller* Spannungsausgleicher
terrific [təˈrɪfɪk] 13 *that's terrific* das ist ganz toll
thermal ['θɜːml] 10/12 thermisch; Wärme-; *thermal mass* thermisch wirksame Masse; *thermal power* Wärmekraft; *thermal efficiency* Wärmewirkungsgrad; *thermal value* Heizwert
thermocouple ['θɜːməʊˌkʌpl] 12 Thermoelement
thermostat ['θɜːməʊstæt] A4 Thermostat
threaded ['θredɪd] 9 mit Gewinde; gewindet
thunder ['θʌndə] A20 Donner
ticket 5/15 *a ticket for speeding* ein Protokoll/Strafmandat wegen Geschwindigkeitsüberschreitung
tile [taɪl] 15 kacheln; mit Fliesen auslegen
timber ['tɪmbə] 4 Holz (= Nutzholz)
tool 16/19/A20 (Computer:) Dienstprogramme (= Hilfsprogramme)
tool extraction [ɪkˈstrækʃn] 16 Werkzeugentnahme
toolmaking ['tuːlmeɪkɪŋ] 1 Werkzeugbau
top up 7 nachfüllen; auffüllen; *the alumina is kept topped up* das Aluminiumoxid wird ständig nachgefüllt
toroidal coil [təˈrɔɪdəl] T2 Ringspule; Toroid
torque [tɔːk] 16/A18 Drehmoment; Drehkraft
touch screen 20 Sensorbildschirm
toughness ['tʌfnɪs] A11 Zähigkeit; Festigkeit; Widerstandsfähigkeit

tow away [təʊ] A3 *tow a car away* einen Wagen abschleppen; *tow away zone* Abschleppbereich (= aus diesem Bereich wird der Wagen abgeschleppt)
track [træk] 6 Bahn; Gleiskette; Spur; Schiene
trackball ['trækbɔːl] 20 (Computer:) Rollkugel
trade name ['treɪd neɪm] 4 Handelsname; Markenname
train captain ['kæptɪn] 14 Zugführer
training facilities T1 Ausbildungseinrichtungen
transaction [trænˈzækʃn] 5 (Computer:) Arbeitsvorgang; Transaktion; Geschäftsvorgang
transformation [trænsfəˈmeɪʃn] A20 Umwandlung; Transformation
transmission [trænsˈmɪʃn] 2 (Auto:) Getriebe; (allgemein:) Übertragung, Übermittlung
transportation [trænspɔːˈteɪʃn] 3 Transport; Beförderung
trap [træp] 11 fangen; einschließen; *so that plating solutions cannot be trapped* so daß die Elektrolyte nicht eingeschlossen werden können
trihydrate [traɪˈhaɪdreɪt] 7 *alumina trihydrate* Aluminiumoxidhydrat
trim shop [trɪm] 6 (etwa:) Ausstattungswerkstatt
tritium ['trɪtɪəm] T2 Tritium (= schwerstes, radioaktives Isotop des Wasserstoffs)
trolley ['trɒlɪ] 6 (hier:) Förderwagen; (auch:) Gepäckwagen; Einkaufswagen; (US auch:) Straßenbahnwagen
truck A8 *in truckload quantities* in ganzen Lkw-Ladungen
trust [trʌst] A6 Vertrauen
tube [tjuːb] A9/A11 Rohr; Röhre
tumour ['tjuːmə] (GB; US: tumor) 20 Tumor
tune [tjuːn] 2/15 *tune a car / tune up a motor* einen Motor richtig einstellen
turn A11 *in turn* der Reihe nach
turnkey installation A10/A19 schlüsselfertige Anlage
turnover 7/A19 Umsatz
turntable 14 Drehscheibe; Plattenteller

twin-track conveyors ['twɪntræk] 19 Doppelbahn-Förderanlagen

U

unauthorized [ʌn'ɔ:θəraɪzd] A3 unbefugt; (hier:) unbefugt geparkte Fahrzeuge

under way 13 *with 1000 programs under way* mit 1000 Programmen, die gerade laufen

undergo T1/7 *how many revolutions does each wheel undergo?* wie viele Umdrehungen macht jedes Rad? *undergo changes* Umwandlungen durchmachen; *undergo training* sich einer Ausbildung unterziehen

unexcelled [ʌnɪk'seld] 16 unübertroffen

uniform ['ju:nɪfɔ:m] A2/19 einheitlich; gleichmäßig

uniformity [ju:nɪ'fɔ:mətɪ] 12 Einheitlichkeit; Gleichmäßigkeit

unitized ['ju:nɪtaɪzd] A6 vereinheitlicht

unloosen [ʌn'lu:sn] T2 lösen; lockern; losmachen

unmatched [ʌn'mætʃt] A16 *an unmatched variety* eine von keinem anderen erreichte Vielfalt

unplug A20 *unplug from the mains* den Stecker aus dem Netz herausziehen

unsurpassed [ʌnsə'pɑ:st] 20 unübertroffen

utilization [ju:təlaɪ'zeɪʃn] A6 Verwendung; Nutzung; Verwertung

update [ʌp'deɪt] A4/5/19 modernisieren; auf den neuesten Stand bringen

upgrade [ʌp'greɪd] 15 modernisieren; auf den neuesten Stand bringen

uppermost ['ʌpəməʊst] 11 oberst; höchst; ganz oben

upright [ʌp'raɪt] 16 aufrecht; senkrecht (stehend)

urban ['ɜ:bən] 3 *urban and regional transportation system* städtisches und regionales Nahverkehrssystem

urgent ['ɜ:dʒənt] 3/A12/16 dringend; dringlich

V

valid ['vælɪd] 10 gültig; stichhaltig

valley ['vælɪ] 20 Tal

value ['vælju:] 5 Wert

variable ['veərɪəbl] 16/A20 variabel; veränderbar; *variable-speed AC motor* Wechselstrommotor mit regelbarer Drehzahl

vector ['vektə] A20 Vektor

verification [verɪfɪ'keɪʃn] A16 Prüfung; Verifizierung

verify ['verɪfaɪ] A16 prüfen; verifizieren

versatile ['vɜ:sətaɪl] 8 vielseitig; anpassungsfähig

victim ['vɪktɪm] 19 Opfer; (hier etwa:) Hilfesuchende/-r

vinegar ['vɪnɪgə] A11 Essig

virtual image ['vɜ:tʃʊəl] 20 virtuelles Bild (= existiert nur im Computerspeicher)

virtual reality ['vɜ:tʃʊəl] 20 virtuelle Realität

virtually ['vɜ:tʃʊəlɪ] A2/A20 im Grunde genommen; praktisch

vital ['vaɪtl] A6 lebenswichtig

voltmeter ['vəʊltmi:tə] 12/15 Voltmeter

volume ['vɒlju:m] 8/13/A17 *volume production* Massenproduktion; *volume of business* (etwa:) Umsatzvolumen

VR → virtual reality

W

waiter ['weɪtə] 1 Kellner

waitress ['weɪtrɪs] 1 Kellnerin

wander ['wɒndə] 20 *wander through shops* durch Geschäfte bummeln

warehouse engineering ['weəhaʊs] A9 Lagertechnik

waste management 13 Abfallwirtschaft

waste-to-energy facilities 13 Einrichtungen, in denen aus Abfall Energie entsteht

water quench [kwentʃ] A9 Härten durch Ablöschen mit Wasser

wear [weə] 11/A16 *it will wear longer* es wird länger halten; *tool wear* Werkzeugabnutzung; *wear and tear* Verschleiß (Abnutzung); *wear index* Verschleißzahl

weather bureau ['bjʊərəʊ] A20 Wetteramt

weight [weɪt] A11 Gewicht

welder ['weldə] A9 Schweißmaschine; Schweißgerät

well-lit screen 5 gut ausgeleuchteter Bildschirm

whiplash effect ['wɪplæʃ] 2 Peitschenhieb-Effekt (z. B. bei einem Autounfall); Schleudertrauma

wholesale ['həʊlseɪl] A8 Großhandel; Großhandels-

wide-field view 20 mit erweitertem Blickfeld

width [wɪdθ] A5 Breite; Weite

wind [waɪnd] (wound [waʊnd] – have wound) 1/14 drehen; aufdrehen; wickeln; *wind a watch* eine Uhr aufziehen; *a self-winding watch* eine Uhr mit Selbstaufzug; *a wind-up toy submarine* Spielzeug-Unterseeboot, das man aufziehen kann

windshield ['wɪndʃiːld] 7 Windschutzscheibe (US; GB: windscreen); (allgemein:) Frontscheibe

wire ['waɪə] A4/A9/20 verdrahten; schalten; *wire rods* Rundwalzdraht; *a wired glove* ein verdrahteter Handschuh

wiring ['waɪrɪŋ] A10/A12/A13 Verdrahtung; Verkabelung; Leitung

workmanship ['wɜːkmənʃɪp] 16 *excellent workmanship* ausgezeichnete Fertigungsqualität

worksheet A20 Arbeitsblatt

workstation 19/A20 (Computer:) Arbeitsplatz, Arbeitsplatzrechner

worth [wɜːθ] 1 *it's worth the risk* das Risiko lohnt sich

worthwhile ['wɜːθ'waɪl] A7 *is such an investment worthwhile?* lohnt sich eine solche Investition?

wrist [rɪst] A18 Handgelenk; (Roboter:) Greifkopf

Y

yield [jiːld] A9 *yield stress* Fließspannung; Streckspannung

Z

zoom [zuːm] 20 zoomen; *I zoomed towards it* (etwa:) ich bewegte mich schnell darauf zu

Not Yet the End – words and phrases

activate ['æktɪveɪt] aktivieren
airlock Luftschleuse
ascend [ə'send] aufsteigen; hochgehen
ascent [ə'sent] Aufstieg
being *a being like himself* ein Wesen wie er
bipeds ['baɪpedz] Zweibeiner; Zweifüßer
blast [blɑːst] *with one blast* mit einer Detonation
bleakly ['bliːklɪ] *they stared at each other bleakly* sie sahen sich mit einem leeren Gesichtsausdruck an
chase [tʃeɪs] (Zeitung:) Schließrahmen (= hier werden die fertigen Bleizeilen zum Drucken festgehalten)
civilization [sɪvɪlaɪ'zeɪʃn] Zivilisation
cloud layer [klaʊd] Wolkenschicht; Wolkendecke
companion [kəm'pænjən] Begleiter/-in; Kamerad
composing room [kəm'pəʊzɪŋ] (Zeitung:) Setzerei
compositor [kəm'pɒzɪtə] (Zeitung:) Setzer/-in
convention [kən'venʃn] (hier:) Konferenz
creature ['kriːtʃə] Kreatur; Lebewesen
cramped [kræmpt] verkrampft
crude [kruːd] *their knowledge is crude* (etwa:) sie haben nur primitive Kenntnisse; *they could not be trained even for the crudest labor* man könnte sie noch nicht mal für die einfachsten Arbeiten ausbilden
cruel ['kruːəl] grausam
cube [kjuːb] Würfel; Kubus
delicate work ['delɪkət] feine Arbeiten
descend [dɪ'send] heruntergehen; herunterkommen
dial ['daɪəl] Zifferblatt; Zeiger; Skala
dissappear [dɪsə'pɪə] *who cares if two monkeys disappeared?* wen interessiert es, ob zwei Affen verschwunden sind?
dissimilar [dɪ'sɪmɪlə] unähnlich

dying off *with the Lounacs dying off* da die Lounacs aussterben
emanate ['eməneɪt] austreten; herauskommen; *nothing visible emanated from the end of the rod* nichts Sichtbares kam aus dem Ende des Stabes heraus
evolve [ɪ'vɒlv] *they'll have evolved enough…* sie werden sich weit genug entwickelt haben…
faceted ['fæsɪtɪd] *a faceted eye* ein Facettenauge (= ein Auge wie bei einem Insekt)
faintly green ['feɪntlɪ] blaßgrün
galley ['gælɪ] (Zeitung:) Setzschiff
glance ['glɑːns] *he glanced at the type* er warf einen kurzen Blick auf die Zeilen; *a single glance* ein einziger Blick; *at a glance* auf einen Blick
greenish ['griːnɪʃ] grünlich; *a greenish, hellish tinge* (etwa:) ein scheußlicher, grüner Farbton
habitable ['hæbɪtəbl] bewohnbar
headsets Kopfhörer
hell [hel] Hölle
honour ['ɒnə] *be honoured* geehrt werden
immobility [ɪməʊ'bɪlɪtɪ] Bewegungslosigkeit
incapable unfähig
inhabited [ɪn'hæbɪtɪd] bewohnt
invisible [ɪn'vɪzɪbl] unsichtbar
launch reprisal raids [rɪ'praɪzl] Vergeltungsangriffe führen
leads [ledz] (Zeitung:) (Blei-)Durchschuß (= dünne Bleistreifen, die früher als Abstand zwischen die Bleizeilen gelegt wurden)
make-up editor (Zeitung:) Metteur (= stellt die Seiten der Zeitung zusammen)
manipulate [mə'nɪpjʊleɪt] manipulieren; handhaben
megrafield ['megrəfiːld] (etwa:) Unsichtbarkeitsfeld
mercy ['mɜːsɪ] Erbarmen; Barmherzigkeit

miracle ['mɪrəkl] Wunder
monkey ['mʌnkɪ] Affe; *Monkey Island* Affeninsel (im Zoo)
muscle ['mʌsl] Muskel
over-set (Zeitung:) überschüssiger Satz (= Zeilen, die man nicht mehr auf die Seite bringen kann)
paired headsets ['peəd] abgestimmte Kopfhörer
pica ['paɪkə] (Zeitung:) Pica (= Maßeinheit für die Zeilenbreite)
pointer Zeiger (eines Instruments)
progress Fortschritte machen
race Rasse
regularly spaced lights Lichter in regelmäßigen Abständen
relative ['relətɪv] relativ
reprisal raids [rɪ'praɪzl 'reɪdz] Vergeltungsangriffe
rose (rise) *he rose* er stand auf
shrug [ʃrʌg] mit der Schulter zucken
slave [sleɪv] Sklave
specimens Exemplare; Muster; (hier:) menschliche Testpersonen

stabilizer ['steɪbɪlaɪzə] Stabilisator
stare ['steə] starren
statuelike ['stætʃuːlaɪk] wie eine Statue
supervise ['suːpəvaɪz] beaufsichtigen; überwachen
threw (throw) *he threw the stabilizer switch* er betätigte den Stabilisatorschalter
tinge [tɪndʒ] Farbton; Färbung
type (Zeitung:) Schriftzeilen (früher aus Blei); *he glanced at the type* er schaute sich die Zeilen kurz an
ultraviolet ['ʌltrə'vaɪələt] ultraviolett
unwinkingly [ʌn'wɪŋkɪŋlɪ] ohne mit den Augenlidern zu zucken
vestige ['vestɪdʒ] Spur; *not even the vestige of a force field* noch nicht mal eine Spur von einem Kraftfeld
visiplate ['vɪzɪpleɪt] (etwa:) Sichtschirm
viviparous [vɪ'vɪpərəs / vaɪ'vɪpərəs] lebendgebährend (also zum Beispiel nicht eierlegend)
waver ['weɪvə] wanken; abgelenkt werden
wipe out [waɪp] auslöschen

American English vocabulary

It is often difficult to say that this word is only used in the USA, the other word only in Great Britain. Therefore, this short list of words is just an introduction. Often, both words are used but one is used more often. The influence of American TV programmes has also changed things a great deal.

AMERICAN ENGLISH	BRITISH ENGLISH
aluminum	aluminium
antenna	aerial
automobile, car	car
back-up lights	reversing lights
box spanner	socket wrench
can (= metal container)	tin
cord (= electric cord)	flex
dead-end (street)	cul-de-sac
divided highway	dual carriageway
downtown	(city, town) centre
drugstore	chemist's (shop)
elevator	lift
engineer (= driver of a railway engine)	driver (of a railway engine)
faucet	tap, water tap
fender	wing, mudguard
first floor	ground floor
flat (tire)	puncture
freeway, superhighway	motorway
freight train	goods train
garbage	rubbish
garbage man, garbage collector	dustman
gas (= gasoline)	petrol
gear shift	gear lever
glaze, glazed frost	black ice
grade crossing	level crossing
ground	earth
ground wire	earth wire
hood	bonnet
kerosene	paraffin
license plate	number plate
muffler	silencer
oil pan	oil sump
parking lot	car park
railroad	railway
scotch tape	sellotape
second floor	first floor

sedan	saloon car
spanner	wrench
spark plug	sparking plug
station wagon	estate car
street car, trolley car	tram
subway	underground, tube
thumb tack	drawing pin
tire	tyre
traffic circle	roundabout
traffic jam	tailback
trailer truck	articulated lorry
trash	rubbish
trash can	dustbin
trash man	dustman
truck	lorry
trucker	lorry driver
trunk (of a car)	boot
underpass	subway, subway crossing
windshield	windscreen

List of common prefixes

PREFIX	EXAMPLES
ab-	abnormal (= not normal, unusual)
counter-	counterclockwise (= in the opposite direction from that in which the hands of a clock move) / counterbalance (= a weight that balances another)
de-	demagnetize (= remove the magnetism) deink (= remove the printing ink from waste paper)
dis-	disconnect (= break the connection) / disassemble (= take apart) disadvantage (= opposite of advantage)
en-	enable (= make possible) / encircle (= form a circle around) enlarge (= make larger)
hyper-	hyperinflate (= inflate very much or too much)
im-	impossible (= not possible) / impure (= not pure)
in-	indirect (= not direct) / ineffective (= not effective)
inter-	interconnected (= connected with all the other parts)
macro-	macromolecule (= very large molecule) macroscopic (= large enough to be seen without instruments)
micro-	microcassette (= very small cassette) / microcircuit (= very small, compact electronic circuit) / microparticle (= very small particle)
multi-	multinational (= concerning more than two nationalities) multiprocessing (= processing of several computer programs)
non-	noncorrosive (= does not corrode) / nonpolar (= not polar)
over-	overload (= put too much load on something) / overheat (= make too hot) / overhead (= over one's head)
poly-	polyaxial (= having many axles)
pre-	precondition (= necessary preparation)
re-	reheat (= heat again) / recharge (= charge again)
semi-	semiautomatic (= not fully automatic)
sub-	subassembly (= assembled unit designed to be used with other units)
super-	supercool (= cool to a very low temperature)
tele-	teleprinter (= printer which uses signals received over a communications circuit)
un-	uncomplicated (= not complicated) / unstable (= not stable)
under-	undercoat (= coat of paint applied as the base for another coat) underestimate (= estimate as being less than the actual size, quantity, or number)

List of common suffixes

SUFFIX	EXAMPLES
-able	washable (= can be washed) / breakable (= can break) machinable (= can be worked on with a machine)
-al	automatical (= having to do with automation)
-ally	structurally (= adverb of "structural")
-ance	acceptance (= noun of "accept") / resistance (= noun of "resist")
-ant	pollutant (= something that pollutes)
-ar	molecular (= having to do with molecules)
-bility	availability (= the fact that something is available)
-en	harden (= make hard) / strengthen (= make strong)
-ent	absorbent (= able to absorb) (also: absorbant)
-er	three-decker (= something that has three decks) / opener (= something used for opening) / reporter (= somebody who reports)
-fold	a six-fold increase (= six times as much)
-ful	powerful (= full of power) / useful (= can be used)
-ible	flexible (= can be bent without breaking; open to change or new ideas) reversible (= can be changed or turned over)
-ify	electrify (= equip for use of electric power)
-ion	insulation (= noun of "insulate")
-ism	magnetism (= property of a magnet)
-ity	polarity (= showing that something is either positively or negatively charged)
-ive	corrosive (= can cause corrosion)
-ivity	resistivity (= property of a conductor)
-ization	standardization (= noun of "standardize")
-ize	aluminize (= treat or coat with aluminium) / magnetize (= make magnetic) / industrialize (= make or become industrial)
-ment	development (= noun of "develop")
-ness	brittleness (= noun of "brittle") / hardness (= noun of "hard")
-or	resistor (= electric component designed to introduce known resistance into a circuit) / translator (= person who translates)
-ous	ferrous (= having to do with or containing iron: ferrous metals) poisonous (= containing poison)
-proof	dustproof (= keeps dust from coming through) / waterproof (= keeps water from coming through) / rustproof (= protected from rust) / shockproof (= not easily damaged by being dropped or hit) / windproof (= protected against wind) / soundproof (= constructed so that sound cannot get through)

Pronunciation of mathematical expressions

x^0	x to the power of zero
x^1	x to the power of one
x^{-1}	x to the power of minus one
x^{-2}	x to the power of minus two
x^2	x squared
x^3	x cubed
x^4	x to the fourth *or:* to the power of four
$x^{-\infty}$	x to the power of minus infinity
$\sqrt{x}$	square root of x
$\sqrt[3]{x}$	cube root of x
$\sqrt[4]{x}$	fourth root of x
x^n	x to the power n *or:* x to the nth power *or:* x raised to n
$(a+b)^2$	a plus b all squared (*or:* a plus b in parentheses squared)
$\dfrac{ab}{cd}$	a times b over c times d
$a'b''$	a dash times b double dash
$[a]$	a in brackets
$[a+b]\,c$	bracket [open] a plus b bracket [close] multiplied by c
(a)	a in parentheses
$a(b+c)$	a parenthesis [open] b plus c parenthesis [close]; a times the sum of b + c
$\{a\}$	a in braces
$\log \sin \beta$	logarithm of the sine [saɪn] of the angle β [ˈbiːtə]
$= \log \sin 29 \cdot 45°$	is logarithm of the sine of the angle of 29 · 45°
$= \log 0 \cdot 4917$	is logarithm of nought point, four, nine, one, seven equals
$= \bar{1} \cdot 6917$	bar one point, six, nine, one, seven
$\log_a m^r$	logarithm of *m* to the *r*th to the base *a* is
$= r \log_a m$	*r* times logarithm of *m* to the base *a*
$R_t = \dfrac{u_t\, U^2\, 10^4}{Sn}$	(capital) R sub small t equals (small) u sub t times (capital) U squared times 10 to the fourth, all over (capital) S sub small n

Signs and symbols

&	(ampersand) and
&c	et cetera; and so forth
@	at; each (three twist drills @ £1.22 = three twist drills at one pound twenty two each)
¢	cent(s)
20°	twenty degrees
⸹	delete; take out
"	ditto marks
$	dollar
#	1) number (if used in front of a figure: the train leaves at 12:25, track # 14) 2) pounds (if it follows a figure: here ist a 10 # sack of cement)
%	percent
‰	per thousand
£	pound Sterling
®	registered trademark
8′	1) eight feet 2) eight minutes
8″	1) eight inches 2) eight seconds
/	oblique (solidus, slash)
\	back slash
}	close brace (right brace)
]	close square bracket (right square bracket)
{	open brace (left brace)
[	open square bracket (left square bracket)
+	plus/and
−	minus/take away
±	plus or minus
×	(is) multiplied by/times (*or, when giving dimensions,* by)
÷	(is) divided by
=	is equal to/equals
≠	is not equal to/does not equal
≃	is approximately equal to
≡	is equivalent to/is identical with
<	is less than
≮	is not less than
≤	is less than or equal to
>	is more than
≯	ist not more than
≥	is more than or equal to
∞	infinity
∝	varies as/is proportional to
3:9::4:12	three is to nine as four is to twelve
$\log_e$	natural logarithm *or* logarithm to the base e
π	pi
r	= radius of a circle
∫	the integral of

Greek alphabet

A	α	alpha	[ˈælfə]		N	ν	nu	[njuː]
B	β	beta	[ˈbiːtə]		Ξ	ξ	xi	[saɪ/gzaɪ/zaɪ]
Γ	γ	gamma	[ˈgæmə]		O	ο	omicron	[əʊˈmaɪkrən]
Δ	δ	delta	[ˈdeltə]		Π	π	pi	[paɪ]
E	ε	epsilon	[epˈsaɪlən/ˈepsɪlən]		P	ρ	rho	[rəʊ]
Z	ζ	zeta	[ˈziːtə]		Σ	σ ς	sigma	[ˈsɪgmə]
H	η	eta	[ˈiːtə]		T	τ	tau	[taʊ]
Θ	θ	theta	[ˈθiːtə]		Y	υ	upsilon	[juːpˈsaɪlən/ˈjuːpsɪlən]
I	ι	iota	[aɪˈəʊtə]		Φ	φ	phi	[faɪ]
K	κ	kappa	[ˈkæpə]		X	χ	chi	[kaɪ/kiː]
Λ	λ	lambda	[ˈlæmdə]		Ψ	ψ	psi	[psaɪ]
M	μ	mu	[mjuː]		Ω	ω	omega	[ˈəʊmɪgə/ˈəʊmegə]

Prefixes for the SI system

Prefix	Prefix symbol	Factor by which the unit is multiplied	Description
atto	a	10^{-18}	GB one trillionth; US quintrillionth
femto	f	10^{-15}	GB one thousand billionth; US quadrillionth
pico	p	10^{-12}	GB one billionth; US trillionth
nano	n	10^{-9}	GB one milliardth; US billionth
micro	µ	10^{-6}	one millionth
milli	m	10^{-3}	one thousandth
centi	c	10^{-2}	one hundredth
deci	d	10^{-1}	one tenth
deca	da	10^{1}	ten
hecto	h	10^{2}	one hundred
kilo	k	10^{3}	one thousand
myria	my	10^{4}	ten thousand
mega	M	10^{6}	one million
giga	G	10^{9}	GB one milliard; US billion
tera	T	10^{12}	GB one billion; US trillion

Fuel consumption

USA: mpg = miles per gallon (1 US gallon = 3.785 litres)
GB: mpg = miles per gallon (1 UK gallon = 4.546 litres)

Conversion factors: l/100 km = 235.215 ÷ mpg (USA)
l/100 km = 282.481 ÷ mpg (GB)

mpg (USA): 235.215 ÷ l/100 km
mpg (GB): 282.481 ÷ l/100 km

Examples: USA: 30 mpg = 7.84 l/100 km
GB: 30 mpg = 9.41 l/100 km

10 l/100 km = USA: ca. 28 mpg / GB: ca. 24 mpg

Engine power

1 PS = 735.498 75 watts = ca. 0.736 kW
1 hp = 745.700 watts = ca. 0.746 kW

Example: 75 PS/CV = ca. 56 kW

The chemical elements

Elements cannot be broken down into simpler substances by using chemicals, but electrons and protons can sometimes be split off from their atoms.

element	symbol	atomic number	element	symbol	atomic number
actinium	Ac	89	mercury	Hg	80
aluminium	Al	13	molybdenum	Mo	42
americium	Am	95	neodymium	Nd	60
antimony	Sb	51	neon	Ne	10
argon	Ar	18	neptunium	Np	93
arsenic	As	33	nickel	Ni	28
astatine	At	85	niobium	Nb	41
barium	Ba	56	nitrogen	N	7
berkelium	Bk	97	nobelium	No	102
beryllium	Be	4	osmium	Os	76
bismuth	Bi	83	oxygen	O	8
boron	B	5	palladium	Pd	46
bromine	Br	35	phosphorus	P	15
cadmium	Cd	48	platinum	Pt	78
caesium	Cs	55	plutonium	Pu	94
calcium	Ca	20	polonium	Po	84
californium	Cf	98	potassium	K	19
carbon	C	6	praseodymium	Pr	59
cerium	Ce	58	promethium	Pm	61
chlorine	Cl	17	protactinium	Pa	91
chromium	Cr	24	radium	Ra	88
cobalt	Co	27	radon	Rn	86
copper	Cu	29	rhenium	Re	75
curium	Cm	96	rhodium	Rh	45
dysprosium	Dy	66	rubidium	Rb	37
einsteinium	Es	99	ruthenium	Ru	44
erbium	Er	68	rutherfordium	Rf	104
europium	Eu	63	samarium	Sm	62
fermium	Fm	100	scandium	Sc	21
fluorine	F	9	selenium	Se	34
francium	Fr	87	silicon	Si	14
gadolinium	Gd	64	silver	Ag	47
gallium	Ga	31	sodium	Na	11
germanium	Ge	32	strontium	Sr	38
gold	Au	79	sulphur	S	16
hafnium	Hf	72	tantalum	Ta	73
hahnium	Ha	105	technetium	Tc	43
helium	He	2	tellurium	Te	52
holmium	Ho	67	terbium	Tb	65
hydrogen	H	1	thallium	Tl	81
indium	In	49	thorium	Th	90
iodine	I	53	thulium	Tm	69
iridium	Ir	77	tin	Sn	50
iron	Fe	26	titanium	Ti	22
krypton	Kr	36	tungsten	W	74
lanthanum	La	57	uranium	U	92
lawrencium	Lr	103	vanadium	V	23
lead	Pb	82	xenon	Xe	54
lithium	Li	3	ytterbium	Yb	70
lutetium	Lu	71	yttrium	Y	39
magnesium	Mg	12	zinc	Zn	30
manganese	Mn	25	zirconium	Zr	40
mendelevium	Md	101			

Paper sizes

ISO Paper sizes (vertical measurement first)

A0	841 x 1189	B0	1000 x 1414		
A1	594 x 841	B1	707 x 1000		
A2	420 x 594	B2	500 x 707		
A3	297 x 420	B3	353 x 500		
A4	210 x 297	B4	250 x 353		
A5	148 x 210	B5	176 x 250		
A6	105 x 148	B6	125 x 176		
A7	74 x 105	B7	88 x 125		
A8	52 x 74	B8	62 x 88		
A9	37 x 52	B9	44 x 62		
A10	26 x 37	B10	31 x 44		

Envelope sizes

C3	460 x 324
C4	324 x 229
C5	229 x 162
C6	162 x 114

Roman numerals

I	1	X	10	C	100	M	1000
V	5	L	50	D	500		

In making up other numbers, a smaller number placed after a larger is to be added to it, and a smaller number placed before a larger is to be taken from it; for example:

I	1	VI	6	XX	20	LXX	70
II	2	VII	7	XXX	30	LXXX	80
III	3	VIII	8	XL	40	XC	90
IV	4	IX	9	L	50	C	100
V	5	X	10	LX	60	CM	900

M	1000
MC	1100
MCD	1400
MDC	1600
MDCLXVI	1666
MDCCLXXXVIII	1788
MDCCCXCIV	1894
MCM	1900
MCMLXXVI	1976
MCMLXXXIX	1989
MM	2000

Common substances used in production and manufacturing

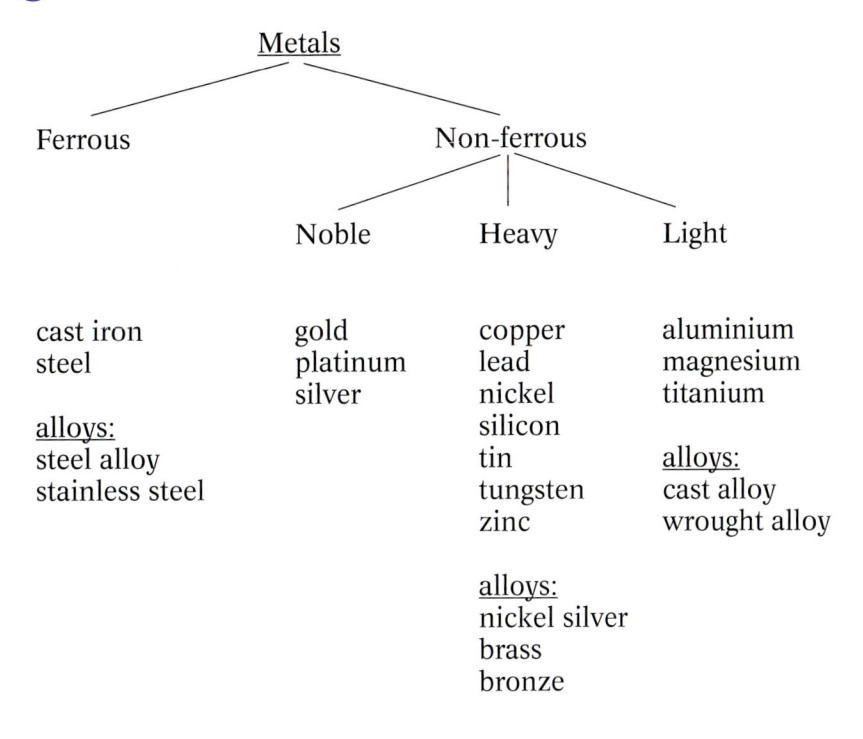

```
                                    Metals
                        ┌─────────────┴─────────────┐
                     Ferrous                   Non-ferrous
                                        ┌──────────┼──────────┐
                                      Noble      Heavy      Light
```

cast iron	gold	copper	aluminium
steel	platinum	lead	magnesium
	silver	nickel	titanium
alloys:		silicon	
steel alloy		tin	alloys:
stainless steel		tungsten	cast alloy
		zinc	wrought alloy
		alloys:	
		nickel silver	
		brass	
		bronze	

Gases

carbondioxide
carbonmonoxide
hydrogen
lighting gas
natural gas
nitrogen
oxygen

```
                                  Non-metals
                        ┌─────────────┴─────────────┐
                    Synthetic                    Natural
                   ┌─────┴─────┐            ┌──────┴──────┐
             Thermoplastic  Thermosetting  Organic     Inorganic
```

Liquids

acid	polyamide	resins:	cork	cement
alkaline	polyethylene	epoxid	cotton	clay
cooling agent	polypropylene	melamine	pine resin	concrete
grease	polystyrene	phenol	rubber	elements
hydraulic fluid	PVC	polyester	silk	glass
lubricants			wax	graphite
mercury		fillers:	wood	mica
		glass fibre		porcelain
oil		asbestos		
paint		carbon fibre		
petrol				
solvents				
varnish				

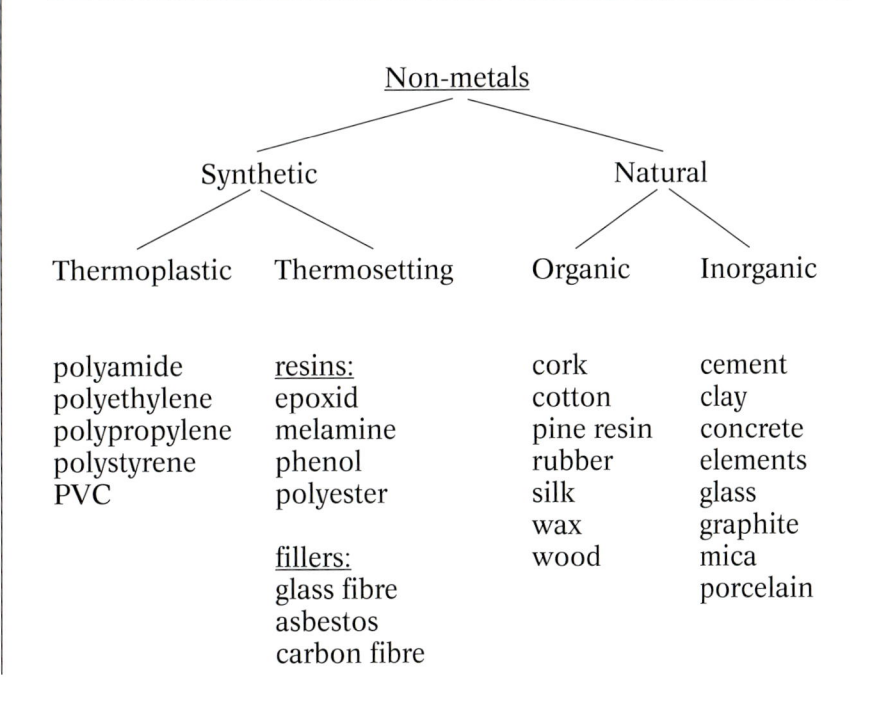

175

Denominations above one million

British system

Name	Value in powers of ten	Number of zeros*	Powers of 1,000,000
milliard	10^9	9	–
billion	10^{12}	12	2
trillion	10^{18}	18	3
quadrillion	10^{24}	24	4
quintillion	10^{30}	30	5
sextillion	10^{36}	36	6
septillion	10^{42}	42	7
octillion	10^{48}	48	8
nonillion	10^{54}	54	9
decillion	10^{60}	60	10
undecillion	10^{66}	66	11
duodecillion	10^{72}	72	12
tredecillion	10^{78}	78	13
quattuordecillion	10^{84}	84	14
quindecillion	10^{90}	90	15
sexdecillion	10^{96}	96	16
septendecillion	10^{102}	102	17
octodecillion	10^{108}	108	18
novemdecillion	10^{114}	114	19
vigintillion	10^{120}	120	20
centillion	10^{600}	600	100

American system

Name	Value in powers of ten	Number of zeros*	Number of groups of three 0's after 1,000
billion	10^9	9	2
trillion	10^{12}	12	3
quadrillion	10^{15}	15	4
quintillion	10^{18}	18	5
sextillion	10^{21}	21	6
septillion	10^{24}	24	7
octillion	10^{27}	27	8
nonillion	10^{30}	30	9
decillion	10^{33}	33	10
undecillion	10^{36}	36	11
duodecillion	10^{39}	39	12
tredecillion	10^{42}	42	13
quattuordecillion	10^{45}	45	14
quindecillion	10^{48}	48	15
sexdecillion	10^{51}	51	16
septendecillion	10^{54}	54	17
octodecillion	10^{57}	57	18
novemdecillion	10^{60}	60	19
vigintillion	10^{63}	63	20
centillion	10^{303}	303	100

*For convenience in reading large numerals, the thousands, millions, etc., are usually separated by commas (21,530; 1,155,465) or esp. in technical contexts by spaces (1 155 465). Serial numbers (as a social security number) are often written with hyphens (042-24-4705).

Guide to English pronunciation

[ə]	number [ˈnʌmbə]	etwa wie *e* in *bitte*
[eə]	where [weə]	*a* zu [ə] gleitend
[e]	best [best]	etwa wie *e* in *fett*
[eɪ]	space [speɪs]	von [e] zu [ɪ] gleitend
[əʊ]	low [ləʊ]	von [ə] zu [ʊ] gleitend
[ɜ:]	early [ˈɜ:lɪ]	etwa wie *ö* in *Segeltörn* (aber ohne *r*!)
[ʌ]	run [rʌn]	etwa wie *a* in *Matsch*
[ɑ:]	last [lɑ:st]	etwa wie *a* in *Kahn*
[aɪ]	file [faɪl]	etwa wie *ei* in *fein*
[aʊ]	brown [braʊn]	etwa wie *au* in *Bau*
[æ]	stand [stænd]	etwa wie *ä* in *lächeln*
[ɪ]	bit [bɪt]	etwa wie *i* in *mit*
[ɪə]	near [nɪə]	etwa wie *ie* in *Bier*
[i:]	beat [bi:t]	etwa wie *ie* in *Miete*
[ɒ]	lot [lɒt]	etwa wie *o* in *Grotte*
[ɔ:]	join [dʒɔɪn]	etwa wie *eu* in *neu*
[ɔ:]	saw [sɔ:]	etwa wie *o* in *Korn* (aber ohne *r*!)
[ʊ]	book [bʊk]	etwa wie *u* in *Futter*
[ʊə]	sure [ʃʊə]	von [ʊ] zu [ə] gleitend
[u:]	tool [tu:l]	etwa wie *u* in *Buch*
[θ]	thing [θɪŋ]	etwa wie gelispeltes *ß* (*Biß*)
[ð]	that [ðæt]	etwa wie gelispeltes *s* (*Sand*)
[ʃ]	shift [ʃɪft]	etwa wie *sch* in *fesch*
[ʒ]	measure [ˈmeʒə]	etwa wie das zweite *g* in *Garage*
[s]	service [ˈsɜ:vɪs]	etwa wie *ß* in *reißen*
[z]	please [pli:z]	etwa wie *s* in *Museum*
[ŋ]	wrong [rɒŋ]	etwa wie *ng* in *bang*
[r]	repeat [rɪˈpi:t]	kein gerolltes *r*! Zunge im Gaumen leicht zurückbiegen
[v]	visit [ˈvɪzɪt]	etwa wie *w* in *Wein*
[w]	wheel [wi:l]	zuerst wie kurzes *u* ansetzen, dann schnell zum nachfolgenden Laut übergehen
[ˈ]	collect [kəˈlekt]	(deutet die stärker betonte Silbe an)

Grammar and subject index

The numbers refer to the pages in the book.

accident report 84
Adverbien 52
adverbs of degree 52
air conditioner 86/88/90/91
aircraft wheels 126
alignment 15
application form 55-57
articles 48
Artikel 48
as 93

because 93
Bedingungssätze → conditional sentences
BROWN Fredric 130/131
bullet train 22

clamp 125
clauses 26
computer 108/109/110/123
conditional sentences 89
continuous form → -ing form
curriculum vitae 59
CV 60
cyberspace 116

design 68
didn't use to 43
die 47
display screen 35
do 100
double 47
double glazing 28
download 110
dummies 14

efficiency 27
engineering 6
-ever 30
extraction 42
extrusion 42

fairly 52
fields of work 11/13
finishing 68
Fragefürwörter → interrogative pronouns
furnaces 74

gear wheels 45
go 33

half 48
head restraints 14, 16
heating systems 28

icon 123
imaging 123
indirekte Rede → reported speech
industrial robots 98/99/102
-ing form 104/111
interrogative pronouns 17

jobs 11/13
job aspects 10

key pad 35
Konditionalsätze → conditional sentences

library 108/110
linear motor 22
lube 15

machining center 92/94/95
Maglev 22
magnetic levitation 22
maintenance centre 82
make 100
memo 12
metal finishing 69
mind 120
monorail 22
motorhome 128/129

need/needn't 59
nuclear fusion 124

own 8

past perfect continuous 71
past perfect simple 84
power and free conveyor 36
present perfect continuous 71
pretty 52
pull down menu 123
puzzle 97

question words → interrogative pronouns
quite 48, 52

rather 52
recycling 78
relative clauses 26
relative pronouns and clauses 26
Relativpronomen → relative pronouns
repair order 15
reported speech 76
rivets 50
robots 98/99/102

safety 14/19
science fiction story 130
science museum 106/114/118
self/selves 8
shop floor 39
simple past perfect 84
since 93
steel 50
steering column 16
such 48

take 80
that 26
tires 126
trash 78
tube furnaces 74
tune up 15
twice 48
tyre balance 15

use(d) to 43
user interface 111

Verlaufsform → -ing form
virtual reality 116
vollendete Vergangenheit → past perfect
VR 116

welding 50/51
what 17
which 17/26
who 17/26
whose 17/26

Quellenverzeichnis

Wir danken den folgenden Personen, Institutionen, Unternehmen und Verlagen für die freundliche Genehmigung von Copyright-Material, soweit sie erreicht werden konnten. Sollten Rechteinhaber hier nicht aufgeführt sein, so sind wir für entsprechende Hinweise dankbar.

Seite 12	Abbildung: Nord/LB, Norddeutsche Landesbank Girozentrale, Hannover, Deutschland
Seite 13	Cartoon reproduced from MICROPHOBIA Honeysett, Century Hutchinson Limited, London, England
Seite 14,16,17,19	Abbildungen und Text: Saab-Scania, Nyköping, Schweden
Seite 21	Foto oben: Underground Construction Co., Inc., Engineering Contractors, Benicia, California, USA; Foto unten: Saab-Scania, Nyköping, Schweden
Seite 22	Foto: Underground Construction Co., Inc., Engineering Contractors, Benicia, California, USA
Seite 25	Cartoon: English Tourist Board, London, England
Seite 29/30	Zeichnungen: "Energy Efficient Renovation of Houses", reproduced with the permission of the Controller of Her Britannic Majesty's Stationary Office, Norwich, England
Seite 32	Abbildung: Westinghouse Systems Limited, Wiltshire, England
Seite 33	Cartoon: English Tourist Board, London, England
Seite 35	Abbildungen: Westinghouse Systems Limited, Wiltshire, England
Seite 36-40	Abbildungen und Text: Conveyors International Limited, Leicester, England
Seite 42/43,46-48	Abbildungen und Text: British Alcan Extrusions Limited, Banbury, England
Seite 50-52	Abbildungen und Text: Nizec Technical Manual, published February, 1990, by British Steel Strip Products Commercial, Newport, England
Seite 59	Foto: Underground Construction Co., Inc., Engineering Contractors, Benicia, California, USA
Seite 63	Karikatur: Der Bundesminister für das Post- und Fernmeldewesen, Bonn, Deutschland
Seite 66	Foto: Lufthansa, Köln, Deutschland
Seite 67	Abbildungen und Text: Conveyors International Limited, Leicester, England
Seite 68	Abbildungen und Text: Ionic Surface Treatments, Warley, England
Seite 70/71	Saab-Scania, Nyköping, Schweden
Seite 72	Cartoon reproduced from MICROPHOBIA Honeysett Century Hutchinson Limited, London, England
Seite 73	Fotos: Edith und Albert Schmitz
Seite 74/76	Abbildungen und Text: Carbolite Furnaces Limited, Sheffield, England
Seite 79/81	Abbildungen und Text: Amoco Chemical Company, Chicago, USA

Seite 82/83	Foto und Text: GEC Alsthom Transportation Projects Limited, Birmingham/Manchester, England
Seite 88-91	Abbildungen und Text: Industrial Air, Inc., Greensboro, North Carolina, USA/Cal-Air Conditioning Company, Whittier, California, USA
Seite 93	Cartoon reproduced from MICROPHOBIA Honeysett, Century Hutchinson Limited, London, England
Seite 94/95	Fotos, Zeichnungen und Text: Kearney & Trecker GmbH, Stuttgart, Deutschland
Seite 98/99, 102/103	Fotos, Zeichnungen und Text: Stäubli Unimation Limited, Telford, England
Seite 109-111	Abbildungen und Text: Cherwell Scientific Publishing Limited, Oxford, England
Seite 112	Foto: Edith und Albert Schmitz
Seite 114	Foto "Puffing Billy": Trustees of the Science Museum, London, England
Seite 115	Foto: Lufthansa, Köln, Deutschland
Seite 118	Foto "Boulton and Watt Rotative Beam Engine 1788": Trustees of the Science Museum, London, England
Seite 119	Cartoon reproduced from MICROPHOBIA Honeysett, Century Hutchinson Limited, London, England
Seite 122	Cartoon reproduced from MICROPHOBIA Honeysett, Century Hutchinson Limited, London, England
Seite 123	Abbildungen und Text: Automatix European Offices, Advanced Tech Centre, Coventry, England
Seite 125	Abbildungen und Text: Cullmann Foto, Audio, Video, Langenzenn, Deutschland
Seite 126/127	Fotos: Lufthansa, Köln, Deutschland; Text: Dieter Vogt, Frankfurt/Main
Seite 128/129	Foto: Autohomes (UK) Limited, Poole, Dorset, England
Seite 130/131	"Not Yet the End", Fredric Brown: Für diese Kurzgeschichte konnte der Rechteinhaber nicht ermittelt werden. Entsprechende Hinweise nimmt der Verlag gern entgegen.